Walking Among our Ancestors

Walking Among
our
Ancestors

Edited by
Rodolfo Jacobo, Ph.D.

Aplomb Media | *Bonita*

Aplomb Media, Bonita 91902
©2018
All rights reserved

Cover front: mural Adelante MEChA Adelante by Ruben Ochoa
Cover back: photo by Daniel Salas

For Karina, Bella, EO, Cheech and Santi

Acknowledgments

I would like to thank everyone that made this work possible. In the academic arena I would like to recognize my mentors, Thomas Davies Jr., Richard Griswold del Castillo, Michael Ornelas, and Isidro Ortiz. All of you have had an enormous influence in my development as a scholar. To all the authors and institutions that collaborated on this project, Raymund Paredes, Richard Griswold del Castillo, Carlos Larralde, Alberto Ochoa, and Henry Lesperance I am grateful for your contributions. To University of Oklahoma Press, the University of Arizona Press and the Journal of San Diego History thank you for your assistance. Finally, to all the team at Aplomb Media thank you for your hard work.

My colleagues and friends at Palomar College who are part of a daily struggle to make our institution and community a better place. I especially want to thank Dr. Jack Kahn and Carmelino Cruz as well as all the members of the Association of Latinos and Allies for Student Success (ALASS).

Finally to my beautiful wife Karina and our children, Isabella, Diego, Cristian, and Santiago. All of you are my UNUM VERBUM. To my father and mother who endured poverty and discrimination to make me and my brothers what we are today. Mom even though you are not with us anymore not a day goes by that I am not influenced by your consejos and guided by your dichos. Gracias Jefa.

Contents

Background Issues I

Michael Ornelas

The Mexican Independence Movement, The Committee of Correspondence, Miguel Hidalgo y Costilla, José María Morelos y Pavon, Chilpancingo, Liberalismo, Secularization, The Northern Provincias, The Mexican Constitution of 1824, The United States Constitution, Adams-Onís Treaty of 1819

At the beginning of the 19th century Spanish sovereignty had been extended into most of the regions of the northern frontier, today's American Southwest. By this time its population, as a result of intensified racial mixture, had become the most heterogeneous group within the entire Spanish colonial empire. They were uniquely self-sufficient colonists due to their distance from Spain's power core center at Mexico City. In some ways they were freer than their countrymen to the south. Their frontier experience was not unlike that of the American frontiersmen. They were freer than their southern counterparts to create agricultural and urban communities adapted to local conditions. This required a healthy regard for the nomadic indigenous groups and a rational allocation of precious natural resources. In some ways, indicated by the presence of communalism in land and resource distribution in the New Mexico region, they developed distinct frontier practices and discarded old ones. The labor and land control institutions imposed throughout the Mexican colony, the encomienda and repartimiento, never took hold in the northern frontier. The frontiersmen were more concerned with survival in the demanding conditions of the frontier.

In central Mexico problems of a different sort surfaced at the turn of the century. Despite many efforts by Spanish colonial officials to maintain a sort of Mexican isolationism, news of events in Europe and among the thirteen American colonies slowly found their way into Mexico and provoked intense debate. Mexicans became aware of the American colonial rebellion against British rule. And they became increasingly interested in revolutionary developments in France which culminated in the first French Revolution. Smuggled copies of the American Declaration of Independence surfaced in Mexico and became the major subject of interest to the emerging 'literary clubs.' One of the most important of these was the Committee of Correspondence. Among its members were Miguel Hidalgo y Costilla, Juan Aldama and Ignacio Allende, prominent participants during the independence movement's early years. They advanced a harsh critique of the Spanish colonial institutions and gave valuable assistance to the Mexican revolutionary movement about to erupt.

The Mexican independence movement of 1810-1821 was the first major international political event on the North American continent in the early 19th century. It culminated decades of discontent with distant and oppressive Spanish rule. Gradually a sense of Mexican nationalism and anti-Spanish privilege had emerged as the overwhelmingly mestizo nation evolved an identity separate from Spain.

For decades prior to these events, mounting discontent with centuries of Spanish oppression had been infused with an unexpected jolt as a result of late eighteenth century colonial reforms. Bourbon reforms of the late eighteenth century had liberalized trade restrictions, opened previously closed areas of the economy to Criollos (Spaniards born in the New World) and unexpectedly nourished a rebellious and independent spirit. With the successful French invasion of Spain and the crown in disarray, some believed, particularly Criollos, that Mexico's independence had already arrived. The Peninsulares (Spanish immigrants in Mexico) maintained that the Spanish crown kept its authority over its colonies. Also of particular interest was the implementation of Spain's new liberalism, and its redefinition of human rights and the fundamental equality of men. Privileged social positions on account of race or birth were undermined and had been targets of the European and American rebellions. Mexican revolutionary leaders followed these events closely.

The Committee of Correspondence, Mexico's first anti-colonial conspiracy, secretly met to discuss these historic victories against tyranny. The French Revolution offered Mexican intellectual leaders the possibility to eliminate government by privileged elites and the American Declaration of Independence, particularly its proclamations against colonial rule, inspired Mexican rebels against their own colonial rulers. Convinced of their need to declare against Spanish colonial rule, members of the conspiracy planned for the uprising to begin in late 1810. The Criollo class, the majority within the Committee of Correspondence, hoped to establish an equal footing with the despised Peninsulares. As a group they cared little for the interests of Mexico's non-Spanish classes and castes. But leaders with more ambitious goals, including massive social and political reorganization, emerged to force the movement into new and radical directions.

Miguel Hidalgo y Costilla emerged as the unlikely leader of the conspiracy to end Spanish colonial rule. Hidalgo, a village priest from Dolores, had contemplated the implications of the American and French Revolutions as a member of the original Committee of Correspondence. And as a fiery opponent of Spanish privilege and an ally of Mexico's countless dispossessed, he rallied the colonial outcasts against the hated gauchupines (derogatory for Peninsulares). Needing little encouragement the castas (non-Spaniards) erupted into vengeful violence against centuries of Spanish oppression. Hidalgo's plan declared for the complete repudiation of Spanish colonial rule and massive social reform including an end to racial privilege and massive distributions of church and privately owned lands. Both proposals were enthusiastically embraced by Mexico's castas but met with fierce opposition from the privileged colonial elite. Following Hidalgo's capture and execution in 1811, an even more unlikely rebel, José María Morelos y Pavón, burst on the scene.

With momentum on his side and thousands of the dispossessed, Morelos streamlined the movement and articulated a set of radical proposals. He called for massive social, economic and political reforms. Not only content to rid Mexico of Spanish authority, he wanted to revolutionize the nation's institutions through a massive reform agenda. At its core was a complete repudiation of all vestiges of Spanish colonial privilege. At the Independence Convention at Chilpancingo in 1813, Morelos and his supporters advocated massive land redistributions, elimination of the racial caste system, expropriation and distribution of the haciendas, republican government with effective suffrage, secularization of Catholic Church properties and taxation of its capital assets. Morelos' grand plan was to lay the basis for an elusive equality at all levels of society for countless generations in the future.

In 1821, after more than a decade of devastating civil war, Spain reluctantly conceded to Mexican Independence in El Plan de Iguala. And in 1822, Juana Machado Wrightington witnessed the changing of the guard and the transition from Spanish to Mexican rule in Alta California. She saw Father Agustin Fernandez de San Vicente order the soldiers to lower the Spanish flag and raise the Mexican tricolor. Amid the assembled soldiers and great fanfare in San Diego's presidio, Wrightington was one of the few eyewitnesses to this momentous occasion. The transition to Mexican rule was official. In the northern regions, Mexicans began the arduous task of implementing the new ideas unleashed during the decade of civil war, embodied in liberalismo. For them it meant more regional autonomy, modernization of the economy through freer trade, elimination of the independent authority and power of the Catholic institutions and trade with foreigners.

Perhaps the single most important result of the new liberalismo was the secularization of church lands, authorized by Mexico's decree of August 17, 1833. The plan to expropriate and distribute church owned properties and lands, underway by the 1830s throughout the northern regions, undermined centuries of Catholic privilege, power and wealth. By the middle of the 19th century secularization had resulted in the distribution of millions of acres of church owned land and elevated hundreds of private citizens to a level of a new landed elite.

Receiving inspiration and direction from the framers of the American Declaration of Independence and the United States Constitution, Mexico fashioned its first Constitution in 1823. Like the American Constitution it included the principle of the balance of powers. The executive, judicial and legislative branches of the federal government were adopted. Mexico also embraced the bicameral legislature, the upper and lower houses, together comprising the Congress. The notion of absolute and proportional representation also became a part of the first Mexican experiment in democracy. And like the Constitution of the United States, Mexicans displayed their fundamental mistrust of the popular will by leaving the election of the Presidential and Vice Presidential offices in the hands of the Electoral College. In sharp contrast to the American Constitution, Mexico sanctioned the designation of Roman Catholicism as its official religion. In addition, the Mexican President was granted unprecedented authority during declared emergencies.

The new Mexican nation inherited sovereignty of Spain's former territories from northern California in the north, to Texas in the far northeast, to the Yucatan Peninsula in the south. Mexico took official possession of the northern frontier zones as a result of the 1831 Treaty of Limits, an international treaty with the United States which reconfirmed the terms of the Adams-Onis Treaty of 1819. The Adams-Onís Treaty of 1819, also known as the Transcontinental Treaty, had previously clarified the western extent of United States possessions acquired through the Louisiana Purchase in 1803 while simultaneously designating the northern extent of Spain's North American territories. In exchange for the United States agreement to relinquish claims to Texas, Spain ceded Florida to the United States. The first Mexican Constitution in 1824 absorbed the northern territories and created the Federal Republic.

The first Mexican Republic originally incorporated 19 states and 4 territories or provincias. The provincias were Tlaxcala in central Mexico, New Mexico in the north, Old California (Baja California) and New California (Alta California). The Texas region, the focus of considerable attention by Mexico and the United States, was absorbed as a part of the state of Coahuila. One of the great tasks before the new nation was the modernization and incorporation of its vast northern territories.

"To people is to govern" was the first Mexican approach to its far northern frontier, a long neglected region under Spanish rule. In response to various domestic and foreign pressures Mexico embraced a number of strategies to modernize the region and encourage settlement into its frontier zones. Some Mexicans encouraged decisive colonization plans to solidify Mexico's grip.

In response to increased international pressure and Mexico's acute interest in protecting the zone, a number of corrective strategies were adopted. First, settlers from the south were offered generous land grants and a chance to begin again in a relatively sparsely populated region. Second, colonization efforts, such as the Hijar-Padres effort, were undertaken during the early 19th century to encourage a Mexican migration into the region. With only modest success in California, the effort was short-lived. Third, to the dismay of California's previous waves of immigrant settlers, exiled criminals were sent to California during the 1830s and 1840s. Fourth, various careful attempts in both New Mexico and California were made to attract limited numbers of foreigners through land grants and other privileges. Ultimately Mexico decided to support a plan for the settlement of American-born Catholics in Texas beginning in 1824. That same year Mexico passed its first decree permitting foreign immigration into the upper regions of the state of Coahuila, in a region later known as Texas.

The 1824 Decree, Haden Edwards, Fredonia, General Manuel Mier y Terán, Tadeo Ortíz de Ayala, Law of 1829, Law of 1830, Counter-Colonization, Anahuac, Lipantíitlan, Tenoxtítlan, The Texas Declaration of Independence, Antonio López de Santa Anna, San Jacinto, The Treaty of Velasco, General José María Tornel y Mendívil, Pedro Bautista Pino, Nueces River, Rio Grande, President James K. Polk, Juan Seguín

For the first time, through the 1824 decree, Mexico permitted each of the northern regions to accept foreign-born immigrants. Offering generous land and tax concessions Mexico's ambitious plan aimed to populate, develop and protect its frontier zones. Immigrants were required to become Mexican citizens, obey *Required* Mexican law and become Catholics. With an eye on American expansionism, Mexico's objective was to erect a barrier in the path of United States expansion. It brought Mexico's northerners in contact with American-born citizens for the first time. And for the first few years, despite vast linguistic, cultural, religious and racial differences, the mestizo population of the frontier and the mostly Anglo Saxon Protestants of North America, cooperated in the first stages of settlement. At first there was little competition over land or resources. The need for common defense also functioned to mitigate against potential conflicts. There was a period of brief and helpful cooperation as they settled the frontier.

However, the period of peaceful coexistence was brief. Tensions between American colonists and the Mexican government surfaced as early as 1826. Haden Edwards, incensed at the Mexican government's unfavorable ruling in a land dispute, declared for a general uprising and Texas independence. It was the first sign of trouble with the American colonists and sent a clear message to authorities in Mexico City. This incident, the "Fredonia Revolt," reminded the Mexican government that the colonists could be dangerous and provoked a reevaluation of the 1824 decree.

In 1827 General Manuel Mier y Terán was ordered to Texas to inspect the region and advise Mexico on a policy that would protect it. He concluded that Mexico should end foreign immigration, counter-colonize with Mexicans and Europeans and enact legislation which would direct more Texas trade to the

Mexican Republic. He asserted that the American settlers were pushing for a separate territorial government apart from the state of Coahuila. His warnings of the potential for an American inspired rebellion were taken seriously by Mexican authorities. The Terán report precipitated the Mexican government's passage of its 1830 decree, curtailing American immigration into the northern frontier. It also called for plans to begin to counter-colonize with Mexican immigrants, economic policies leading to stronger trade with Texas and a stronger military presence in the region.

Slavery in Mexico had already been declared illegal in Mexico through the 1829 decree. Mexican officials expressed hope that this measure would also discourage Americans from coming to Texas. Some Mexican officials, such as Tadeo Ortíz de Ayala, elevated concern when he informed Mexican authorities of Texas' vast economic potential. Its natural resources and agricultural potential were unmatched anywhere in the Mexican Republic. The region was an indispensable part of Mexico's long-term modernization. Its loss could be devastating to the Mexican economic future and forever relegate Mexico economically subordinate to the United States, wrote Ortíz de Ayala.

The 1829 and 1830 decrees polarized Mexicans and Americans, a condition exacerbated by questions of loyalty and other political differences. Mexico's growing concern about its new immigrants and looming United States expansionism. Mexico took another step and used counter-colonization strategies aimed at the zone through the creation of three cities, Lipantitlan, Anáhuac and Tenoxtitlán, in southern Texas. The plan encouraged a northern migration of southern Mexicans in order to create a more balanced population of Mexicans and Americans. From the Mexican view this would discourage or prevent American rebellion from going any further. But the plan failed to attract a large northern migration. For Mexicans the frontier was not an attractive alternative and offered little advantage over their home regions.

According to Arnoldo De León, the American immigrants rebelled against Mexico for reasons unrelated to specific political questions. They had determined that Texas was run and inhabited

[handwritten margin note: No slaves]

8

by a people who were incapable or unwilling to progress beyond the present state of "disorder and primitivism." Mexicans were a particularly lethargic and unremarkable people that could not measure up to the Anglo American. And Mexico, in particular Texas, was plagued by political and economic indolence. The need to invert the political order from a people unwilling to progress and civilize the wilderness was a common concern on the minds of many Texians (American-born Texas settlers). And the Americans kept arriving, despite the new restrictive legislation and their well documented discomfort with alleged flaws in the Mexican character. American-born Texians numbered nearly 35,000 by the middle 1830s, while Mexicans numbered 5,000. For the first time Mexicans in the northern frontier were outnumbered by foreign-born immigrants. Consequently the need for counter-colonization and other measures.

In direct violation of Mexican law, Texas rebels organized conferences at Washington-on-the-Brazos in March, 1836, and wrote their Declaration of Independence. At first they had hoped to negotiate differences with the Mexican government including repeal of the 1829 and 1830 decrees. The 1829 decree was especially troubling to the Texians. They regarded it as a violation of their private property, even though Mexican law made no such guarantees. They had also determined that it violated the 1824 law which had permitted Texians to bring their slaves. For a complete summary of the Texians' grievances against the Mexican government see the Texas Declaration of Independence in this section. Mexico remained firm. The foreign immigrants had agreed to obey Mexican law and defiance of Mexican law amounted to sedition. The Texians claimed that they lacked political representation in the Coahuila state legislature. Rebellious Texians also charged Mexico with a failure to provide civil and constitutional protections. The Mexican government claimed that such guarantees were never a part of the 1824 immigration law. The Texians, the Mexican government argued, had traveled to a foreign country with copies of their American Constitution and blatantly defied Mexico's authority.

The rise to power by Centralist Antonio López de Santa Anna

was an important development for relations with the rebellious Texians. Determined to eliminate the Texas insurgency, Santa Anna advanced to the Texas frontier at the head of an army estimated at 3,000-6,000 men to destroy the seditionists. In San Antonio he found about two hundred Texians and several Tejanos (Spanish-speaking Texans) had taken refuge in the old mission site called the Alamo. After defeating them he moved on to Nacogdoches and Goliad where the poorly organized Texians were wiped out. The Texians retreated and the brief war appeared to be over. But at San Jacinto, Santa Anna's troops, in a surprise attack led by Texas revolutionary leader Sam Houston, were defeated. Santa Anna was taken prisoner by Houston. Under the threat of execution, he was forced to sign the Treaty of Velasco.

The treaty enumerated the conditions of the Mexican surrender and withdrawal from Texas. A copy of the treaty is included in this section. The treaty, highly controversial and disputed by many Mexican political leaders, virtually assured Texas autonomy in 1836. As a result of internal chaos and nationalistic opposition to the conditions of the treaty, it was never officially ratified by the Mexican Congress. To many major Mexican newspapers, intellectuals, political opponents of Santa Anna and the military the notion of Texas independence was unthinkable. Other opponents of the treaty would question its constitutionality under Mexican law. They argued that no Mexican authority could alienate the national territories. Furthermore, Santa Anna had signed the treaty under the threat of execution.

Despite the Mexican refusal to ratify the Treaty of Velasco, Texas independence was virtually assured. Many of Mexico's most prominent political voices, such as General José María Tornel y Mendívil, not only believed that the Treaty of Velasco was invalid but that the Texas independence movement was part of a larger United States conspiracy to realize its Manifest Destiny. The Tornel commission in 1836 concluded that more Mexican territories would be lost if Texas continued to remain independent. Tornel had predicted a sort of nineteenth century domino effect if Texas independence was not reversed. Other important territories, Tornel suspected, could fall to American expansionism. The United States, after all, had expressed a strong desire to acquire the California province and other regions from Mexico.

For decades prior to the Texas Revolt, Mexicans had been alerted to United States expansionistic designs on their northern territories. As early as 1812 prominent northern officials, such as Pedro Bautista Pino, a strict Spanish protectionist, made repeated appeals to the central government for financial and military support to prevent the loss of the northern territories. Pino had also predicted that the Mexican failure to enact and enforce stringent protectionist measures in the north could result in territorial loss to the United States or some other European power. Despite the warnings of the American scheme for conquest and appeals by the Mexico's northern officials, Texas became the Lone Star Republic in 1836. Between 1836 and 1845 statehood within the United States was delayed because of its status as a slave state. Mexican opposition under the threat of war was an additional factor which may have delayed Texas statehood.

Further complicating relations between the Texas Republic and the Mexican government was the conflict regarding Texas' southern boundary. According to Mexican surveys and maps dating to 1767, the southern boundary of Texas was placed at the Nueces River, approximately 120 miles north of the Rio Grande (called the Rio Bravo del Norte by Mexico). Despite evidence to the contrary, Texas maintained its largely insupportable claim for the Rio Grande, based on Article 4 of its secret agreement in the Treaty of Velasco with Antonio López de Santa Anna. The disputed territories represented approximately one-third of the current state of Texas. The United States, upon admission of Texas as a state in 1845, agreed to support Texas claims to the Rio Grande. This disputed territory was the focus of numerous diplomatic exchanges and the site of the principal military confrontation which prompted President James K. Polk to request a declaration of war against Mexico. Not until 1848 and the signing of the Treaty of Guadalupe Hidalgo was the Rio Grande validated as the boundary separating northern Mexico and southern Texas.

Why then would Mexico invite and encourage foreign immigration into a region so vulnerable and coveted by competing foreign nations? The answer rests in the Mexican conviction that if strict adherence to the provisions of the law were respected including the adoption of Roman Catholicism, Mexican citizenship, regard for Mexican traditions and the law, colonists would be sufficiently 'Mexicanized' in order to erect a barrier in the path of American expansionism. Mexico believed that these hijos del país (sons of the country) would help to diversify the Texas economy, orient trade toward Mexico and most of all, remain loyal Mexican citizens.

The hopes of the Mexican government were shattered when American-born Texians began a campaign of blatant disregard for Mexican authority. The disputes with Mexicans and their government also included racial, sexual, political, class and ethnocentric dimensions which colored the earliest contacts between the two people. A complete accounting of the relationship between Anglo Americans and Chicanos in the northern frontier must include these aspects of their earliest contact. These disputes, in part due to historic anti-Mexicanism, continued unabated throughout the nineteenth century and were a primary feature of the relationship between Mexicans and Anglo Texians for decades to come. Raymund Paredes' survey of early anti-Mexicanism, explores the complex origins of anti-Mexican sentiment as it is transmitted to the border region through the nineteenth century.

Chicanos in the region undoubtedly endured a multitude of mixed emotions as events unfolded around them. Some Texas Mexicans such as José Antonio Navarro, Ignacio Zaragoza and Juan Seguín were open and public about their political differences with the Mexican government. Although they did not originally advocate an open defiance of Mexican authority, ultimately they came to support the revolutionary cause. But this position emerged only after attempts for Texas statehood within the Mexican Republic had failed. For the most part, the majority of Tejanos became victims of the Mexican and American conflict. Some like Juan Seguín repeatedly proved their allegiance to the Texas revolutionary cause. He was forced to leave, under the threat of a lynch mob, on the allegation of disloyalty when Mexico tried to retake Texas in 1842.

The Lone Star Republic, Thomas Catesby Jones, James K. Polk, hijos del paiz, John Slidell, General Zachary Taylor, Spot Resolutions, General Winfield Scott, General Stephen Kearney, The Bear Flaggers, Andres Pico, Nicholas Trist, The Treaty of Guadalupe Hidalgo, Article V, VIII, IX, and X, The Protocol of Querétaro, McKinney v. Saviego, Texas-Mexico Railroad v. Locke, California Land Act of 1851, Court of Private Land Claims

Events over the next decade following the Texas Revolt drew the United States and Mexico invariably closer to armed conflict. The struggle for sovereignty over Texas and the suspicion of the inexorable expansion of the United States into regions of the Mexican Republic quite naturally contributed to increased international polarization. Chicanos, by virtue of the signing of the Treaty of Guadalupe Hidalgo, the Protocol of Querétaro and the Supreme Court's systematic erosion of the intent of these documents would be the ultimate losers in the confrontation. For the most part the residents of the Mexican frontier remained apart from the major diplomatic and war maneuvers. But within a short time their lives would be enveloped by developments after the middle 19th century. Conflicts over territory and colliding interests would have serious ramifications for the first generation of Chicanos in the United States. The Mexican American War, which culminated decades of Mexican and American conflict, is the defining event of the Chicano experience. The Treaty of Guadalupe Hidalgo promised unprecedented civil, political, religious and property to the newly adopted citizens of the United States following the war.

Despite the Texas Declaration of Independence and the defeat of the Mexican army at San Jacinto in 1836, many issues remained unsolved. Texas established the Lone Star Republic and maintained its sovereignty until its admission into the United States in 1845. The Texas boundary question continued to remain a major irritant to relations between the Lone Star Republic and Mexico. While the Lone Star Republic claimed territories to the Rio Grande, Mexico continued to insist on a boundary 120 miles to the north, at the Nueces River. The United States administration of President James

K. Polk agreed to support Texas territorial claims. The admission of Texas as a slave state into the United States in 1845, despite Mexico's insistence that this was tantamount to an act of war, caused Mexico to break off diplomatic relations with the United States and brought the nations to the brink of war. The United States had always supported Texas territorial claims to the Rio Grande. It now moved to go to war to make it official.

Mexican and American relations, prior to the admission of Texas to the United States, had periodically reached crisis levels. In 1842, Thomas Catesby Jones, based on misinformation that the United States and Mexico had gone to war, captured the California provincial capital at Monterey. He declared California an American protectorate, lowered the Mexican flag and raised the American. Later he realized his mistake and shamefacedly removed the American flag and apologized to Mexican officials. The seriousness of this brief episode, and warnings from California officials led to the enactment of a new law in 1843 authorizing the expulsion of foreigners from the northern regions, including California, Sonora, Sinaloa and Chihuahua. But northern Mexican officials moved slowly or not at all. The law was least effective in the northern regions. In 1842, Texas invaders attempted to "liberate" New Mexico but were promptly defeated and arrested. That same year the Mexican army invaded Texas and briefly occupied the city of San Antonio and areas to its south. The United States government had made no secret of its desire to obtain Mexio's northern regions and Mexico made it clear it would defend them.

The direct threats to Mexican sovereignty in the region caused alarm but few effective measures which solidified Mexican control over the northern provinces. Mexico encountered aggressive negotiations as well as additional occupations of portions of its northern frontier. The Mexican government attempted to strike a delicate balance between the urgency to populate the region while insisting upon the political loyalties of foreign immigrants. Northern officials, such as New Mexican provincial governor Manuel Armijo, undertook the delicate task of encouraging a controlled flow of foreign immigrants while simultaneously ensuring the continuation of Mexican political authority. Similar problems emerged in the California province where officials tried various solutions, including, to the distress of the native population, the forced exile of convicts from various Mexican prisons in the 1820s and 1830s. Mexico had also permitted a small number of Americans and Europeans to reside there.

Mexican political instability also contributed to the deterioration of relations with the United States. The struggle for power between Centralists and Federalists bred internal political chaos and hindered an effective campaign to reclaim Texas. Effective diplomatic responses to problems with the United States became nearly impossible. The Mexican political strategy of concentrating political authority in the hands of the federal authorities may have also contributed to growing political discontent which contributed to open rebellion.

The election of Democrat James K. Polk for President of the United States in 1844, a southerner with grand plans for American expansion, brought matters to a critical point. The Polk administration would epitomize the climax of American expansionism during the 19th century. Elected on pro-slavery and pro-expansion platform, Polk had decided to seek the admission of Texas as a slave state and support Texas claims for the Rio Grande boundary. Polk also pursued the acquisition of the Oregon Territories from Great Britain, a feat accomplished in 1846.

Polk made no secret of his desire to acquire or seize California from Mexico. He had unsuccessfully proposed to purchase it through diplomatic exchanges. He formulated two more belligerent plans to realize his objective. He had instructed United States Consul to California, Thomas Larkin, to fashion his "California Plan," a scheme to encourage Californio (Spanish-speaking Californians) support for an American military occupation. The hijos del paíz, a collection of early California settlers principally from the United States, functioned as a seditionary front line for the plan. That same year John Slidell was sent to Mexico City on a secret mission to present various American demands, including the purchase of Mexico's vast northern provinces, California and New Mexico.

The John Slidell mission in 1845 created the illusion of a United States strategy to pursue a diplomatic resolution to the Texas boundary question. Its purpose was to convince Mexico to finally agree to the Rio Grande boundary. And Slidell was prepared to offer up to $25 million for the purchase of the California and New Mexico provinces, virtually the entire American Southwest. Incensed by Slidell's audacious proposals and an American sponsored Texas Independence, Mexican officials rejected the Slidell proposal.

Mexico was aware of reports which placed American General Zachary Taylor in southern Texas. While Slidell was in Mexico trying to negotiate an end to the territorial dispute, the American forces had already prepared to seize it. But the Slidell mission was a daring political maneuver for the Polk administration. Polk's strategy had worked. The United States Congress could now be persuaded to believe that the administration was attempting a diplomatic resolution of its troubles with Mexico. Mexico, in contrast, appeared to reject peaceful negotiation.

Mexico's most immediate concern was the presence of American General Zachary Taylor in the disputed region in southern Texas. Taylor was poised to launch an attack on northern Mexico. By March, 1846, under specific instructions from President Polk, Taylor advanced south of the Rio Grande and blockaded the Mexican port city at Matamoros, an act which not only violated international law but also caused an armed Mexican response which resulted in American bloodshed.

When news of the incident reached Washington D.C., Polk prepared his war message to Congress. He asserted that the United States had no choice but to declare war since Mexico had invaded American territory and "shed American blood on American soil." Sensing a conspiracy of Southern slave states and attempting to prevent a war declaration against Mexico, Congressman Abraham Lincoln introduced the "Spot Resolution." Lincoln's proposal demanded the identification of the exact spot where American blood had been spilled. Unable to assemble a majority vote, the initiative failed. Polk, some historians argue, had already unfolded his war strategy. The exchange of fire between American and Mexican troops provided the ground for Polk's plea for war with Mexico. He used the incident to convince Congress of a Mexican invasion of American territory. On May 13, 1846, Congress accepted Polk's argument and declared war. Polk's war of territorial conquest had begun.

The Polk war strategy advanced along three fronts. General Winfield Scott arrived in Mexico by sea at Vera Cruz and he began an arduous and costly march toward Mexico City. After several decisive battles on southern Mexican soil he would eventually force peace terms on the Mexican government through the Treaty of Guadalupe Hidalgo. What remained of the Mexicans troops near Texas were cleared out of northeastern Mexico by General Zachary Taylor. General Stephen Kearney, in command of the Army of the West, occupied New Mexico and moved west to merge with the "Bear Flaggers," as they sat poised off the California coast prior to the war.

In New Mexico and California American military forces met stern armed resistance from Mexican citizens as they tried to prevent American occupation. At San Pascual Pass, in southern California, Stephen Kearney's troops confronted fierce resistance from loyal Californios led by Andres Pico and were forced to retreat to New Mexico in 1847. In New Mexico, opposition to American occupation surfaced frequently during and after the war, primarily in the north. Despite the promises of a bright American future many displayed their strongest apprehensions toward the American occupiers. The natives had come to view themselves as occupying a homeland and had evolved a strong identification with the region. They displayed their loyalty to Mexico by organizing resistance to American occupation. Perhaps their vivid displays of loyalty to the Mexican Republic are better understood in light of the uncertain future they faced in a nation already influenced by anti-Mexicanist thought. Periodic resistance was almost certainly a sign of their disenchantment with the prospects of an American takeover of Mexico's northern frontier zone.

By September, 1847 General Winfield Scott drove into Mexico City and made peace offers to Mexico. Nicholas Trist, sent to Mexico as peace commissioner, opened negotiations with Mexico. Despite being recalled by President Polk, due to Polk's insistence on more Mexican territory and a reduced financial settlement, Trist began negotiations which ultimately resulted in the Mexican ratification of the Treaty of Guadalupe Hidalgo on February 2, 1848. Polk, furious with Trist and sensing growing opposition to the war and the treaty, had no choice but to submit the treaty to the Senate for its approval. On March 10, 1848, the United States Senate, by a 28-14 vote, ratified the treaty.

For Chicanos the treaty is the most important document defining their constitutional, civil and property rights in the United States. Richard Griswold del Castillo, in an article in this section, documents the complex task involved in the negotiations among the national representatives which resulted in the final document. Negotiations with Mexico included the attempted acquisition by the United States of the regions of Sonora, Baja California, Chihuahua and access to the Isthmus of Tehuantepec in southern Mexico. American negotiator had insisted on the inclusion of the Isthmus as a point where trade goods and other transactions could occur. Most alarming to Mexican officials was the movement to absorb the entire Mexican republic, a virtual obliterating of Mexico. The movement, known as the "All of Mexico" movement gained momentum and became a distinct possibility. However, in an ironic twist of history, southern racists opposed the annexation of the entire republic on the grounds that the United States would inherit an additional race problem and be compelled to absorb over 12 million Mexicans of diverse racial compositions. Senator John C. Calhoun was blunt and forceful, declaring that the United States was founded as a white nation for white people and the inclusion of millions of Mexicans would forever taint the republic. Ultimately the United States negotiators agreed to the provisions of Article V.

Article V forced Mexico to surrender its vast northern provinces including California and New Mexico. It also redefined the border between Texas and northern Mexico at the Rio Grande. Through Article V the United States had acquired the Southwest. This region comprises the current states of California, Arizona, Nevada,

Colorado, and New Mexico. It also included regions of the current states of Texas, Utah and Wyoming. These new boundaries would remain unchanged until the United States, under the threat of seizure and occupation, forced the sale of Mexico's Mesilla Valley, known as the Gadsden Purchase. It extended southern Arizona's territory beyond the Gila River, 120 miles farther south.

For Mexico, the Treaty of Guadalupe Hidalgo was a bitter humiliation and the subject of considerable political debate. Some Mexican political analysts believed the territorial surrender was unconstitutional. The Mexican Constitution, in their view, did not authorize the alienation of the national territories. In their view, Article V violated the Mexican Constitution. Some Mexican politicians such as Benito Juarez and Manuel C. Rejón encouraged a protracted guerilla war to resist the treaty and save the Mexican Republic. To others it meant the economic, political and cultural subordination of Mexico to the United States. To them, Mexico would forever remain a defeated nation with bitter memories of United States imperialism. It also forced Mexicans to examine the failures of their leaders. Others reminded Mexico that resistance or continued warfare could mean the complete obliteration of the Mexican nation. The United States, they argued, could strike back and absorb the entire Mexican nation, a position promoted by the All of Mexico movement. The issue was settled when Mexico, in a state of unprecedented disarray, ratified the treaty and it was forwarded to the United States Senate.

Mexicans in favor of the treaty pointed to the unprecedented political, civil, religious and cultural protections extended to the former Mexican citizens now residing on the lost lands. Under Article VIII, approximately 120,000 former Mexican citizens living in the acquired regions were allowed to continue to reside in their old homelands or move south across the new border into Mexico. They could retain Mexican citizenship or accept United States citizenship. But they had to make their decision within one year of the ratification of the treaty, or around May, 1849. A "substantial number," principally New Mexicans, decided to declare their intent to retain Mexican citizenship. And according to studies by Richard Griswold del Castillo, approximately five thousand people returned to Mexico, principally due to a planned Mexican repatriation campaign to create a defensive border buffer against further American expansionism.

⌠The vast majority decided to stay and take their chances with the new American administration. For the first time in the history of the United States, citizenship was granted to non-whites. Proponents of the treaty, Miguel Atristain and Bernardo Couto, were optimistic that the new United States citizenship as well as property and civil provisions would protect the former Mexican citizens. The treaty also appeared to offer attractive guarantees for their properties, including civil and religious protections.

Article VIII permitted the new citizens to retain their properties of all kinds. Many of the former Mexican citizens possessed lands and properties granted to them under Mexico's secularization decrees of the early 19th century. As many as thirty million acres of land had been distributed to private land holders in the twenty years following Mexican Independence. According to the treaty they could retain these properties, or sell them without any restriction. In addition they were also protected in the free exercise of their Catholic faith.

Article IX expanded upon the guarantees confirmed through Article VIII. Not only was United States citizenship guaranteed, Article IX extended all the rights of citizenship according to the principles of the Constitution to the new Americans. But these guarantees only became effective when the territories were incorporated as states. Until then citizenship provisions were in force but any additional rights would remain unmet until Congress authorized the inclusion of the territories as states. For the Californios this occurred in 1850, soon after the treaty was signed. For others, in the regions which eventually became the states of Arizona and New Mexico, the extension of all the rights of citizenship was delayed until 1912. In theory this meant that the fully incorporated new citizens enjoyed the right to vote, run for public office, testify in court and sue on their behalf. These were unprecedented guarantees which were withheld from most residents of the United States. In practice, however, Mexicans faced constant challenges to these protections. In California, for example, considerable time and debate was spent trying to exclude Mexicans from voting on the grounds that they had Indian ancestry. And as late as the 1920s attempts were made to classify Mexicans as Indians in order to legally segregate them in public schools in the Southwest. Indians were virtually without rights in the United States and excluded from citizenship protections of the treaty.

In other regions of the Southwest, particularly in Texas, these guarantees were never seriously considered or upheld. Texas had previously declared, during the 1830s, that Mexicans who had not voluntarily taken an oath of allegiance to the Republic of Texas had forfeited their land rights. In general, they were never considered citizens of the Republic or the state. Texas officials had taken the position that provisions and protections under the Treaty of Guadalupe Hidalgo did not apply to their state. This argument was based upon their unique history as an independent republic and Texas admission to the United States prior to the Treaty of Guadalupe Hidalgo. According to the state of Texas citizenship protections did not apply. Texas officials hinged their belief on a Supreme Court decision known as McKinney v. Saviego (1856). In this case, the justices determined that Texas was not part of the Treaty of Guadalupe Hidalgo since its independence and statehood had both occurred prior to the Mexican American War. Later rulings, such as Texas-Mexican Rail Road v. Locke (1889), overturned this decision and pointed to specific references to Texas in the Treaty of Guadalupe Hidalgo and the Protocol of Querétaro. For Mexicans in Texas these rulings, exacerbated by prevailing anti-Mexicanism, quickly evaporated any hopes of equal treatment as citizens or property holders in the state of Texas.

Important to Mexican negotiators in the Treaty of Guadalupe Hidalgo were protections of Spanish and Mexican land grants. Estimated at between twenty and thirty million acres across the Southwest, the grants had been obtained by private citizens principally through Mexico's early 19th century secularization decrees. The original version of Article X had asserted that all land grants made by the Spanish and Mexican authorities were considered valid. However, under heavy pressure by President James Polk, who insisted that Article X would complicate land disputes in Texas, the United States Senate omitted it. Mexican officials protested and demanded an explanation. American and Mexican officials agreed to place in writing the substance of their understanding with regard to the omission of Article X. This language, known as the Protocol of Querétaro, contains the statements of clarification regarding the legal status of land grants in the Southwest. The treaty could not validate land titles, argued the American negotiators, only the courts could.

As a result, the California legislature passed the California Land Act of 1851. The law empowered a panel of judges, the California Land Commission, to decide on the validity of Mexican owned land grants. Mexican land owners were required to present their case for ownership within three years. But the process never worked as smoothly as anticipated. Within twenty years, due to the tremendous cost of litigation, fraud, thievery and organized bands of squatters, the Californios had lost millions of acres of their ancestral lands. Richard Griswold del Castillo, in an article in this section, documents how this process worked in more detail. The Mexicans in New Mexico and Arizona had a similar experience with the American courts. The Court of Private Land Claims, established in 1891, decided on the validity of land claims in these two regions. Prior to 1891 land grant validation was directed by the Office of the Surveyor General of the Territory of New Mexico. The record clearly indicates that the United States courts, over the course of at least fifty years, seriously eroded not only the purpose of the treaty but its spirit as well. The systematic erosion of the guarantees contained in the treaty is the core of the Chicano experience in the United States following the Mexican American War.

1

The Origins of Anti-Mexican Sentiment in the United States

Raymund A. Paredes

Traditionally, when scholars have treated the development of anti-Mexican sentiment in the United States, they have focused on the first large-scale encounters between Mexicans and Americans in the early 19th century as the source of bad feelings."[1] The cultures of the two peoples, goes the conventional wisdom, were so dissimilar that misunderstanding and resentment grew rapidly and hardened into a tradition of prejudice. Samuel Lowrie, in his study of American-Mexican relations in Texas, found that a "culture conflict" developed immediately after American colonists entered Mexican Texas in 1821[2] while Cecil Robinson, the well known scholar of American literary images of Mexico, describes the "inevitable collision" between two nations competing for the same stretches of land.[3] The weakness of these studies, and others of their type, is that they have little to say about the attitudes American travelers and settlers carried into Mexican territory that largely determined their responses to the natives. The enmity between the two peoples may well have been inevitable but not exclusively for reasons of spontaneous culture conflict and empire building.

Rather, American responses to the Mexicans grew out of attitudes deeply rooted in Anglo-American tradition. Americans had strong feelings against Catholics and Spaniards and expected their evils to have been fully visited upon the Mexicans; after all, had not the Mexicans been subjected to nearly three hundred years of Catholic-Spanish oppression? The logic may have lacked a certain finesse but the fact of its application is inescapable. Secondly, although Americans in the early 19th century knew little about the contemporary people of Mexico, they held certain ideas about the aborigines --- and the natives of Latin America generally -- that affected their judgments.

The purpose of this essay is to trace the nature and history of those attitudes and images that shaped early American assessments of the Mexicans. Anti-Catholic sentiment and hispanophobia will be considered first, inasmuch as these prejudices operated in Anglo-American culture from the earliest days and exerted the most immediate influence on American attitudes. Next, I will discuss the more desultory career of the Mexican aborigines in early American thought. Finally, I will consider how these notions merged, in effect forming a mode of perception which rendered unlikely the possibility that 19th-century Americans would regard the people of Mexico with compassion and understanding.

The English settlement of America commenced at a time when hatred of Catholicism and Spain had been building for over fifty years. Widespread dissatisfaction with the Roman Church, based on charges of corruption and complacency, appeared in England shortly after 1500, crystallized during the Reformation, and intensified as Protestantism drifted leftward.[4] Propagandists denounced the Mass as blasphemous, indicted the clergy for the encouragement of superstition and ignorance, and assailed the Pope as the anti-Christ. Eventually, resentment of Catholicism transcended religious issues. Englishmen came to regard the Roman Church as a supra-national power which sought to overthrow their government. Reports of Catholic plots circulated regularly in England after the mid- 16th century, some warning of tangible dangers such as the Desmond revolts in Ireland and the fantastic Gunpowder Plot of 1605, while others -- the constant rumors of Jesuit intrigues, for example -- only demonstrated how closely English fears of Catholic political adventures verged on hysteria. It was in the context of this fear that English anti-Catholicism intersected and merged with a nascent hispanophobia. As every Englishman knew, Spain was the most powerful of Catholic nations and the self-proclaimed champion of the Roman Church. The Spanish military forces -- the "popist legions" -- were the very instruments of Catholic tyranny. The

Catholic-Spanish alliance was regarded by many Englishmen as a partnership conjured by Satan himself and thus one that possessed an unlimited capacity for mischief. Englishmen were well aware of the most notorious product of this collaboration, the Spanish Inquisition.

Although Englishmen disliked Catholics in the lump, the Spaniard was considered the worst of the breed for reasons not altogether related to religion. The spirit of nationalism surged in the Elizabethan era and England's attempts to assert itself as an international power placed it directly across the gun barrel from Spain. Countless military engagements, the most spectacular of which was with the Armada in 1588, maintained animosities at a high pitch until well into the 18th century. During the Revolt of the Netherlands (1555-1609), an event closely followed in England, Dutch nationalists conducted an impassioned "paper war" against their Spanish rulers, vilifying them for their cruelty, avarice, arrogance, and immorality.[5] In 1583, *The Spanish Colonie* by Bartolomé de Las Casas appeared in England and reported how the Spaniards, in an astonishing display of brutality, managed to reduce the native population of America by twenty million souls. By the end of the decade, the "Black Legend" had been firmly planted in the English mind and the Spaniard had displaced the Turk as the greatest of English villains.[6]

There is one other feature of 16th-century English hispanophobia that bears mention here. As Englishmen traveled more widely -- particularly to Africa on slaving expeditions -- they became increasingly aware of human differences, the most obvious of which was complexion. The color "black" had already acquired a number of negative connotations in the English mind, and eventually, the Elizabethans formulated a scale of human beauty ranging from the blond perfection of the northern European to the ebony hideousness of the African.[7] The Spaniard was placed near the bottom of the scale. In an era when Englishmen increasingly esteemed purity not only in a religious sense but also in an incipient racial context, the Spaniard was manifestly "impure," being the product of European Moorish miscegenation which had proceeded for hundreds of years.

This well-known phenomenon disturbed many Englishmen who used the terms "Moor" and "Negro" almost interchangeably.[8] Quite simply, the Moor was an African, so that in the mixture of bloods on the Iberian peninsula the odium of blackness was transferred to some extent to the Spaniard.

The colonial record provides ample evidence that prejudices against Catholics and Spaniards traveled across the Atlantic intact. Indeed, they may well have been more intense among the immigrants than in the general English public. After all, many of the colonists derived from the most anti-Catholic element in England, the radical Puritans, and to a man the settlers were ardent nationalists who regarded their role in the struggle with Spain with high seriousness. They saw themselves as guardians against Spanish penetration into the northern regions of the New World, as economic rivals intent on undermining the fragile structure of Spanish mercantilism, and as Protestant missionaries who would carry the Gospel unperverted to the American savages.

Always in contact with their homeland, the colonists received a steady influx of anti-Catholic and hispanophobic literature from England. One of the most popular works among the settlers was John Foxe's *Book of Martyrs,* a study of Catholic persecution which described vividly the numerous outrages of the Spanish Inquisition.[9] The collections of Richard Hakluyt and Samuel Purchas, the two great literary champions of English imperialism, were also well known to the settlers. By the late 17th century, the denunciations of Spanish activity in the *New World by Las Casas* and Thomas Gage had appeared on colonial booklists.[10]

The settlers themselves produced a conspicuous body of anti-Catholic and hispanophobic literature. In one of the earliest colonial works, *Of Plymouth Plantation,* William Bradford cited the corrupting influences of "popish trash" as a major reason for the Separatist emigration. He also railed against the jealousy and cruelty of the Spaniards and speculated that the colonists would have no greater trouble with the American savages. Bradford's history gave voice to Separatist hispanophobia which had been exacerbated during sojourns in Dutch sanctuaries where memorials to Holland's struggle with Spain were everywhere in evidence. During Bradford's tenure as governor of Plymouth Colony, the citizens allied with the Dutch settlers of New Amsterdam "the better to resist the pride of that common enemy, the Spaniard, from whose cruelty the Lord keep us both, and our native countries."[11] Like most of his co-religionists, Bradford believed that God protected Protestant true-believers from the evil designs of the Spaniards.

As it turned out, Bradford's invective was temperate when measured against other expressions of colonial anti-Catholicism and hispanophobia. The greatest denunciators were ministers who raged against their enemies from the pulpit and in religious tracts. The renowned John Cotton, for example, described the Roman Church as "worldly and carnal" and the Spaniards as a belligerent nation possessed by Satan. The Spanish Inquisition, he proclaimed, was "incomparably more bloody than any other Butchery."[12] Thomas Hooker outlined a history of Catholic treachery and corruption in the preface to his *Survey of the Summer of Church Discipline* (1648) and characterized the Pope as the incarnation of evil and his followers as "wretched rabble." Such assaults extended beyond religious literature. Colonists read anti-Catholic doggerel in their almanacs and heard anti-Spanish ballads on the streets.

A well-known poem in New England during the late 17th century was John Wilson's "Song of Deliverance." Wilson, a Boston minister, claimed, with appropriate modesty, no great merit for his verses but explained that they were intended to help children "learn and rehearse." One section of the "Song" treats the wicked intentions of the Spanish Armada and indicates how precisely and firmly Elizabethan prejudices were planted in the colonies:

Besides, great store and company
of tearing torturing Whips,

And instruments of cruelty,
provided in their Ships;

As meaning not to be so kind,
our blood at once to spill,

But by our lingring pain, their mind
and bloody lusts to fill.

From seven years old (or if not so,
from ten and so forth on)
All had been kill'd, both high and low
their Sword could light upon.

Virgins had dyde, when they had first
the Virgins honour lost:

Women unript, on Spears accurst,
had seen their Infants tost.

The children, whom they meant to save,
with brand of Iron hot,

Were in their face (like Indian slave,)
to bear a seared spot.

Their Soul (alas) had been a spoyle
to Soul-destroying Pope;

Their bodyes spent in restless toyle,
without all ease or hope.[13]

It is difficult to say how widely Wilson's poem was used as a pedagogical tool but we can say that colonial schoolchildren were exposed to a barrage of anti-Catholic and anti-Spanish propaganda. One of the most popular of early American textbooks was the *New England Primer* which over a period of one hundred and fifty years sold three million copies. Early editions contained excerpts from *The Book of Martyrs* and poems which admonished their readers to

"Abhor that arrant Whore of Rome,/ And all her Blasphemies."
Children learned basic anatomy lessons by studying a figure of that
"man of sin," the Pope, whose various body parts were indicated with
such captions as "In his Heart,...Malice, Murder, and Treachery" and
"In his Feet...Swiftness to shed Blood."[14]

The literary campaign against Rome and Spain continued
throughout the colonial period and beyond, engaging some of the
most able and influential figures in the settlements. Cotton Mather
inveighed eloquently against the traditional enemies of the Puritans
while publishers of popular almanacs such as Nathaniel Ames (both
father and son) and Nathaniel Low issued a stream of anti-Catholic
and anti-Spanish materials. In the mid-18th century, the first
Anglo-American magazines appeared and took up the fight. The
Dudleian lecture series was established at Harvard in 1750, a part of
which was given over to "the detecting and convicting and exposing
of the idolatry of the Romish church: their tyranny, usurpations,
damnable heresies, fatal errors, abominable superstitions, and other
crying wickedness in her high places."[15]   One could easily recite the
details of these various tirades, but to little purpose; suffice it to say
that the character and vehemence of literary anti-Catholicism and
hispanophobia continued virtually unchanged.[16]

Colonial resentment of Rome and Spain was not confined to
the printed page but found expression in a number of statutory
and military actions. As the settlers desired to see Catholicism
removed from the continent, many of the colonial legislatures passed
exclusionary and restrictive laws.[17] In 1641-42, the Virginia House
of Burgesses ruled that no "Popish recusants" could hold colonial
office. Massachusetts Bay banished priests and Jesuits under penalty
of execution. In 1698, New York forbade Catholics to hold weapons
and required that they deposit bond as security of good behavior.
Even in Maryland, originally established as a Catholic settlement,
Protestants became dominant, turned out the colony's founder, Lord
Baltimore, and decreed that "none who profess to exercise the Popish
religion...can be protected in this province."[18]

The colonists were no less vigorous in their campaigns against
the Spaniards. In the 1630s, New Englanders helped to establish

a Puritan colony off the Mosquito Coast to be used as a base for English penetrations into Central America. Many colonists, including John Cotton and Roger Williams, supported Cromwell's "Western Design," according to which the English would drive the Spaniards from the West Indies. In 1655, colonists participated in the assault on Jamaica, the first recorded venture against the Spaniards by English-Americans.[19]

Soon thereafter, English- and Spanish-Americans were battling on the mainland, particularly as the English colonists pushed southward and westward and found themselves, as the saying went, "in the chops of the Spaniards."[20] The settlers of Jamestown lived under constant threat of attack and in 1686, the Spaniards razed the Scottish settlement at Port Royal; predictably, Carolinians vowed to redress this "bloody insolency." After 1700, hostilities intensified as the enemies became embroiled in lengthy, bloody disputes involving titles of possession, buccaneering, and runaway slaves. English colonists complained constantly that the Spaniards provoked the Indians against them; the Spaniards countered with similar charges. One episode in 1702 exemplifies the character of the rivalry. As an opening blow in Queen Anne's War, Governor James Moore of Carolina organized an attack on the Spanish garrison at St. Augustine. Moore himself led the naval contingent of the expedition while a force of some five hundred Englishmen and Indians approached St. Augustine overland, ravaging enemy outposts along the way. The town fell without resistance, the residents having retreated nearby to the Castillo de San Marcos. Moore then lay siege to the fort and waited for heavy artillery to arrive from Jamaica. Still without cannon after seven weeks, the colonial forces withdrew hastily when the sails of Spanish warships appeared on the horizon.[21] This engagement, like many others between English-Americans and Spaniards, was as significant as an exhibition of long-standing hostilities as for any inherent military importance.

It is no exaggeration to characterize the 18th century as a period of incessant military and political conflict between English-Americans and Spain. The establishment of Georgia in 1733 greatly agitated the Spaniards who laid plans to destroy the colony.

England, for its part, was itching for a fight and found an excuse five years later when Captain Robert Jenkins appeared in the House of Commons to tell how the Spaniards had severed his left ear as punishment for a trumped-up charge of illegal trade in the West Indies. The wronged officer dramatized his tale by exhibiting the remnant of his humiliation, still remarkably well-preserved after several years.[22] The spectacle was too much for the politicians who, after the fashion of their breed, had an appreciation of the theatrical; after an extended debate, they finally declared war. English colonists leaped to the fray -- known, of course, as the War of Jenkins' Ear -- engaging the enemy along the Georgia-Florida frontier and in an abortive assault on the South American port of Cartagena. Moving to the revolutionary period, we find that many Americans were angered by Spain's delay in granting recognition of independence, stubbornly unsympathetic to Spain's fear that such an act would be considered an inducement to rebel by its own restive colonies. Perhaps the greatest controversy between the two peoples involved navigation rights on the Mississippi. Anglo-Americans traditionally had traveled the river freely but after 1782 Spain moved to interdict illegal trade and incursions into its northern territories. Americans responded with threats of war against their "natural and habitual enemy."[23] The dispute was settled by the Treaty of San Lorenzo in 1795 but bitterness and suspicion remained. Eleven years later, Thomas Jefferson surveyed the history of Anglo-American relations with Spain and concluded: "Never did a nation act towards another with more perfidy and injustice than Spain has constantly practiced against us."[24] To some extent, Jefferson's resentment was justified but it was also a product of a long tradition of hispanophobia. Like most of his compatriots, the great Virginian was more inclined to remember Spanish vices than Spanish virtues.

The political and military conflicts combine with the mass of literary evidence to reveal that prejudices against Catholics and Spaniards, transported to the New World at the end of the Elizabethan era, persisted among Anglo-Americans for two centuries without significant modification. The colonists believed the Roman Church to be corrupt and ostentatious, an institution that demanded blind allegiance and thus fostered ignorance and superstition. As for the Spaniards, they were the perfect adherents of Popery, cruel, treacherous, avaricious, and tyrannical, a people whose history was an extended intrigue. As Americans gazed southward with increasing interest, they saw yet another episode of that history unfolding and they could not but believe that the Mexicans had been blighted by their participation in it.

Concerning their impressions of the Mexican aborigines, the early English-American colonists had virtually nothing to say but such notions as they held were unquestionably those of their contemporary homebound compatriots. Although questions related to the character and culture of the Mexicans -- and of all the American Indians -- were not issues of pressing concern to 17th century Englishmen, information on these subjects had been accumulating since the 1550s. During that decade, Richard Eden, an obscure civil servant with a Cambridge education, tried to awaken his countrymen to the advantages of overseas exploration and settlement. Eden's method was to gather in two collections summaries of the early voyages of Columbus and Vespucci, portions of Peter Martyr's monumental chronicle of the New World, *De orbe novo*, and selections from the highly regarded histories of the Spaniards, Oviedo and Gómara.[25] Eden had one eye on the economic potential of distant lands, but the other on national glory; he earnestly believed that the conquest of the New World was an undertaking of such immense ambition and daring that no nation aspiring to greatness could risk exclusion from it. Unfortunately for Eden, his own ambitions for England were ahead of his time so that his works never achieved the desired impact. But they did alert later writers to the certain rewards of western travel.

In learning about Mexico and other regions of the New World, Englishmen were at a severe disadvantage when compared to citizens of other European countries. Continental interest in America had been mounting, not spectacularly but steadily, from the moment Columbus' celebrated letter on his first voyage to the Indies began circulating in 1493. Moreover, mainland Europeans were exposed not only to a selection of letters, histories, and narratives on American subjects but also to illustrations, New World artifacts, and an assortment of live aborigines kidnapped by travelers and delivered to Europe for public display.[26] Owing to an early series of unprofitable voyages to North America and a certain degree of cultural isolation, England had been virtually untouched by the first wave of continental interest in the New World.[27]

This situation began to change in 1577 when Richard Willes enlarged Eden's "Decades" to include, among other things, Martyr's account of the conquest of Mexico and published the volume as *The History of Travayle in the West and East Indies.* The following year, an English edition of Gómara's *Conquest of the Weast India* appeared, this too featuring a treatment of Cortés' destruction of the Aztec empire. The major breakthrough came in 1589 with the publication of Richard Hakluyt's *Principall Navigations,* a collection of travel narratives touching on English exploration. Hakluyt, as indicated earlier, was the greatest literary champion of English imperialism and as he urged his compatriots across the Atlantic, he described what to expect on the other side. The "Voyages" (as Hakluyt's work was generally known) was extremely popular and undoubtedly provided many Englishmen with their first glimpse of Mexico and other American regions. Samuel Purchas, Hakluyt's successor as literary imperialist and hispanophobe, issued two works, *Purchas his pilgrimage* (1613) and *Hakluytus Posthumus* (1625), which circulated widely and provided new information on Mexico. By the time their program of colonization was well underway, Englishmen had access to as much general information about Mexico as any people in Europe with the possible exception of the Spaniards.[28]

The image of Mexico that emerges from these works is marked by a distinctive cleavage characteristic of general European responses to the Mexicans. On the one hand, European writers expressed admiration for the relatively advanced civilization of the Mexicans as compared with other New World aborigines. The Mexicans generally eschewed nakedness -- a trait that most 16th and 17th century writers regarded as a certain sign of savagism -- and instead wore bright cotton garments. The Mexicans were gifted craftsmen and created exquisite pieces of jewelry from the plentiful supplies of gold, silver, and precious stones to be found in their country. A number of Spanish writers noted their astonishment upon approaching Mexican cities which were marvels of planning and architecture. Especially notable was Tenochtitlán, the capital city of the Aztecs which sat in a salt lake and supported more than half a million residents.[29] The conqueror Cortés was especially impressed by the numerous temples of the city, monuments, he wrote, that were built with perfect art.

Moreover, English readers learned that Mexican cities pulsed with a variety of civilized activities. The Mexicans had established a sound educational system and instructed their children affectionately in the virtues of humility and respect for authority. Using a distinctive system of pictographs, native scholars recorded the traditions of their people in books made from the leaves of the maguey plant. A number of Europeans noted that the Mexicans lived according to a body of laws while the learned Jesuit, José de Acosta, found that they selected their rulers through democratic elections.[30] Perhaps the most gratifying news about the Mexicans to reach English readers was their quick receptivity to Christian instruction. Pedro Ordoñez de Cevallos reported that the Mexicans "very much honored priests and monks" and "when the Bell rings to Sermon, the Indian Boyes run up and down the streets crossing their foreheads."[31]

As to other positive qualities of Mexican character, English readers learned that the natives were hospitable, courteous and understanding, possessed of an ingenuousness all but extinct among Europeans. Acosta observed a contemplative aspect in the Mexicans, while another Spaniard, Martin Pérez, applauded the Mexicans for their valor. The greatest champion of the Mexicans, as for all the Indians, was Las Casas, who particularly admired the aborigines of Yucatan for their prudence and the general "uprightness" of their lives.[32]

Las Casas' diligent, indeed obsessive, campaign notwithstanding, the preponderance of European and, consequently, English opinion weighed heavily against the Mexicans.[33] Virtually every writer declaimed on their indolence, while others reported that the Mexicans were given to drunkenness, polygamy, and incest. The

Mexicans were vilified for their hostility to the Spaniards and their refusal to acquiesce promptly in the moral and cultural superiority of their conquerors. Their rapid degeneration under colonial rule also adversely affected European judgments. Ultimately, the Mexicans were regarded as a depraved race whose defects were only slightly mitigated by the grandeur and opulence of their cultures. Acosta, whose history of the Indies evinces a combination of erudition and fair-mindedness remarkable for his time, nevertheless portrayed Mexican history as a grotesque interplay of tribal jealousies, warfare, and heathenism. Acosta sanctioned a widespread European belief when he observed that the Mexicans had developed "customs more superstitious and...inhumane" than any ever seen or spoken of.[34]

No European writer on Mexico failed to note the terrible forms that heathenism had assumed in that land. Witches, sorcerers, and other agents of Satan fairly overran the countryside and held the natives in thralldom. Believing that their deities lived on human blood, the Mexicans had devised elaborate rites of sacrifice. Sullen priests led children, virgins, and prisoners of war to altars where they ripped open the chests of their victims, removed the still-beating hearts, and smeared blood on the marble lips of their idols. The priests would next burn the entrails in the belief that their gods enjoyed the smoke from such offerings. Finally, the priests ate various parts of the victims' bodies, including the arms and legs.[35] English readers learned that human sacrifices in Mexico sometimes reached the astonishing total of fifty thousand a year.[36] López de Gómara, who was perhaps the harshest and most influential writer on Mexico in the 16th century,[37] seemed to find the perfect symbol of Mexican culture in the Great Temple of Tenochtitlán. As architecture, the structure was the equal of the finest buildings of Europe but the Mexicans created their greatest art in celebration of their implacable savagery. Inside the Temple, priests offered up their victims to insatiable gods. An unmistakable stench emanated from the sacrificial chambers where blood ran several inches deep on the floor and the walls were stained red. It was a spectacle to make so stout a warrior as Cortes -- who had his own genius for barbarism -- turn away in revulsion.

As a writer of history, Gómara possessed various qualities unlikely to enhance his objectivity. He was a sedentary scholar with no experience in the New World and a hero-worshiper who had served as private secretary to Cortés. As an ardent nationalist, he sought to justify the violence of the Conquest and the subsequent subjugation and exploitation of the natives. Finally, Gómara embodied all the defects of a Renaissance European absolutely certain of his cultural and moral superiority. Still, Gómara's assessments, and those of writers of similar persuasion, had their impact, and Europeans came to regard the Mexicans as the most depraved of American aborigines. How could one condone, after all, such uniquely massive and reprehensible practices of human sacrifice and cannibalism among a people obviously intelligent and creative? Human sacrifice occurred in other regions of the New World and, of course, cannibalism was rampant, but of all the Americans, the Mexicans should have known better. A European might more easily accept the pure savagery of the Brazilian Tupinambá who wore not so much as a fig leaf, mindlessly devoured their enemies, and displayed not a trace of civilization.

As I have said, English images of Mexico derived largely from general European notions, mainly Spanish. There was, to be sure, a small irony in Englishmen accepting rather uncritically the views of their greatest enemies. But Englishmen had little experience in Mexico themselves and they took information where they found it. A small number did travel and live in Mexico, however, and a few even wrote about their experiences. Some of these early reports were collected by Hakluyt; together they provide a somewhat different perspective on the Mexican situation from the Spanish.

These early accounts form a tissue of fantasy, distortion, and occasionally acute observation. Some of the visitors emphasized the physical greatness of Mexico while others were most immediately struck by its sheer strangeness. Henry Hawks, a merchant who spent five years in Mexico, described the recurrent earthquakes, the "burning mountains," and the remarkable fauna. He wrote of a "certain gnat or fly which they call a musquito, which biteth both men and women in their sleep" and caused death. He reported too the existence of a "monstrous fish" -- presumably a crocodile

-- which was a "great devourer of men and cattle."[38] Other travelers insisted that lions and tigers roamed the forests of Mexico. Here was a land where anything seemed possible.

As the travelers made clear, the inherent exoticism of Mexico was conspicuous in the natives. John Chilton, another merchant with over seventeen years experience in Spanish America, observed that the Mexican aborigines went about naked, painted their bodies blue, and wore their hair "long downe to their knees, tied as women use to do with their haire-laces."[39] Miles Philips, a survivor of the Hawkins debacle at San Juan de Ulúa in 1568, confirmed Chilton's description, only adding that the Mexicans painted their faces green, yellow, and red as well as blue. The Mexicans seemed, all in all, a sight terrible to behold. Interestingly, Hakluyt's travelers had little to say about the Mexican customs of devil worship, human sacrifice, and cannibalism, all of which were already disappearing under the cruel efficiency of Spanish colonialism.

As to the character of the natives, the English travelers had little good to report. Miles Philips came to regard the aborigines as pleasant and compassionate, but none of his compatriots shared his affection. More typical was the reaction of Henry Hawks who described the Indians as "void of all goodness." More than one writer found the Mexicans to be cowardly and drunken. John Chilton observed that for a bottle of wine, an Indian would sell his wife and children. But the most persistent charge against the Mexicans was indolence. English travelers were appalled that the natives had so little exploited their land. In noting the great fertility of the area around Mexico City, Robert Tomson commented "that if Christians had the inhabitation thereof, it would be put to a further benefit."[40] It was not much of a step to conclude that because the Indians had so little utilized their land they hardly deserved to keep it, a principle that later generations of Englishmen and Anglo-Americans would invoke frequently.

The English travelers, writing in an age of rising hispanophobia, were quick to note that Spanish conduct was as reprehensible in the New World as the Old. Tomson, for example, described how he was slapped into a Mexican prison on false charges of heresy and released only after numerous humiliations. Miles Philips and Job Hortop, whose unintended sojourns in Mexico were caused by Spanish "treachery," found themselves subjected to the outrages of the Inquisition tribunals which had been established in Mexico in 1571. Still, Philips and Hortop at least survived their ordeals in the grip of the Holy Office, as other marooned veterans of the Hawkins expedition did not.[41] Philips and Hortop also fared better than the native Mexicans who, by English estimates, had been reduced to absolute misery. Significantly, the English writers never had much praise and sympathy for the Indians but when they compared them to the Spaniards.

Indeed, the Indians had been so terribly abused that insurrection hung in the Mexican air and hardly an English traveler failed to catch its scent. Henry Hawks, in a rare instance of understatement, remarked that the aborigines "loved not the Spaniards" but he doubted that their courage and military prowess matched their resentment. John Chilton, who witnessed two rebellions during his stay in Mexico, noted that the Indians killed their conquerors at every opportunity and liked to wear Spanish scalps around their necks. The travelers went so far as to suggest that the Indians would welcome any interventionists who delivered them from their oppressors. This sort of oblique propaganda appears throughout the "Voyages" and served Hakluyt's great purpose of arousing his countrymen to challenge the Spaniards' domination of the New World. In support of this goal, Hakluyt graciously provided information about defense fortifications throughout Spanish America.

Hakluyt's "Voyages" was very popular in England but the collections of Samuel Purchas were even more so. Purchas' major work, Hakluytus Posthumus (generally known as the "Pilgrimes"), considerably advanced English knowledge of Mexico. The long excerpts from Acosta's Natural and Moral History of the Indies, for example, provided Englishmen with their first close look at pre-colonial Mexican society. Again, the exoticism of the Mexicans stands out. Acosta described how native priests beat themselves and slashed their legs to the bone in heathen rites of penitence, smearing blood on their faces and temples. Englishmen learned that the gods of Mexico were half man and half beast with bizarre names like Quetzalcóatl and Vitzliputzli. In the original edition of his "History," Acosta had maintained that the Mexicans -- and all the Indians -- were descended originally from unknown Old World peoples who had wandered to America across an as yet undiscovered strait or land bridge.[42] But English readers of his work were unlikely to detect any trace of blood-ties between the Mexicans and themselves. As always, the Mexicans seemed an alien and degenerate race whose very humanity was an issue much in doubt.

Certainly the most dramatic treatment of Mexican subjects to appear in the "Pilgrimes" was the partial reproduction of the Codex Mendoza, the first example of Mexican picture writing to be published in England.[43] It provided no important new information but it vividly illustrated various aspects of Mexican history and culture. The Codex depicted such mundane matters as parents instructing and disciplining their children but also represented various aspects of native warfare, including the disembodied heads of slain warriors. The human figures in the Codex were drawn in a primitive style and were distinguished by the almost formless faces, at once aloof and inscrutable.[44]

Purchas presented various other accounts of Mexican life including brief narratives by Cabeza de Vaca, Martín Perez, and Pedro Ordoñez de Cevallos and longer excerpts from Gómara, Oviedo, and Las Casas.[45] The first group of reports, although minor, are interesting inasmuch as they reveal 16th-century Europeans vacillating in their assessments of the Mexicans and finally settling into a bewildered contempt. Although many English readers were already familiar with the major writers represented in the "Pilgrimes," their response to Las Casas deserves a further comment here. As we have seen Englishmen eagerly accepted his testimony regarding Spanish atrocities in the New World, largely because it confirmed their prejudices and suited their purposes. But the friar's equally adamant defense of the Mexicans and other Indians fell on deaf ears because it did neither. Purchas himself, although an admirer of Las Casas, was inclined to emphasize not Mexican virtues but their "Man-eatings, Sodomies, Idolatries and other vices."

Within a span of three-quarters of a century, English translators, scholars, and propagandists had presented to their countrymen a substantial body of literature on Mexican subjects. The images that emerged from these works were not distinctively English but belonged to a broader European tradition. In any case, they did little to enhance appreciation of the Mexicans, grounded as they were in distortion, fantasy, and simple confusion.[46] As Europeans passed through Mexico, they carried ideological equipment which essentially precluded true understanding of the natives. The Aristotelian perspective of many Spanish writers, for example, required that the Mexicans exhibit recognizable systems of laws and social organization lest they be deemed savages. Their classical training also led a number of Spaniards to conclude that the stout aborigines were created for hard labor, which is to say to be slaves. English and Spanish writers alike were handicapped in their evaluations of Mexicans by the prevailing European fashion of travel reporting. Travelers and scholars had long insisted upon the exoticism and inherent inferiority of foreign societies, the rule of thumb being the more distant the people, the more striking these qualities. The benighted state of European ethnology in this period was exemplified by the enduring popularity of the "Travels" of Sir John Mandeville (which Hakluyt extracted in the first edition of the "Voyages" but judiciously omitted in the second), a preposterous chronicle of races of giants and headless people with eyes in their chests. Many of the Mexican narratives, with reports of strange beasts and natural wonders, bear traces of the Mandeville legacy. When European writers were not declaiming on the strangeness and barbarism of Mexico, they occupied themselves by trying to force the natives into conventional contexts of understanding and belief. Thus we see that the descriptions of the Chichimeca tribe manifest a strong resemblance to the *wilder Mann* of medieval thought. We note too the powerful influence of Biblical authority which maintained that all men, no matter how depraved, were receptive to Christianity; as a consequence, Europeans dutifully reported -- sometimes against their better judgment - the Mexicans to be so. Unable to deal with the Mexicans on their own terms and surveying the Americas in a haze of ethnocentrism, European writers in effect "invented" a species compatible with their traditions of savagism.[47]

The evidence regarding early colonial images of the Mexicans is primarily inferential. As indicated earlier, the collections of Hakluyt and Purchas were well-known to many colonists, perhaps even a majority. Probably the same percentage was acquainted with Thomas Gage's *The English-American*, the first book-length treatment of America by an English eyewitness and a work which managed to excoriate simultaneously the Spanish conquerors, the Catholic missionaries, and the hapless aborigines of Mexico and Guatemala. Gage added nothing new to available knowledge about Mexico except his pervasive malice but his work was quite popular in England and the colonies nonetheless.[48] Las Casas was also known to many colonists while the works of other major Spanish historians, notably Acosta, were read by a few intellectuals. Two other considerations should be borne in mind here. As a group, the colonists -- particularly the New Englanders -- were unusually well educated and alert to intellectual fashions in England and on the Continent. Secondly, given their powerful hatred of Catholicism and Spain, they were unlikely to disregard completely so important an area of activity for their enemies. It seems reasonable to conclude, therefore, that the early settlers held images of the Mexicans such as were circulating in contemporary England. Unquestionably, these images were not so clear, widespread, or fixed as those of Catholics and Spaniards, but still they lived in the minds of the colonists and grew more vigorous as time passed.

The first signs of active colonial interest in Mexico emerge near the end of the 17th century in the papers of Samuel Sewall, a devout Puritan whose commercial interests were pushing him subtly towards secularism; not surprisingly, Sewall's interest in Mexico was partly religious, partly economic. His earliest mention of Mexico occurred in a telling diary entry for September 26, 1686. That day, Sewall had attended a sermon during which the preacher, a Mr. Lee, "said that all America should be converted, Mexico overcome, England sent over to convert the Natives, look you do it."[49] Sewall took the charge seriously, read Las Casas and Gage, and came to imagine that he had located the New Jerusalem in Mexico City. He listened to every report of revolt in Mexico in the hope that the aborigines would overthrow the Spaniards and thus leave the way clear for his intended pilgrimage. But such reports were invariably "shams"[50] and Sewall decided to move matters along himself. In 1704, he urged Henry Newman to "set on foot the printing of the Spanish Bible in a fair Octavo; Ten Thousand Copies: and then you might attempt the Bombing of Santo Domingo, the Havana, Porto Rico, and Mexico itself."[51] Sewall's grandiose, if foredoomed, scheme apparently had the support of other New Englanders including Cotton Mather, who set about learning Spanish when he too received word of revolution in Mexico.[52]

Sewall's recurrent disappointments never dissuaded him from his interest. He pounced upon any tidbit of information about Mexico and wrote letters asking about such matters as the tides on the lake surrounding Mexico City. As a merchant, Sewall was dazzled by the reputed wealth of Mexico and the possibility of trade. He wrote of the "magnificence" of the capital city in which were found "1500 Coaches drawn with Mules." Sewall prayed long hours for Mexico and beseeched God to "open the Mexican Fountain."[53] Clearly, his words carried a double meaning. After the banishment of the Spaniards, Sewall expected that indigenous regimes would be receptive not only to Protestantism but to English-American traders.

Sewall's excited pursuit after news from Mexico suggests some of the difficulties any colonist interested in the subject would encounter. For the dearth of colonial writing on Mexico was not so much a function of indifference as of the sheer inaccessibility of such information. Although by 1700 colonists had established trade relations -- mostly illegal -- with various Spanish-American regions,[54] Mexico remained almost impenetrable. Spain regarded Mexico as the jewel of its colonial empire and guarded it assiduously against foreign economic exploitation -- a task simplified by the concentration of shipping in the single port of Veracruz -- until the moment of independence in 1821. Furthermore, overland travel from the English colonies to Mexico was impracticable because of great distances, rugged terrain, and hostile Indians. When colonists managed to elude Spanish defenses, as they did in the early 18th century on log-cutting expeditions to Yucatan and later on trading sorties into Texas, their business was conducted quietly and quickly.[55] Such incursions were not likely to stimulate studious treatments of Mexican life. In any event, because their ventures were both illegal and profitable, traders were disinclined to publicize them for fear of Spanish reprisals and intensified competition.

With the advent of local newspapers, word of contemporary Mexican affairs began to circulate more actively among the colonists. Mostly, it treated mundane issues and shed little light on the Mexicans themselves. Reports of native insurrection, widespread among Englishmen since the initial publication of Hakluyt's "Voyages," appeared occasionally, and if Sewall's and Mather's enthusiasm is any indication, were followed closely. *The Boston News-Letter*, the earliest established newspaper in the colonies, published this item in its second issue of April 24, 1704: "There was an Indian come from the Mainland of New Spain, complaining to the Governour of Jamaica, of bad usage they had met with from the Spainards [sic] and if His Excellency would send Forces, that the Indians would joyn them, and destroy the Spainards."[56] Colonists read that the Jesuits, living up to their reputation for mischief, also fomented revolt. Other types of reports, generally of a commercial nature, appeared in colonial newspapers. *The Boston News-Letter*, which advocated the opening of trade with Mexico as early as 1704, published lists of Mexican exports and noted the exchange value of Mexican currency. Needless to say, the Mexican gold and silver mines aroused great curiosity among Anglo-Americans and colonial newspapers regularly noted the immense quantities of these minerals being loaded in Veracruz for shipment to Spain. Where there was Spanish treasure there also were English pirates ready to pounce. Colonial newspapers reported on such activity with thinly-disguised approval.[57]

Although commercial news predominated, colonial newspapers provided other types of information about Mexico. They told of earthquakes and plagues in the country and changes in the governmental hierarchy. Around the middle of the 18th century, several newspapers carried articles speculating on the origins of the Mexicans. A piece in *The New York Weekly Post-Boy* argued that the Mexicans had descended from ancient Chinese or Japanese voyagers.[58]　In 1740, *The Boston News-Letter* printed an article entitled "The CROWN of England's Title to America prior to that of Spain..." which resurrected the Elizabethan legend of Madoc ap Owen, a Welsh prince who allegedly planted a settlement in Mexico in the 12th century.[59] The story was sheer fantasy but its publication in a major New England newspaper indicates the intensity with which the colonists sought to wrench away from the Spaniards a portion of Mexican and southern American riches.[60]

The significance of these newspaper accounts is three-fold. First, the willingness of newspapers to publish Mexican items, no matter how trivial, inaccurate, or fanciful, suggests a considerable curiosity among colonists about the country. Secondly, the nature of the reports reflects the abiding Anglo-American interest in the economic exploitation of Mexico. Figures such as Sewall and Mather may have been motivated to learn about Mexico primarily for religious reasons, but other settlers had a different priority; in any case, colonial concern for the salvation of the aborigines seems to have receded quickly. Finally, and most importantly, the information received by the colonists contained nothing to challenge traditional images of Mexico as established by Spanish and English writers in the Elizabethan and Jacobean ages.

Actually, traditional images of Mexico underwent a period of revitalization after the mid-18th century. In 1758, for example, *The English American* by Thomas Gage re-emerged not once but twice. Samuel Nevill, a notorious imperialist and hispanophobe, serialized the work in his *New American Magazine* while James Parker issued the first American edition of Gage's diatribe. Both reproductions appeared under the title "The Traveller" and they not only stirred up sentiment against the Spaniards[61] but vivified colonial images of Mexican depravity. Colonists read of Montezuma's harem of one thousand concubines, and his menagerie of crocodiles and great snakes nourished on human flesh and blood. Gage described the superstition of Mexico City as the greatest in the world, exceeding even that of Rome. And, of course, there was mention of the aboriginal rites of human sacrifice. Gage told how Aztec priests concocted a paste out of seeds and children's blood to be used in their ceremonies. Colonists learned that around the Great Temple of Tenochtitlán were displayed the skulls of sacrificial victims, Gage estimating the total at 136,000.[62] Under Spanish rule, the Mexicans had improved not at all but regressed, retaining many of their old vices and absorbing some from the Spaniards as well. Gage argued that the Professed conversion of the Indians was mere pretense to placate their masters. Away from Spanish eyes, the Mexicans practiced devil worship and witchcraft.

Over the next generation, other conventional treatments of Mexican character and culture came into Anglo-American hands, notably *The History of the Conquest of Mexico* by Antonio de Solís who relied heavily on the accounts of Cortés and Gómara and thus inevitably disparaged the Indians.[63] The travel collection of John Harris and Edmund Burke's *Account of the European Settlements in America* were other representative works found on colonial booklists which treated the Mexicans with varying degrees of antipathy.[64]

By all odds, the most important study of Mexico to reach English Americans in the 18th century was William Robertson's *History of America*. This work, originally issued in London in 1777, remains with William Prescott's books the classic treatment of the Spanish Conquest in the English language. The "History" made an immediate impact in Britain and was soon transported to the United States where its influence was enormous.

Robertson gracefully recounted an historical episode which he regarded as one of the greatest of human adventures. He chronicled the exploits of the heroic Columbus, the ambitious Cortés, and the villainous Pizarro, all the while condemning what he perceived as the tragic flaw of Spanish character, an avarice so boundless that it compelled the conquerors to an unprecedented succession of outrages. Robertson allowed that the Conquest was effected for the most part by the dregs of Spanish society, an army of scoundrels all but banished from their homeland, and he warned about drawing unfair inferences about Spanish character from their actions. But Robertson's qualifications were unconvincing and the reported barbarism of the Conquerors spoke for itself. In any event, Robertson's low estimate of the American performance of the Spaniards was no surprise, coming as it did from a Scottish Presbyterian and a licensed minister at that. More interesting, and ultimately of greater importance, were Robertson's comments on the Mexican aborigines.

Robertson moved to his assessment of the Mexicans from a broader consideration of the character of the New World aborigines. Writing in an age when the idea of the noble savage had gained wide currency, he vigorously rejected the concept.[65] He found nothing in his researches to conclude that the Americans were innocent and generous, a race that had luxuriated in a western paradise before the intrusion of the Spaniards. Instead, Robertson argued that their pre-Columbian way of life was less an example of dignified repose than a case of extraordinary indolence. A strict environmentalist influenced by Buffon and de Pauw, Robertson believed man was particularly affected by climate. All the great peoples and cultures, he noted, were found in the temperate zones; other factors being equal, the closer one lived to the equator, the less likely the possibility of human development. Thus, Robertson described the North American Indians as being "more robust, more active, more intelligent and more courageous" than those in the southern regions where the sultry climate had stifled the native molecules into a perpetual lethargy.[66] But such praise as he offered the northern aborigines was only relative; as a group, the Americans were brutal, treacherous, and cruel: in a word, "savages" without any mitigating adjectives. They were given to drunkenness and cannibalism and the only activity likely to shake them from their indolence was war. In sum, the Americans exhibited few of the traits that distinguish man from beast.[67]

Robertson's aborigines were not only defective morally and intellectually but physically. The Americans lacked robustness and sexual desire and were decimated by the ordinary diseases of the Old World. Here again, the Americans were victimized by the environment. Because of the constant heat, the Americans could not summon the energy to cultivate the land. This in turn caused the air to stagnate, the water to give off "putrid exhalations" and the land to be full of "noxious maladies." The climate of America was consequently "remarkably unhealthy" and the "principle of life" necessarily "less active and vigorous than in the ancient continent."[68]

While Robertson characterized the Americans as altogether a bad lot, some were worse than others and the supreme villains, by any measure, were the Mexicans. Unlike earlier writers such as Acosta, Robertson did not soften his denunciations with concessions to the cultural achievements of the Mexicans. He argued instead that their institutions "did not differ greatly from those of other inhabitants of America." They fought incessantly, were vengeful, and never learned to temper their rage, a certain sign of savagism. Robertson concluded that "we cannot but suspect their degree of civilization to have been very imperfect."[69]

What did distinguish the Mexicans was their sophisticated religious system which contrasted with the primitive rituals of other Indians. But it was sophisticated essentially in its capacity for a brutality and sordidness which shaped the very character of the Mexican natives:

> From the genius of the Mexican religion we may...form a most just conclusion with respect to its influence upon the character of the people. The aspect of superstition in Mexico was gloomy and atrocious. Its divinities were clothed with terror, and delighted in vengeance. They were exhibited to the people under detestable forms, which created horror. The figures of serpents, of tigers, and of other destructive animals, decorated their temples. Fear was the only principle that inspired their votaries. Fasts, mortifications, and penances, all rigid, and many of them excruciating to an extreme degree, were the means employed to appease the wrath of their gods, and the Mexicans never approached their altars without sprinkling them with blood drawn from their own bodies. But, of all offerings, human sacrifices were deemed the most acceptable. This religious belief mingling with the implacable spirit of vengeance, and adding new force to it, every captive taken in war was brought to the temple, was

devoted as a victim to the deity, and sacrificed with rites no less solemn than cruel. The heart and head were the portion consecrated to the gods; the warrior by whose prowess the prisoner had been seized, carried off the body to feast upon it with his friends. Under the impression of ideas so dreary and terrible, and accustomed daily to scenes of bloodshed rendered awful by religion, the heart of man must harden and be steeled to every sentiment of humanity. The spirit of the Mexicans was accordingly unfeeling; and the genius of their religion so far counterbalanced the influence of policy and arts, that notwithstanding their progress in both, their manners, instead of softening, became more fierce. To what circumstances it was owing that superstition assumed such a dreadful form among the Mexicans, we have not sufficient knowledge of their history to determine. But its influence is visible, and produced an effect that is singular in the history of the human species. The manners of the people in the New World, who had made the greatest progress in the arts of policy, were, in several respects, the most ferocious, and the barbarity of some of their customs exceeded even those of the savage state.[70]

Later in his study, Robertson compares the other great civilization of the Americas, the Incan, to the Mexican. In nearly every respect the Incas are described as more civilized and more humane. Particularly in that notable American institution, the art of war, the Peruvians were less barbarous: "the wars in which the Incas engaged were carried on with a spirit very different from that of other American nations. They fought not, like savages, to destroy and exterminate; or, like the Mexicans, to glut blood thirsty divinities with human sacrifices. They conquered in order to reclaim and civilize the vanquished, and to diffuse the knowledge of their own institutions and arts."[71]

Ultimately, Robertson presented an extremely gloomy assessment of the Mexicans, greatly underestimating their cultural achievements while exaggerating the uniqueness of their barbarism.[72] In his mind, the Mexicans stood as the fiercest and most detestable of the New World peoples, inferior culturally to the Incas and in qualities of character to the North American natives.[73] By also arguing that the Spaniards who were attracted to America were the most undesirable elements of their society, Robertson offered to his readers a Mexico populated by two extraordinary breeds of scoundrels already mixing their bloods.[74] In an era when revolutionary movements in Latin America were at last beginning to gather real support, Robertson's Mexico seemed an unlikely setting for the flourishing of humane, republican institutions. To those readers acquainted with traditional portraits of Mexican life, Robertson's depictions were all too familiar; his claims of objectivity and originality notwithstanding, he essentially took old images and couched them in a variety of 18th-century scientism.

The History of America had its critics of course, both in Europe and in America. Francisco Clavigero, another historian of Mexico but one with broad experience in the country, attacked Robertson for his biases and his imperfect use of available sources.[75] Thomas Jefferson, who disagreed not with his depictions of the southern aborigines but with his generalizations about the American environment, rebuked Robertson for his slavish reliance on Buffon and de Pauw. Still, the "History" withstood such attacks and remained the most popular and influential study in its field until the publication of Prescott's *Conquest of Mexico* in 1843. It was serialized in numerous American journals and sold briskly in several editions, including a paperback. Prescott himself called Robertson "the illustrious historian of America" and prominent writers such as Joel Barlow, Washington Irving, and William Gilmore Simms came under Scot's influence. Indeed, Frederick Stimson wrote that for early American writers both historical and fictional, Robertson "seems to have been the chief source for all things pertaining to the Spanish in the New World."[76] Confirming traditional prejudices and vague premonitions, *The History of America* found a broad readership in the young republic.

The popularity of Robertson's "History" served to bring into play the final component necessary to form an ideological prism through which Americans would view contemporary Mexicans in the 19th century. As we have seen, anti-Catholicism and hispanophobia were clearly defined and pervasive in Anglo-American culture long before 1777; more than any previous event or literary work, *The History of America* helped to codify and disseminate anti-Mexican sentiment and raise it to a more nearly equal level of importance. These various antipathies eventually linked and merged as Americans came to recognize the phenomenon of cultural and racial fusion between Indian and Spaniard which had been proceeding since the Conquest.

When Americans began actually to encounter Mexicans in Texas, Santa Fe, and other Mexican territories after 1821, their initial responses were conditioned primarily by the traditions of hispanophobia and anti-Catholicism. Many American travelers in Mexico called the natives "Spaniards" and assigned to them, almost reflexively, the familiar defects of the Black Legend.[77] Josiah Gregg, a trader on the Santa Fe Trail, observed that the New Mexicans "appear to have inherited much of the cruelty and intolerance of their ancestors and no small portion of their bigotry and fanaticism."[78] Other travelers called the Mexicans "priest-ridden." Richard Henry Dana, a visitor to California, attributed Mexican indolence to their Catholicism which subordinated work to the celebration of an interminable series of religious holidays. The primacy of hispanophobia and anti-Catholicism in early American treatments of the Mexicans was partly the result of their sheer tenacity in the national consciousness but it was also a function of the traditional European belief that advanced cultures (which is to say their own) invariably overwhelmed primitive ones. Robertson lent support to this view when he contrasted the awesome hegemony of the Spaniards with the languid acquiescence of the Mexicans.

About 1840, racialist thought emerged to focus attention on the "inherent" characteristics of the Mexicans rather than those acquired during their long subjugation to the Catholic Spaniards. Here again, we note a natural line of development and the force of traditional images. The core of Anglo-American notions about the Mexicans had always been an assumed depravity and certainly the racialists retained this idea. It is striking how closely their depictions of contemporary Mexicans resemble Robertson's portrayal of pre-Conquest aborigines: there is the same indolence, duplicity, melancholy, violence, and cruelty. I am not suggesting that racialists generally bore the direct influence of Robertson but that his views of the Mexicans represent a traditional mode of perceiving them that persisted into the mid-19th century with only slight modifications. To be sure, racialists discarded Robertson's environmentalism as an insufficient explanation of human differences just as he had rejected earlier concepts of savagism. But his fundamental assumptions about Mexican character, some of which are traceable to Gómara, endured.

Of all racialist theories, the doctrine of miscegenation, which held that the progeny of racially-different parents inherited the worst qualities of each, had the greatest impact on American views of Mexicans. Racialists regarded mixed-breeds as impulsive, unstable, and prone to insanity.[79] The Mexicans, as the most conspicuous products of mass miscegenation, inevitably were assigned these qualities. Still, we recall that Gage had attributed part of the aborigines' decline to their intermarriage with the Spaniards and Robertson had noted that the Mexicans were given to sudden springs of violence. Moreover, in its emphasis on the vices of the Mexicans' progenitors, the doctrine of miscegenation led back to hispanophobia. Other 19th-century responses to Mexicans reveal the same process: old images received new justifications and lived on. Some are with us still.

Notes

1. I am grateful to the American Council of Learned Societies for a research grant during 1976-77 which allowed me to complete this study.

2. Culture Conflict in Texas, 1821-1835 (New York: Columbia University Press, 1932).

3. Mexico and the Hispanic Southwest in American Literature, 2nd ed. (Tucson: University of Arizona Press, 1977), pp. 17-18. A longer but still incomplete view of anti-Mexican sentiment in the United States is presented in Karl M. Schmitt, Mexico and the United States, 1821-1973 (New York: John Wiley & Sons, 1974). pp. 11-31.

4. The literature on anti-Catholic attitudes in England is voluminous but particularly useful to this study are Sister Mary Augustina (Ray), American Opinion of Roman Catholicism in the Eighteenth Century (New York: Columbia University Press, 1936), pp. 11-35; Arnold O. Meyer, England and the Catholic Church under Queen Elizabeth (London: Paul, Trench, Trubner, 1916); and William Haller, Foxe's Book of Martyrs and the Elect Nation (London: Cape, 1963).

5. See a condensation of the "Apologia" by William of Orange in Charles Gibson, ed., The Black Legend: Anti-Spanish Attitudes in the Old World and New (New York: Alfred A. Knopf, 1971), pp. 42-47.

6. The term "Black Legend" refers to a system of beliefs which holds that Spaniards are uniquely depraved. For a more extensive discussion of this phenomenon see William S. Maltby, The Black Legend in England (Durham, N. C.: Duke University Press, 1971); and Philip Wayne Powell, Tree of Hate (New York: Basic Books. 1971).

7. See Winthrop Jordan, White Over Black (Chapel Hill: University of North Carolina Press, 1968), pp. 3-43 for a thorough treatment of this phenomenon.

8. Ibid., p. 5. See also Robert R. Cawley, The Voyagers and Elizabethan Drama (Boston: D. C. Heath, 1938), p. 31 and Marvin A. Breslow, A Mirror of England: English Puritan Views of Foreign Nations, 1618-1640 (Cambridge: Harvard University Press. 1970). p. 73.

9. Louis B. Wright commented that "no one can calculate the enormous influence of Foxe's descriptions of persecutions by Catholics in keeping alive hatred of Romanism in the breasts of American Protestants." See his The Cultural Life of the American Colonies, 1607-1763 (New York: Harper & Row, 1957), p. 133.

10. See Thomas G. Wright, Literary Culture in Early New England, 1620-1730 (New Haven: Yale University Press, 1920) and C. A. Herrick, "The Early New Englanders: What Did They Read?," The Library, 3rd series, 9, No. 33 (1918), 1-17.

11. Of Plymouth Plantation, ed. Samuel E. Morison (New York: Knopf,

1952), p. 380.

12. *The Powring Out of the Seven Vials: or, An Exposition of the Sixteenth Chapter of the Revelation, With an Application of It to Our Times* (London: n.p., 1645), p. 44.

13. "The Song of Deliverance" in *Handkerchiefs from Paul,* ed. Kenneth B. Murdock (Cambridge: Harvard University Press, 1921), p. 32.

14. See Paul L. Ford. The New England Primer (New York: Dodd, Mead, 1897), pp. 45, 90, 247-48.

15. Quoted in Ray Allen Billington, *The Protestant Crusade, 1800-1860* (1938; reprinted, Chicago: Quadrangle Books. 1964). p. 16.

16. There are several excellent studies of early American attitudes toward Catholicism and Spain. In addition to Billington and the Sister Augustina study cited earlier, see Arthur J. Riley, Catholicism in New England to 1788 (Washington, D.C.: Catholic University of America, 1936) and Stanley T. Williams, The Spanish Background of American Literature (New Haven: Yale University Press, 1955), I, 3-20.

17. See Augustina, pp. 212-61, Billington, pp. 4-19, and Riley, pp. 217-60.

18. Quoted in Billington, p. 6.

19. Harry Bernstein, Origins of Inter-American Interest, 1700-1812 (Philadelphia: University of Pennsylvania Press, 1945), p. 2. See also Charles M. Andrews, The Colonial Period of American History (New Haven: Yale University Press, 1934), 111, 6-34.

20. For examples of hispanophobic documents from the Southern colonies, see Alexander S. Salley, ed., Narratives of Early Carolina, 1650-1708 (New York: Charles Scribner's, 1911), pp. 185-86, 204-09, and Alexander Brown, The Genesis of the United States, 2 vols. (New York: Houghton-Mifflin. 1890), passim.

21. Charles W. Arnade, The Siege of St. Augustine in 1702 (Gainesville: University of Florida Press, 1959).

22. J. Leitch Wright, Anglo-Spanish Rivalry in North America (Athens: University of Georgia Press, 1971), p. 87.

23. See G. L. Rives, "Spain and the United States in 1795," American Historical Review, 4 (1898), 62-79; for other treatments of American-Spanish problems in the period, see Arthur P. Whitaker, The Spanish-American Frontier: 1783-1795 (Boston: Houghton-Mifflin, 1927) and Whitaker, The Mississippi Question, 1795-1803 (New York: Appleton, 1934).

24. The Writings of Thomas Jefferson, ed. H. A. Washington (New York: Riker, 1857). V, 64.

25. Eden's major works, A treatyse of the newe India (1553) and the Decades of the newe worlde (1555) are reprinted in The First Three English Books on America, ed. Edward Arber (Birmingham: Turnbull & Spears, 1885).

26. See Hugh Honour's marvelous study, profusely illustrated, The New

Golden Land (New York: Pantheon, 1975), esp. pp. 3-83.

27. See David Beers Quinn, England and the Discovery of America, 1481-1620 (New York: Alfred A. Knopf. 1974). passim.

28. There are several useful studies of English responses to America during the period under consideration: Franklin T. McCann, English Discovery of America to 1585 (New York: King's Crown Press, 1952); John Parker, Books to Build an Empire (Amsterdam: N. Israel, 1965); and Colin Steele, English Interpreters of the New World from Purchas to Stevens (Oxford: Dolphin Books, 1975). A bibliography of books related to the New World published in England to 1600 may be found in George B. Parks, Richard Hakluyt and the English Voyages, 2nd ed. (1928; reprinted, New York: Ungar. 1961), pp. 270-76.

29. See Eden, "Decades," p. 342. Here, Tenochtitlán is called "Temixtitan."

30. José de Acosta, The Natural and Moral History of the Indies, ed. Clements R. Markham (1604; reprinted, London: Hakluyt Society, 1880), II, 411. The impact of the 1604 English edition of Acosta's monumental study was greatly enhanced by Purchas who extracted long sections in Hakluytus Posthumus.

31. "Notes of the West Indies," in Hakluytus Posthumus, or Purchas His Pilgrimes (Glasgow: MacLehose, 1906), XVII, 213.

32. "A briefe Narration of the destruction of the Indies by the Spaniards," in Purchas, XVIII, 120.

33. Howard Mumford Jones treats in admirable fashion the ambiguity of general European images of the Americans in A Strange New World (New York: Viking, 1964), pp. 1-70.

34. "Mexican Antiquities," in Purchas, XV, 240.

35. See Eden, "Decades," p. 189.

36. Francisco López de Gómara, The Conquest of the Weast India (1578; reprinted, New York: Scholars' Facsimiles & Reprints, 1940), p. 110.

37. See Benjamin Keen, The Aztec Image in Western Thought (New Brunswick, N.J.: Rutgers University Press, 1971), pp. 49-172, for a broad treatment of European attitudes towards the Mexicans in this period.

38. See Hawks, "A relation of the commodities of Nova Hispania," in Hakluyt, Principall Navigations (Glasgow: MacLehose, 1904), IX, 378-97. This modern publication of Hakluyt's work is based on the second edition which began appearing in 1598. The later edition dropped a narrative by a traveler in Mexico, David Ingram. This holds no importance for the present study because Ingram's report contains virtually no information on Mexico

39. "A notable discourse of M. John Chilton..." in Hakluyt, IX, 371.

40. "The voyage of Robert Tomson Marchant..." in Hakluyt, IX, 357.

41. At least two of the Hawkins party were burned at the stake and many others—of over a hundred put ashore—were punished for heresy. See Richard Greenleaf, The Mexican Inquisition in the Sixteenth Century (Albuquerque:

University of New Mexico Press, 1969), pp. 163-67.

42. The origins of the Mexicans and other New World aborigines became a subject of considerable debate among European intellectuals and theologians soon after the Discoveries. Generally speaking, Europeans, like Acosta, sought to develop theories consistent with the biblical doctrine of monogenesis. Oviedo speculated that Americans were descended either from Carthagenians or ancient Spaniards; Las Casas argued for an East Indies origin. Gómara offered the mythical continent of Atlantis as the homeland of the Americans. Ever the nationalists, Hakluyt and Purchas both published the whimsical legend of Madoc ap Owen, a Welsh prince who allegedly planted an American colony about A.D. 1170. See Lee Huddleston, Origins of the American Indians: European Concepts, 1492-1729 (Austin: University of Texas Press. 1967).

43. Steele, p. 43.

44. The portions of the Codex are presented in Purchas, XV, 412-504. For a look at the way sixteenth-century European artists depicted the Mexicans, see Honour, pp. 59-62.

45. For a survey of Mexican materials in the "Pilgrimes," see Steele, pp. 40-49.

46. The following remarks draw heavily from these works: J. H. Elliott, The Old World and the New, 1492-1650 (Cambridge, Eng.: Cambridge University Press, 1970), pp. 1-53; Margaret Hodgen, Early Anthropology in the Sixteenth and Seventeenth Centuries (Philadelphia: University of Pennsylvania Press, 1964); and John H. Rowe, "Ethnography and Ethnology in the Sixteenth Century," Kroeber Anthropological Society Papers, 30 (1964), 1-19.

47. See Edmundo O. Gorman, The Invention of America (Bloomington: Indiana University Press, 1961).

48. In discussing the Spanish Conquest of Mexico, Gage plagiarized long passages from Gómara. See J. Eric S. Thompson's introduction to Gage's work in Thomas Gage's Travels in the New World (Norman: University of Oklahoma Press, 1958), xix.

49. The Diary of Samuel Sewall, ed. M. Halsey Thomas (New York: Farrar, Straus, Giroux. 1973). I, 122.

50. Ibid., pp. 397-98.

51. "Letter-Book of Samuel Sewall," Collections of the Massachusetts Historical Society, 6th series, 1 (1886), 297.

52. See "Diary of Cotton Mather, 1681-1708," Massachusetts Historical Society Collections, 7th series, 7 (1911), 284. Mather eventually published a Protestant pamphlet in Spanish, "La Fe del Christiano."

53. "Diary," I, 462. For further discussion of Sewall's interest in Mexico, see Harry Bernstein, Making an Inter-American Mind (Gainesville: University of Florida Press. 1961). pp. 6-10.

54. See Bernstein, Origins of Inter-American Interest, pp. 15-32.

55. Ibid., esp. pp. 16-19, and J. Leitch Wright, p. 118. The trade to Campeche in Yucatan was especially significant. Bernstein reports that in one month in 1714, twenty ships weighed anchor from Boston to Campeche. A number of years later, New Englanders were cutting so much Campeche wood that they drove down the English price by as much as eighty percent.

56. For another typical example of this type of report see New York Gazette, 31 January 1737, p. 3.

57. See, for example, New York Weekly Post-Boy, 25 April 1743, p. 1.

58. New York Cazette, 11 March 1754, p. 1. The same article, reprinted from The London Daily Advertiser, also appeared in The Boston News-Letter, 7 February 1754, p. 1.

59. The Boston News-Letter, 12 June 1740, p. 1.

60. The legend was reprinted in the second issue of Benjamin Franklin's General Magazine, February 1741, pp. 80-83. For a brief discussion of the Madoc legend, see Samuel Eliot Morison, The European Discovery of America: The Northern Voyages (New York: Oxford University Press, 1971), pp. 84-87.

61. Towards this end, Nevill published another series in his magazine, "The History of the Continent of America," which drew from Hakluyt and Purchas to celebrate the English presence in the New World.

62. The Traveller (Woodbridge, N. J.: James Parker, 1758). See pp. 34-40.

63. For an evaluation of Solis' treatment of the Mexicans see Keen, pp. 176-79.

64 Harris' work, Navigantium arque Itinerantium Bibliotheca, drew its Mexican material from Solis. See Keen. p. 258.

65. See Honour, pp. 118-37. A standard, although flawed study on the subject of the romantic primitive is Hoxie N. Fairchild's The Noble Savage (New York: Columbia University Press, 1928). See also Edward Dudley and Maximilian Novak, eds., The Wild Man Within (Pittsburgh: University of Pittsburgh Press, 1972).

66. See The History of America (1777; reprinted, New York: J. Harper, 1832), pp. 195-96.

67. As a devout Christian, Robertson was obliged to accept the Americans as fellow humans but he occasionally characterized them as "melancholy animals" (p. 188).

68. Robertson, p. 127. For a brilliant treatment of the ideas of Buffon and de Pauw and Robertson's adherence to them, see Antonello Gerbi, The Dispute of the New World, trans. Jeremy Moyle (Pittsburgh: University of Pittsburgh Press, 1973), esp. pp. 165-69. Buffon posited the inferiority of animals in the New World because of climatic influences while de Pauw extended the theory to the aborigines.

69. Robertson, p. 324.

70. Ibid., p. 329.

71. Ibid., p. 333.

72. Other scholars, Hugh Honour and Benjamin Keen for example, would not agree with my assessment of Robertson's depictions. Honour (p. 132) calls Robertson "more judicious" than many of his predecessors while Keen (pp. 275-85) argues that he paid respect to the Mexicans' cultural achievements. The issue is complicated by Robertson's habit of contradiction. As indicated before, he accepts the aborigines as fellow humans yet calls them animals. Certainly, Robertson notes the cultural superiority of the Mexicans over other aborigines but the admiration is purely relative, always qualified and not deeply felt. His truer feelings seem to emerge in the long passage quoted here in which he, a highly disciplined rationalist, nevertheless comes close to passionate excoriation.

73. The notion of the superiority of the North American Indians to the Mexicans in Anglo-American thought goes back to Hackluyt who in a letter to Walter Raleigh described the northern Indians as being of "better wittes" than the Mexicans. See Hakluyt, VIII, p. 443. This idea received great currency in the United States during the nineteenth century and has become part of the national mythology. See, for example, Walter Prescott Webb's remark that compared to that of the Plains Indians the blood of Indians in Mexican territory was "as ditch water." See Webb, The Great Plains (Boston: Ginn, 1931), pp. 125-126.

74. Robertson correctly identified the product of Spanish-Indian miscegenation as the mestizo. The term was not unknown to American readers. Miles Philips used it in his sixteenth-century narrative as did Thomas Gage in the next century. The phenomenon of miscegenation was to have a highly negative effect on American attitudes toward Mexico after 1840. See my "The Mexican Image in American Travel Literature, 1831-1869," New Mexico Historical Review, 52 (January 1977): 5-29.

75. Clavigero's work, The History of Mexico (1787) is far more balanced than Robertson's. Clavigero does not condone Mexican atrocities but juxtaposes them with the many humane and meditative aspects of Mexican life that Robertson ignores. Clavigero's book was also known in the United States but its influence was restricted to intellectual and scholarly circles.

76. See Stimson, "William Robertson's Influence on Early American Literature," Americas, 14 (1957), 37-43. Surprisingly, Robertson's influence on American attitudes toward Mexico has been all but overlooked by scholars. One exception is David J. Weber in his Foreigners in Their Native Land (Albuquerque: University of New Mexico Press, 1973). pp. 52-61, 68-69.

77. As Harry Bernstein and Stanley Williams explain, there was a small group of scholars and intellectuals who sought to enhance appreciation of Spanish culture, to stimulate, as it were, "a white legend." But the movement was small and had no significant effect on popular attitudes in the period under consideration.

78. Commerce of the Prairies (1844; reprinted, Norman: University of Oklahoma Press, 1954), p. 154.

79. The legacy of the doctrine of miscegenation has persisted into the present century. In explaining the rash of Mexican rebellions in the Santa Anna era, the respected historian Wilfrid Callcott wrote: "For one thing, the Mexican was a new ethnic combination and as such had not become standardized as a product either physically or mentally. No plant or animal breeder will risk his cash or reputation by guaranteeing standard results as to types, color or characteristics of plants or animals secured from a new blend. The more emotional and less stable new racial blend, the new Mestizo, had vague longings for equality and justice, but as a class lacked the stamina and courage of his own convictions. He would start out boldly, but, at the first reverse, his old fear of the 'master' would return, and panic-stricken, he would give up the contest." See Santa Anna (Norman: University of Oklahoma Press, 1936), p. 116. In American fiction there are numerous Mexican characters who, suddenly and inexplicably, go temporarily crazy. One thinks, for example, of "Spanish Johnny" in Willa Cather's The Song of the Lark and Danny in Steinbeck's Tortilla Flat.

2

The U.S.-Mexican War in San Diego, 1846-1847

Richard Griswold del Castillo

Little has been written about the American military conquest of San Diego during the U.S.-Mexican War, 1846-1848. The survey histories of San Diego, while mentioning the Battle of San Pasqual, do not discuss the ways in which the conflict here divided the Californio population. Neither is it appreciated that the majority of the Mexican population valiantly fought against the American occupation of their town and succeeded, for a time, in recapturing San Diego from the U.S. Army and in besieging the Americans throughout the winter months of 1846. The final capture of San Diego was not at all an easy affair. It was accomplished only after a major resistance movement by the Mexican partisans. A closer look at this period of conflict in San Diego can give us a better appreciation of the evolution of our Mexican American community.

On May 11, 1846, the Congress of the United States voted to declare war on the Republic of Mexico. President James K. Polk justified his war message saying that Mexico had attacked American troops and invaded the United States and that the Mexican government had not been cooperative in negotiations over the Texas boundary issue. The first battles between U.S. and Mexican troops occurred in the area just north of Matamoros, a few miles north of the Rio Grande (Bravo), in an area that had been part of the state of Coahuila for decades. In reality the Mexican "invasion" occurred in territory which was not conclusively American soil. Many Americans at the time saw the declaration of war as a legitimate and natural expression of America's Manifest Destiny to acquire the western territories reaching to the Pacific Ocean. Merchants and commercial men saw California's ports as part of a commercial expansion leading to the lucrative China trade. Strategically the U.S. government worried that the British or perhaps the Russians might annex California and that this would jeopardize national expansion.

San Diego's port was well known as one of the best in California after San Francisco. For years American merchant ships had visited these ports selling manufactured goods to the Mexican Californios. The occupation of these ports became a priority during the first few months of U.S.-Mexican War. On July 9, 1846, Commodore John D. Sloat occupied the California capitol port of Monterey and turned over command to Commodore Robert F. Stockton, who ordered Lieutenant John C. Frémont to occupy the town and port of San Diego. Sailing on the sloop-of-war Cyane with 160 men, the Americans arrived in San Diego harbor on July 29, 1846. After they captured the Mexican brig Juanita, the American troops occupied San Diego and raised the American flag on July 30, 1846. According to the Americans they got a friendly reception and the Californios offered no resistance. After a week Frémont set out with about 120 men from San Diego to assist Stockton in his capture of Los Angeles, leaving behind a garrison of about 40 men.

As was true elsewhere in California, the Mexican elite divided over whether or not to accept American military rule. On one hand, some of the Californio landholders had married their daughters to Americans and family loyalty counted a great deal in their culture. Also some Californios stood to gain economically by the links they had forged with American traders, and they believed that future prosperity would be assured under an American administration. On the other hand, the Californios felt a love of their *patria chica*, their homeland, and were fearful of what these foreigners would do to them and their families. Very few had abstract political loyalties to the Mexican government but most had a strong identity as Mexicans based in their language and culture.

Thus the Californios were of ambiguous and torn loyalties during the Mexican War. In San Diego many of the leading families supported the American occupation including the Bandinis, the Arguellos, the Pedrorenas, and the Carrillos. At the same time many of the *hijos de pais* in the countryside did not such as the Osunas, the Ibarras, the Cotas, the Machados. Some families were split with relatives on both sides, as was the case in the Carrillo household. Henry Delano Fitch, a wealthy merchant had married Josefa Carrillo, and he supplied the American troops in San Diego during the occupation. Meanwhile members of the Carrillo family fought against the Americans at the battle of San Pasqual. Economic ties, friendships, and family loyalties were the strongest forces binding individuals to one side or the other and inevitably, personalities and hurt feelings emerged.

The American Occupation

The American occupation of San Diego lasted from July 29, 1846 until the first week in October. Stockton ordered an election to solidify Californio support for the occupation. As a result, the San Diego Mexicans elected Miguel de Pedrorena, a Spanish merchant, as Justice of the Peace and Pedro Carrillo as the customs collectors. Later an election was held for municipal justices and, using the Mexican system of electors and the pueblo elected Joaquin Ortega as justice of the first instance and J. D. Wilson as justice of the second. This gave some of the Californio families a stake in the U.S. occupation.

As they had in Los Angeles, the Americans then decreed martial law requiring all people to be within their houses from 10 p.m. until sunrise. On August 17, 1847, Pedrorena issued an order forbidding citizens or their servants from leaving the city and the next day he relayed an announcement issued by the U.S. military which was propaganda intended to make the Californios more cooperative. Pedrorena announced that "this territory is actually invaded by a party of fanatic adventurers called Mormons, who arrived by sea at San Francisco in order to form a large number of others who come by land well armed with the purpose of taking this country by force." Also that, "we are threatened by another party of five hundred Indians called Piutes, who are already in this territory intent upon our complete destruction."[2] Accordingly, Pedrorena called for volunteers and a donation of horses from the Californios, promising that the

Americans would pay for the horses. He requested that all rancheros give all possible assistance. The fear of the threat of the mysterious Mormons and an Indian invasion probably strengthened the local Californio perceived need of the American army for protection. Pedrorena, who was pro-American and who would later be a San Diego delegate to the California Constitutional Convention, was aware of the tensions that were being built up by the American occupation. He wrote in English to his compadre, Henry D. Fitch, on August 8, 1847:

"... Some of our friends (Californios) did not like to stay... the Señores retired to their Farms—Marron was the only man left I could speak to. (sic) However we managed in the old Fashion way and nobody dare insult us....I find my friend Aguirre so much like a lamb in my presence is taking every opportunity of speaking against me and wounding my feelings in very possible way and manner. I hope that he and I will meet again and if there is not hot water enough to scald one of us it is a pity I forgave him once on account of Family relationship but that will not avail him again".[3]

Another account of the American occupation of San Diego in the fall of 1846 is given by Helen Elliott Bandini, based on stories she had heard as a child growing up in San Diego. She remembered that her family and the Arguellos had given the Americans "a hearty welcome, and much needed assistance...."[4] According to her, the patriarch Juan Bandini escorted some of the Americanos to his rancho in Baja to get cattle and food. While the Americans were there, his own family had to leave the rancho. Following the family legend Commodore Stockton asked Señora Bandini to make him an American flag. "From the handbag on her arm came needle, thimble, thread and scissors, and from the clothing of her little ones the necessary red, white, and blue cloth."[5] Thus the Bandinis could claim to be as loyal as the descendants of Betsy Ross.

Events to the north would change the political situation in San Diego and lead to further warfare. On September 27, 1846, the Californios in Los Angeles revolted against the Americans and succeeded in recapturing the pueblo on October 4, 1846. Then from Los Angeles Captain José María Flores sent Francisco Rico and Serbulo Varela with fifty men to recapture San Diego. Captain Ezekiel Merritt and John Bidwell, who were in charge of the American garrison in San Diego, feared that they would be overrun and so the Americans and a few of their Californio supporters decided to abandon the town. The Californios went to their ranchos, the Americans and a few allies boarded the whaling ship Stonington anchored in the harbor. Others like Jose Antonio Estudillo and his large extended family proclaimed their neutrality in the affair and stayed in the pueblo. Without firing a shot the Mexicans recaptured San Diego from the Americans in early October 1846.

The Mexican partisans held on to San Diego for three weeks until October 24, 1846, when the American army moved to recapture the pueblo. An American soldier sneaked ashore and spiked the Mexican cannons on the hill where the old presidio had been (Presidio Hill). Then the American volunteers charged the Mexican defensive positions. The Mexican commander, Serbulo Varela had been ordered to send most of his men back to Los Angeles to protect that town from an expected attack and so was outnumbered. After a brief skirmish the Americans took possession of the town and hauled down the Mexican flag. But before it could touch the ground María Antonia Machado rushed to save it from being trampled. She clutched it to her bosom and cut the halyards to prevent the American flag from being raised. This emerged as a counter legend to offset that of the Bandini's.[6]

The Siege of San Diego

Two days later on October 26, 1846, Captain Leonardo Cota and Ramon Carrillo arrived with 100 men and laid siege to the Americans and their sympathizers in San Diego. Stockton arrived a few days later with reinforcements. Don Juan Bandini, one of the leading Californios in San Diego, welcomed Commodore Stockton into his home, which became the American military headquarters. During the occupation it was the scene of frequent fiestas held in honor of the Americans.

For the next several months the Americans were trapped inside the pueblo. Skirmishes were a daily occurrence. Commodore Robert Stockton reported:

> "The situation of the place was found to be more miserable and deplorable.... On the afternoon of our arrival the enemy came down in considerable force and made an attack; they were, however, soon driven back with the loss of two men and horses killed and four wounded. These skirmishes, or running fights, were of almost daily occurrence. Since we have been here we have lost as yet but one man killed and one wounded."[7]

As described by Stockton, Arguello and Pedrorena helped lead a counter attack. Arguello, "though wounded in the leg, drove the Californian, under Hermosillo, from their position. They made a new stand behind the ruins of the old Presidio walls, but soon retreated toward the mission. Capt. Pedrorena went in pursuit, and about a mile up the valley met and exchanged some shots with the advanced guard under Leandro Osuna. From this time...many began to come in and give themselves up. Dances and festivities followed."[8]

Eventually more than 700 American troops would enter San Diego in preparation for the build up for the recapture of Los Angeles. Nevertheless the siege remained effective. The Americans sent out Indian scouts to assess the Californio strength and received reports that there were about fifty of them located at San Bernardo (20 miles from San Diego), but that many more surrounded the pueblo.

The Americans and Californios who were inside old town were constantly harassed by snipers, who shot into the town every night, especially when the U.S. flag was raised and lowered. A Californio partisan shot at Miguel de Pedrorena and the bullet passed through his hat. Meanwhile the Americans dragged the old cannons from Ft. Guijarros at the end of Point Loma to the west end of the town and built a barricade using adobes from the town.[9] The Californio strategy was to drive all the cattle and edible stock into the hills while laying siege to the pueblo, hoping to starve the Americans out. They guarded the roads out of the town to prevent "spies" from escaping to locate food for the population. These spies were undoubtedly Californios or Indians who had joined the Americans. Finally with the help of a local Indian chief, the Americans secured about 600 sheep who were herded onto an island that was connected to the mainland at low tide.[10]

The Californios continued harassing and besieging the pueblo for the next month. The deaths mounted. On November 1, 1846, Commodore Stockton arrived with reinforcements and sent out a patrol twenty miles south of San Diego, past present day Tijuana, to "acquire" a herd of cattle but was unsuccessful. On November 18 the Californios staged an unsuccessful attack on the American positions in the pueblo. They were led by José Antonio Carrillo with a force of between 80 and 100 men. During the battle three Californios were mortally wounded. Following the attack, there were sporadic encounters. An American soldier who strayed 300 yards from the protection of the town to water his horse was lanced by a Californio soldier and died. An Indian was killed while he was herding sheep destined for the American troops.

During the siege the Americans built an earthen fort on top of Presidio Hill and even built a draw bridge for an entrance. On December 1 the Americans inside the pueblo learned that General Stephen Kearney's dragoons were about eighty miles away at Warner's Pass so Commodore Stockton mounted an escort of fifty men commanded by Captain Archibald Gillespie to march north to meet him. The joint command, comprising about 150, men soon encountered about ninety-three Californios led by Andrés Pico at the Battle of San Pasqual, the bloodiest of the war in California.[11]

A Californiana Account of the War: Felipa Osuna de Marron

Perhaps the best account of this period from the point of view of the Californios in San Diego is the reminiscence of Doña Josefa Felipa Osuna de Marron. When historian Hubert Howe Bancroft's assistant, Thomas Savage interviewed Doña Felipa in 1878 she had been a widow twenty-five years and was sixty nine years old.[12] Her father had been a soldier in the presidio during the Spanish administration and at the age of twenty she married a rancher, Juan María de Marron. He became the administrator of mission San Luis Rey following the secularization of the missions in the Mexican period.

Doña Felipa remembered that she was still living at Mission San Luis Rey in the summer of 1846 when General Frémont and the American troops arrived looking for the Californio leaders whom they desired to capture. The Americans questioned her as to where her husband was and who else was at the mission. As it happened Don María Matias Moreno, the secretary to the California government, was staying with the Marron family at the time. When the Americans appeared, Doña Felipa decided to disguise him as a sick cousin and succeeded in fooling the Americans who left without him. As soon as they had departed, Don Matias, who had recognized his good friend Don Santiago Arguello riding with the Americans, sent a messenger to catch up with Arguello to tell him to return so he could join him. This sudden switching of allegiances angered Felipa since it put her delicate situation in jeopardy. She ordered Don Matias to leave the mission immediately.

This episode revealed some of the schisms among the Californios regarding the American conquest. Some supported the U.S. occupation and others were opposed. Switching sides, at least in the case of Don Matias, was prompted by friendship more than ideology. Indeed Doña Felipa and her husband were later forced into changing sides.

Soon after this incident at the mission she accompanied her husband to their rancho and later she traveled alone to San Diego for safety. This was during the second American occupation of the town. She recounted how in San Diego Don Miguel Pedorena, Don Santiago E. Arguello, and Don Pedro C. Carrillo, were allied with the Americans. The Californios who were still opposed to the Americans asked her husband to join them which he did. The leader of those against the Americans were Leonardo Cota and José María Alipaz.[13]

Doña Felipa remembered that while she was in San Diego, the Californios continued to harass the American troops, hiding in the hills near the pueblo and shouting "challenges, threats and insults." Others entered San Diego at night and occasionally shot into the pueblo.[14] After a time, her husband sent word to her to leave San Diego and join him on their rancho. Felipa recounted what happened:

> We women, all of us left our houses and met in the Estudillo adobe. The Californios against the Americans (los del pais) approached the pueblo above the fort that the Americans had built on the hill. I wanted to leave to join my husband and I had sent a message to Alipaz and Cota to come and get me. So they sent my husband under a white flag thinking that since he was such good friends with Pedrorena, Arguello and Carrillo, they would let him pass. So he approached under a white flag and Pedrorena and a party of Americans rode to meet him- they took his horse and arms and put him in jail. Since he was detained several days without returning to the countryside with me (Felipa), los del pais suspected that he had gone over to the Americans and they became very angry with him.[15]

Felipa, in her words, feared the Americans who she thought were not disciplined soldiers and soon she and her husband were allowed to leave after swearing that they would not continue hostilities. They were given a safe conduct pass in case they were detained by other American troops. With their children they fled San Diego and returned to their rancho where they found the Californios "furious with her husband" accusing him of working as a courier for the Americans. They even threatened to shoot him. Instead they took all their horses and the family as prisoners to another rancho, Agua Herivida, located near present day Carlsbad. Here they left Felipa and their children and took Juan, her husband, along with their Indian servants. Juan Marron became sick and the Californio partisans left him on his rancho and let her return to San Diego. Every day the "fuerzas del pais" descended on the Marron rancho to take what they needed, so that finally "most of what we had was taken from us including the cattle that had been given to me by Fr. Zalvidia."[16]

When the war ended they barely had enough to eat and the Californios continued to accuse Felipa and her husband of being pro-American. Their bad treatment finally forced the Marrons to ask for protection from the American commander of San Diego. After indications that they would be welcome and not mistreated they departed for San Diego. Traveling with the Marron party were several Californio lancers who had been at San Pascual, inlcuding Felipa's brother Leandro who had killed an American in that conflict. On the outskirts of the town her husband raised a white flag and they entered the pueblo leaving their few remaining livestock outside. She reported that some Americans in San Diego were angry at the return of these former enemies but finally did nothing.

The narration of Doña Felipa de Marron Osuna is most interesting for its account of the problems that her family had in being loyal to Mexican California. Circumstances forced them to rely on the Americans for protection from suspicious countrymen. Her account serves as a critique to those who might simplify the issue of loyalty during the war.

The Battle of San Pascual

During the fall of 1846 a large contingent of Californios in Southern California continued to resist the American occupation. In Los Angeles the Mexicans continued to hold on to their recaptured city while in San Diego, the Americans and their supporters were besieged. The country-side belonged to the hijos de pais. The Battle of San Pascual in December 1846 marked the high water mark of the Californio resistance during the war. It was the bloodiest battle fought in California and was a victory for the partisan forces. Nevertheless the Americans were able to reinforce the San Diego garrison and eventually use it as a basis for an overland march to retake Los Angeles.

About a month after the American recapture of San Diego, the Mexican governor of California, José María Flores, sent Andrés Pico to the San Diego region to watch for American troop movements. Pico established a base at Mission San Luis Rey and assisted Captain Leonardo Cota in keeping the Americans in San Diego from foraging the countryside for food. Pico had an informant within the city, his sister Margarita who told him of the American movements. From here he learned that Gillespie had set out from the town toward the Indian rancheria of San Pascual intending to join another group of Americans. These were General Kearney's troops coming from the east, after having marched overland from Santa Fe. Many of the Angelenos who were with Pico were anxious to fight Gillespie since he earned a reputation as a Mexican hater when he had been in charge of the occupation of Los Angeles. Early in December Pico's men, numbering about seventy-two men, marched to the Indian rancheria of San Pascual (called Kamiai by the natives) to intercept Gillespie's troops. A local Diegueño Indian named Felicita remembered their entry:

"a great company of these soldier men came up the valley. We seized our baskets and ollas of food and ran to the hills as before to wait until they passed, but they did not pass. The Californios then took what foraging they could from the village for their horses and entered into the empty Indian huts to build fires for cooking. They slaughtered some of the surrounding cattle for food.

My father, Pontho the chief, was brave, so he went to talk with the soldiers; their head man was called General Pico, and to him my father spoke. This man said we might come and live in the huts the soldiers did not need, so at night we crept back, for it was cold, and the rain was falling. There were few houses left for so many, and little food, but we said nothing."[17]

Upon arriving at the village Pico commanded the lancers to practice their tactics. Pablo Vejar, one of the soldiers who was later captured by the Americans, remembered that "we concluded that they were sufficiently adept to go into combat."[18] Pico then ordered the horses put into pasture to be guarded by the local Indians. The horses were some distance from the Indian village; he discounted reports given by the natives that there was an American force nearby. Meanwhile some members of the Californio lancers were suspicious of Pico's motives in all of this—even to the point of thinking that perhaps he was preparing to turn them over to the Americans. One solider, Juan Bautista Moreno, remembered, "It had been some days that we had suspected that Don Andrés wanted to turn us in. He received continuous correspondence from Los Angeles but he would not tell us anything. This case of the horse made us more suspicious still."[19]

Meanwhile the American troops under Gillespie and Kearny had joined forces near the present day city of Ramona, in the Santa Maria valley. Kearny's men numbered about 150, including Delaware Indians with Kit Carson and African American slaves of the officers and drovers. Gillespie's party had thirty nine soldiers including Rafael Machado, a local Californio. The total American force was about 179. The Californios under General Andrés Pico had about 100 men.[20]

The American commanders debated whether to engage Pico's troops at San Pascual or bypass them on their way to San Diego. Finally, over objections from some of the officers, Kearny decided to scout the Californio positions and sent out a party led by Rafael Machado, a local Californio deserter. Machado succeeded in entering the San Pascual village and learned of the Californio strength. But the American troops grew impatient with him and advanced making enough noise to wake people in the camp who came out "crying Viva California, abajo los Americanos."[21] Soon after that the Californios sent out a patrol and they retrieved a US Army blanket—proof that the Americans had been near. When this was discovered Pico ordered the horses retrieved from the distant pasture and the Californios to prepare for battle.

Early in the morning of December 6, 1846, the American force charged the Californio army camp in the Indian village of San

Pasqual. During the long charge the Americans became strung out in a long file, with those on stronger mules and horses far outdistancing others who were on tired mounts. The few gunshots exchanged were in this first charge, as the Californios met the early arrivals some distance from their camp. Captain Johnston was the first man to be killed. Then the Californios raced away being chased for about three-fourths of a mile. The Californio troops turned and charged at the Americans with their lances. It had been raining off and on for several days and Kearny's troops had damp powder and had to fight with their sabres. The Californios were armed with long lances that they were expert at using in slaughtering cattle. In the hand to hand combat the Californios had the advantage of superior mounts, weapons and battle preparation. José F. Palomares, one of Pico's men at the battle recalled:

> "With our lances and swords we attacked the enemy forces, who could not make good use of neither their firearms nor of their swords.... We did not fire a single shot, the combat was more favorable to us with our sidearms (swords). Quickly the battle became so bloody that we became intermingled one with the other and barely were able to distinguish one from the other by voice and by the dim light of dawn which began to break."[22]

Felicita, the San Pascual Indian woman recalled:

> "The Americans did not shoot their guns many times: perhaps the rain had made the powder wet. They struck with their guns and used the sword, while the Mexicans used their long lances and their riatas. The mules that the Americans rode were frightened and ran all through the willows by the river. After them rode the Mexicans on their swift horses, striking with the lance and lassoing with the riata; it was a very terrible time."[23]

Only about half of the American force of 179 were involved in the actual battle. The rest were in reserve guarding their supplies and baggage. The Americans had trouble loading their newly-issued carbines with the small firing caps in the dark and cold. The two groups fought for about a half an hour mostly in the semi-dark and fog. Gillespie was struck twice. One lance threw him from his horse and another pierced his chest. According to one Californio account Andrés Pico engaged in hand-to-hand combat with Captain Moore. Another version put him and Leonardo Cota and Tomás Sánchez a mile away on a hill observing the battle. One Californio solider recalled that Juan Lobo, a twenty-three year old vaquero from Mission Vieja, led the main Californio assault on Kearny's forces. During the battle the Californios captured one of the American cannons when the mules pulling it bolted and ran towards them. Finally the Americans brought up another howitzer which they fired at the Californios causing their retreat.[24]

Dead on the field of battle were nineteen American soldiers. Two more died later from their wounds. Kearny himself had suffered three lance wounds and temporarily relieved himself of command. The Californios had eleven wounded and one, Pablo Véjar, was taken prisoner. Juan Alvarado was wounded in the back by a rifle ball. Some American deaths may have resulted from friendly fire. Lieutenant Emory recalled finding the body of Captain Johnston; he had been shot in the head. He was the only American to be killed by a bullet wound. The American wounded were taken with the remnants of the U.S. troops to a camp on a hill near San Pascual. The dead were buried in a mass grave and a messenger sent to Commodore Stockton in San Diego to ask for help.[25] The next day, December 7, Kearny's troops resumed their march to San Diego followed by the Californios who constantly harassed them.

When the Americans reached Rancho San Bernardo a larger group of Californios attacked them, and Kearny made the decision to establish a fortified camp on a hill. They were unable to advance further because of the wounded and the increased Californio attacks. On what became known as Mule Hill, the Californio lancers surrounded the remnants of Kearny's and Gillespie's command

and because of hunger they were reduced to eating mule flesh, also they had no water. The Californios captured the messenger the Americans had sent to San Diego when he was returning and, under a flag of truce, he was exchanged for the only Californio prisoner, Pablo Vejar. Kearny then learned that Stockton was not able to come immediately because of the lack of horses.

By December 8, 1846, the Americans decided to send out another party to inform Stockton of the urgency of their situation. One of the three messengers sent was a Native American, possibly from the San Pascual tribe. They arrived in San Diego after walking thirty miles and Stockton set out that same day to rescue the Americans. Meanwhile Pico received orders from Governor Flores to abandon his siege of the Americans and return to Los Angeles to rescue him from an insurrection from within the Californio ranks. So Pico and his men departed before Stockton's led by Lieutenant Gray's troops, arrived on December 11. Finally Kearny's troops were able to move on toward San Diego in safety, arriving on the afternoon of December 12.[26]

Later General Kearny wrote that the battle of December 6th had been a "victory" and that the Californios had "fled from the field." This view was challenged by one U.S. soldier, who wrote that they had been saved from decimation by the Californios' capture of the American howitzer, an act that made the Californios "consider themselves victorious, which saved the balance of the command." Later at the court martial of John Charles Frémont, Kearny admitted that the rescue party from San Diego had saved them from disaster. Generally the Navy officers, headed by Stockton, considered the Battle of San Pascual a defeat for the U.S. Army. Of course the Californios considered this engagement a victory and news of it spread throughout the district.[27]

Kearny's defeat was a product of his overconfidence in the condition of his own men and an underestimation of the Mexicans will to fight. When in New Mexico, Kearny had expressed his contempt for Mexicans, writing, "the Mexicans are physically, mentally and morally an inferior and 'low flung' race." The Californios for their part did not follow up their initial advantage.

General Andrés Pico had divided his forces prior to the battle, not expecting to encounter Kearny's troops. Moreover he knew that the Californios could not fight a conventional war. They lacked the military training, firearms and supplies. Under these circumstances the most effective tactics was guerrilla warfare. He wrote after the battle on April 15, 1847, "the morale of the people had fallen, due to the lack of resources... together with my compatriots we made the last efforts, notwithstanding the extreme lack of powder, arms, men and all kinds of supplies."[28] The battle of San Pascual proved that despite internal dissention and division many Californios were willing to die to defend their homeland from the American invasion.

Aftermath

During the hostilities between the Americans and the Mexicans, the local native populations were by and large neutral. They composed the majority of the population of Southern California and their loyalty towards the Mexican government was not very solid—having experienced the loss of mission lands and various injustices at the hands of Mexican Californios. Nevertheless, many natives who had assimilated the Spanish language and religion and had become separated from their traditional villages and were living in and around the pueblo of San Diego. Many of them worked as servants and laborers or were casual migrants in search of food. In the back country, away from the coast, the natives were subject to misinformation and manipulation by both sides. An example of the resentments against the Californios affecting the war was the infamous Pauma massacre.

During the Mexican War, some Luiseño, Diegeño and Cupeño bands raided Californio ranchos, taking advantage of the weakened defense. The Californios considered the raiding bands as inspired by the Americans but the majority were probably the work of opportunists who were taking advantage of the war-time chaos. A major event involving the Native Americans of San Diego during the war was the Pauma massacre.

A few days after the battle of San Pascual eleven Californio men and youths took refuge in an adobe house on Rancho Pauma owned by José Antonio Serrano. While they were there they were tricked into allowing themselves to be captured by Luiseño Indians led by Manuelito Cota. The Indians took all the men prisoner and then took them to Warners Ranch. There they consulted with a Mexican named Yguera and William Marshall an American who had married the daughter of a local Indian chieftain. What happened next is subject to some debate. According to Doña Juana Machado de Ridington, Marshall instigated the massacre that followed by telling the Indians that they would be rewarded by the Americans. After a short captivity the prisoners were put to death by a torture of red hot spear thrusts. Doña Juana Machado de Riddington reported that, at the time, she had heard rumors that the Americans had authorized the Indians to kill and rob Californios, but that these rumors turned out to be false.[29] Another Californio rumor was that Bill Marshall hated José Maria Alvarado, who was among the prisoners, because he had married Doña Lugarda Osuna, who Marshall had loved.[30] José Antonio Estudillo remembered that the killings were carried out by Indians from Mission San Luis Rey and that other natives from San Pascual had set out to rescue these captives but had arrived too late.[31] Later Marshall was implicated in the Garra Indian uprising in 1851 and executed. His actual role in the Pauma massacre is not clear since during his trial no mention was made of the atrocity and he was not linked to the massacres until 1878, more than twenty years after the event.[32]

Immediately after learning of the capture of the Californios a punitive force of twenty-two Californios set out, led by José del Cármen Lugo and with a force of friendly Cahuilla Indians. They ambushed the Luiseño force and killed more than a hundred and took twenty captive who were later killed by their Cahuilla allies, according to their custom.[33]

The Pauma massacre illustrated the persistence of native animosities towards the Mexicans and the possible manipulation of Indian hatreds by the Americans. It also depicts how later reminiscences by Californios attributed a prime role to the Americans in the massacre. News of the massacre along with the fact that in 1847 the Indians vastly outnumbered the Californios and Mexicans may have worked to demoralize the Californio resistance movement in San Diego County.

Despite the Californio successes at San Pasqual, Dominguez Rancho, and Chico Rancho in Southern California, the U.S. forces were able to force the Californios to surrender and an armistice was signed on January 13, 1847. With the Americans reoccupying Los Angeles and San Diego the guerilla forces in the countryside disbanded. The war was officially over for the Californios and their conflicts with the Americans now went underground to resurface in banditry and other forms of resistance.

The Mexican War in San Diego County was a period that divided the Californio society into those loyal to the Americans and those who resisted with arms. This division persisted into the next decades making it even harder for the Mexicans to unite politically against the many injustices they experienced during the American takeover. The U.S.- Mexican War in San Diego was a small chapter in a much larger conflict, however it illustrated the resistance of the Mexican population to the American conquest and that the issue of loyalty was indeed a complex one.

Notes

1. Donald M. Grugal, "Military Movements into San Diego from the Mexican War to Statehood, 1846-1850," Masters thesis, History, San Diego State University, 1950, pp. 3-6.

2. Miguel de Pedrorena, August 17, 18, 1846 in Benjamin Hayes, Documentos para la historia de california, Ms, Bancroft Library, Berkeley, California.

3. Miguel de Pedrorena to H.D. Fitch, 8 August 1847, Henry Delano Fitch, Documentos para la historia de California, 1827-1858, Bancroft Ms., Berkeley, California.

4. Helen Elliott Bandini, History of California (NY: American book co., 1908), p. 145.

5. loc. cit.

6. Both flag stories are retold in George Tays, "Plaza in Old San Diego," typescript 1937, California Historical Landmarks Series, Bancroft Library, Berkeley, California mF 864. C136 no. 63. Later Antonia Machado and her family had to flee to a rancho in Baja California to escape retribution for their deed. See Carl H. Heilbron, History of San Diego County (San Diego: San Diego Press Club 1936), p. 66.

7. Ibid., p. 66.

8. Ibid., p. 66.

9. "Duvall's Log of the Savannah," Quarterly of the California Historical Society, Vol. III, no. 2 (July 1924): 119.

10. Ibid., p. 120.

11. Ibid., passim. Andrés Pico was Pío Pico's brother. He had been born in San Diego in 1810 and had gotten his military training as an officer in the San Diego Company. He had been the administrator of the San Luis Rey mission lands and had a rancho at Santa Margarita, San Juan Capistrano and Temecula. Later he would be elected, at various times, a state senator from San Diego, San Bernardino and Los Angeles Counties.

12. "Recuerdos de Doña Felipa Osuna de Marron: Natural de San Diego donde vive acutalmente con various papels oriniales..." 1878 Bancroft Library, MSS C D 120.

13. Ibid., p. 14.

14. "...daban gritos y echaban amenazas y desverguenzas," Ibid., p. 20.

15. "Nosotras las mujeres, todas dejamos nuestras casas, y nos reuníamos en la de los Estudillos Venian los del pais arriba del fortin que habían lavantado en la loma yo quería ir a unirme con mi marido, y hubo de conseguir el con Alipaz y Cota licencia para venir a sacarme para eso pusieron alla una bandera blanca Alipaz y Cota dijeron a Marron que el no sería agarrado por los Americanos porque llevaba mucha amistad con Pedrorena, Arguello y Carrillo Los de aqui le dejaron entrar, porque los Californios me venían con una bandera blanca. Luego

que entro me puso, porque salieron Pedrorena y un partido de Americanos a recibirlo le quitaron su caballo y armas y lo llevaron al cuartel. Como se tardo aqui varrios dias sin volverse a campo de los Californios conmigo, sospecharon aquellos que el se había pasado a los Americanos, y se pusieron muy enojados con el. Ibid., p. 15.

16. "Estabamos muy ansianos de ir a unirnos con nuestros paisanos, porque yo les tenía mucho miedo a los Americanos, que no era tropas disciplinados. Al fin logramos salir bajo palabra de honor de no hacer armas contra los Estados Unidos." And: "asi se acaba gran parte del nuestro, y el que me había dado el P. Zalvidia," Ibid., p. 16 .

17. As told to Elizabeth Judson Roberts and published in Indian Stories of the Southwest (San Francisco: Harr Wagner Publishing Co., 1917), p. 222 in Eileen M. Hook and Mary A. Helmich, "San Pasqual Battlefield State Historic Park, Interpretive Plan," Review Draft (Sacramento: Office of Interpretive Services, California State Parks and Recreation, May 1985), 136-7.

18. Eileen M. Hook and Mary A. Helmich, p.137; see Allen Olmstead Véjar and Pablo Véjar, Californios—one Portola Soldado de cuera's Family in California (1769 1877) (San Franicsco, Ca: private printing, 1989) for Vejars complete reminiscence.

19. Ibid., p.137 quoted from Juan Bautista Moreno, "Vida Militar," Ms. 1887, Bancroft Library, p. 27.

20. Sally Cavell Jones, "The Battle of San Pascual," Master's Thesis, USD, 1973, p. 72. Various estimates of troops sizes are discussed in this work. A partial list of the Californios soldiers commanded by Andrés Pico at San Pascual are as follows (from Grugal, "Military Movements into San Diego," p. 114)

Andrés Pico, Commander
Leonardo Cota, officer
Tomás Sanchez, officer
José Aguilar
Dionisio Alipas
José Alipas
José María Alvarado
Juan Alvarado
Pablo Apis
Felipe or Salvador Canedo
Ramon Carrillo
José Duarte
Gabriel Garcia
Franciso Higuera
José María Ibarra
Francisco Dorio Lara
Juan Lobo Mariano

Santiago Lobo
Cristobal Lopez
Jesus Machado
Juan Manirquez
Juan Bautista Moreno
Isidoro Olivares
Leandro Osuna
Ramon Osuna
Felipe or Rafael Peralta
Pedro Perez
Gregorio Santiago
Casimiro Rubio
José Antonio Serrano
Joaquin Valenzuela
Pablo Vejar
Miguel or Pedro Verdugo
Domingo Yorba
José Antonio Yorba III
Romualdo Young

21. Ibid., p. 139

22. Ibid., p. 175 found in José Francisco Palomares, "Memoria," Ms. June 21, 1877, Transcribed by Carlos N. Hijar, Bancroft Library, Berkeley, California, pp. 91-92.

23. ibid., p. 176 in Roberts, p. 224.

24. Sally Cavell Jones, "The Battle of San Pascual," Masters Thesis, USD, 1973, p. 83-93. See Benjamin Hayes, "Notes on California Affairs," Ms., n.d. in Bancroft Library.

25. Ibid., pp. 164-6.

26. Ibid., p., 173.

27. Ibid., pp. 130-31.

28. Ibid., p. 140; Nile's National Register, November 7, 1846 p 146 in George Tays, "Pío Pico's Correspondence with the Mexican Government," California Historical Society Quarterly, XIII (June, 1934), p. 132.

29. Juana Machado de Ridington, "Los Tiempos pasados de la alta california: recuerdos de la Sra. Doña Juana Machado de Ridington, Bancroft Ms. 1878, C D 119; see also Raymond S. Brandes, trans. "Times Gone By in Alta California: Recollections of Senora Doña Juana Machado Alipaz de Ridington," Historical Society of Southern California, Vol. 41 (1959) pp. 195-240.

30. General John Bidwell, Echoes of the Past.... (Chico: Chico Advertiser, n.d.), p. 72; Bidwell was a resident of San Diego during this period.

31. José Maria Estudillo," Datos Historicos sobre la Alta California,"

Bancroft Ms., 1878 c D 76, p. 48. He listed some of the victims as José Maria Basualado, José Lopez, José Maria Alvarado, Dona Lugarda Osuna, Jesus Serrano, Santiago Osuna, and José Rosario Alipaz. Estudillo calls Bill Marshall, Bill Matador.

32. See Leland E. Bibb, "William Marshall," Unpublished Research Paper, San Diego Historical Society.

33. R. W. Brackett, A History of the Ranchos (San Diego: Union Title Insurance and Trust Co., 1939), p. 59.

3

Finalizing the Treaty, 1848 - 1854

Richard Griswold del Castillo

*We remain as free, after accepting the treaty, to look to
our own interests and to hold to a purely Mexican policy, as
we were the moment we became independent. The loss we
have sustained in this adjustment of peace was necessary and
inevitable.*

REPORT TO THE SUPREME GOVERNMENT
OF THE COMMISIONERS WHO SIGNED THE
TREATY OF PEACE WITH THE UNITED STATES,
IN SIGLO XIX, JUNE 2, 1848

The final stage in the making of the Treaty of Guadalupe
Hidalgo lasted from the signing of the treaty on February 2, 1848, to
the exchange of the ratification on May 30, 1848. During this period
both Mexican and U.S. statesmen deliberated over the articles in the
treaty. The U.S. Congress made several significant changes that the
Mexican government accepted only after a protocol was drafted. In
its final form the Treaty of Guadalupe Hidalgo was still an imperfect
document. Ambiguities and errors in the treaty led to boundary
disputes, a near renewal of warfare, and the drafting of another
treaty, in 1853, that ceded even more territory to the United States.

U.S. RATIFICATION

An immediate consequence of the signing of the treaty on
February 2, 1848, was to initiate a debate in Washington, D.C.,
over the desirability of ratification. President Polk, after a long

consultation with his cabinet on Sunday and Monday, February 20 and 21, decided to accept the treaty and to ask Congress to ratify it. This was a decision based primarily on his appraisal of the likelihood of continued congressional support for the war. Polk's view was that Congress would probably reject requests for further war appropriations and that this would lead to an even less favorable treaty. [1] In his message to Congress he recommended not only ratification but also the deletion of Article X, which dealt with land grants (see Appendix) and a secret article relating to the extension of the period for ratification.

Article X was an explicit statement protecting Mexican land grants, particularly those in Texas. Polk objected to the provisions on the grounds that it would revive old land grants and throw into question the grants made by the Texas government since their declaration of independence in 1836. Further, Polk argued, "public lands within the limits of Texas belong to that state, and this government has no power to dispose of them, or to change the conditions of grants already made." [2]

Even with the president's endorsement, when the treaty came before the Senate, it was not assured of passage. Secretary of State Buchanan and Secretary of the Treasury Walker openly opposed it because it would not gain enough territory for the Republic. The opposition party, the Whigs, were against the treaty for the opposite reason: It would annex too much territory, which eventually would increase the slavocracy's power in Congress. Upon a motion by Sam Houston the Senate voted to conduct its deliberations in secret and as a result there are no exact records of the debate. [3]

One roadblock to a speedy passage of the treaty was the possibility that the Senate Foreign Relations Committee, which had to issue its report prior to the debate, might recommend rejection of the document on the basis that Nicholas Trist had been an unauthorized agent. Only Polk's personal intervention with the committee chair, Ambrose H. Sevier, resulted in a noncommittal rather than a negative report.

Finally, on February 28, the Senate met in executive session. For eleven days the various factions traded arguments. The Whigs led by Daniel Webster, who feared a growth of the southern section and slavery, opposed the treaty. Some northern Democrats rejected the treaty because they were morally against the war. Some opposed it because they were political rivals of the president. Others like Sam Houston and Jefferson Davis did not want the treaty because it did not annex more of the Mexican territories; Houston favored retaining the territory as far south as the state of Vera Cruz while Davies wanted to annex most of the northern Mexican states.

The treaty remained largely intact because of each faction's opposition to the proposals of the others. Motions to modify, to either expand or retract, the boundary were defeated. The Senate defeated an attempt to insert the language of the Wilmot Proviso, restricting slavery in the new territories. Article X was stricken as recommended by the President; language in Article IX was changed by substituting language from the Louisiana and Florida treaties; Article XI was changed to allow the United States to sell arms and ammunition to Indians in its territories; and the secret article lengthening the time allowed for ratification was omitted. The Senate made a few other minor changes that did not affect the substance of the treaty. During the debate, President Polk exerted his influence on a number of senators by personal visits and pledges of support. Just before the final vote, a powerful opponent of the treaty, former President John Quincy Adams, died. This removed a major rallying point for the opposition, and the mourning period that followed delayed the Senate debate long enough for the senators to assess the mood of public opinion, which was strongly in favor of the treaty and an end to the war.

On March 10, 1848, the Senate voted to ratify the modified version by a vote of 38 to 14, four more than the required two-thirds majority. The vote followed sectional rather than party lines, with the majority of northerners opposing. [4]

MEXICAN RATIFICATION

It now remained for Mexico to ratify the treaty. Buchanan attempted to gain Mexican acceptance by writing a letter of explanation to the Mexican minister of foreign relations, Luis de la Rosa. Buchanan argued that changes in Article IX dealing with the rights of citizenship were primarily the result of the Senate's wish not to violate precedents established in treaties negotiated with France and Spain. Article IX in its original form forcefully maintained the civil and property rights of the former Mexican citizens (see Appendix). The key portion of that article originally read:

> The Mexicans who, in the territories aforesaid, shall not preserve the character of citizens of the Mexican Republic, conformably with what is stipulated in the preceding Article, shall be incorporated into the Union of the United States as soon as possible... In the meantime, they shall be maintained and protected in the enjoyment of their liberty, their property, and the civil rights now vested in them according to the Mexican laws. With respect to political rights, their condition shall be on an equality with that of the inhabitants of the other territories of the United States.[5]

The U.S. Senate struck this language from the treaty and replaced it with a more general and ambiguous statements:

> [Mexicans not choosing to remain citizens of Mexico] shall be incorporated into the Union of the United States and be admitted, at the proper time (to be judged of by the Congress of the United States) to the enjoyment of all the rights of citizens of the United States according to the principles of the Constitution; and in the meantime shall be maintained and protected in the free enjoyment of their liberty and property, and secured in the free exercise of their religion without restriction. [6]

Buchanan maintained that the Senate amendment of the original was justified because in Florida and Louisiana, "no complaint has ever been made by the original or other inhabitants that their civil or religious rights have not been amply protected."[7] In this he chose to ignore the litigious territorial history of Louisiana where there had been numerous public complaints and lawsuits by the native French against the American administration of New Orleans in the early years. [8] Buchanan's overestimation of the benefits of protection afforded ethnic minorities under the Constitution extended to his rationale for the deletion of Article X from the treaty. In its original form, Article X had read:

> All grants of land made by the Mexican government or by the competent authorities, in territories previously appertaining to Mexico....shall be respected as valid, to the same extent if said territories had remained within the limits of Mexico. But the grantees of lands in Texas... [who] may have been prevented from fulfilling all the conditions of their grants, shall be under the obligation to fulfill the said conditions within the periods limited in the same respectively; such periods to be now counted from the date of the exchange of ratifications. [9]

This article struck to the heart of a question that would be the basis for hundreds of lawsuits and many instances of injustice against the former Mexican land holders. The treaty makers knew well that most of the Mexican citizens occupying land grants in the ceded territories did not have perfect title to their lands and that the majority were in the process of fulfilling the requirements of Mexican law. Frequent changes in political administrations, the notorious slowness of the Mexican bureaucracy, and many individual circumstances had made it difficult for Mexican landholders to obtain clear title in an expedient way. Article X would have allowed them to complete the process under an American administration. The article specifically recognized the unique condition of the Mexican land-grant claimants in Texas, most of whom had been dispossessed of their lands by Anglo Texans following Texas Independence. The article would allow them to resurrect their claims and fulfill the conditions of Mexican law. [10]

In his letter to the Mexican minister, Buchanan said that

Article X was so outrageous that if it were a part of the treaty "it would be a mere nullity" and that "the Judges of our courts would be compelled to disregard it." He went on in prolix fashion: "It is to our glory that no human power exists in this country which can deprive the individual of his property without his consent and transfer it to another. If the grantees of lands in Texas, under the Mexican government, possess valid titles, they can maintain their claims before our courts of justice." [11] The language of Article X applied to New Mexico and California as well. For the next five decades the territorial, state, and supreme courts would be occupied with sorting out "perfect" and "imperfect" land grants and dispossessing those who occupied the land in 1848. The absence of specific treaty protections for the holder of unperfected grants threw them on the mercy of the American courts. In 1848 Buchanan had an unbridled optimism about the ability of the judicial system to dispense justice; subsequent decisions, however, created a heritage of ill will between Mexican settlers and Anglo immigrants.

Realizing that these amendments and deletions might prevent the Mexican Congress from ratifying the treaty, President Polk sent with the modified document two commissioners to explain the changes and to accept the Mexican ratification on the spot. Senator Ambrose Sevier, chair of the Senate Foreign Relations Committee, and Nathan Clifford, the attorney general, arrived in Mexico in mid-April, and on May 3, 1848, the Mexican Congress convened to debate the modified version of the treaty.

In the period following the signing of the treaty, a vocal opposition formed. Before the congressional debates, the opponents of the treaty, led by Manuel Crescencio Rejon, published their arguments against ratification and stimulated debate over whether to continue the war. Rejon, a liberal from Yucatan, had helped draft the 1824 constitution and had served as minister of relations under Herrera and Santa Anna. Rejon believed that Mexico could win a protracted guerrilla war. Other liberals such as Melchor Ocampo and Benito Juarez, shared this view and opposed the Treaty of Guadalupe Hidalgo.

Rejon's opposition was published in an 1848 broadside

entitled "Observations on the Treaty of Guadalupe Hidalgo." [12] His argument against the treaty was contained in fifteen closely reasoned juridical sections of this treatise. Rejon believed that the treaty would mean the inevitable economic subordination of Mexico by the United States. He predicted that the new boundary, by bringing American commerce closer to the heartland of Mexico, would lead the Americanization of Mexico. He said, "We will never be able to compete in our own markets with the North American imports.... The treaty is our sentence of death." [13] Rejon criticized those who thought that the Mexican citizens in the ceded territories would be protected. He believed that American racism would prevent their being treated justly: "The North Americans hate us, their orators deprecate us even in speeches in which they recognize the justice of our cause, and they consider us unable to form a single nation or society with them." For Rejon the treaty would only delay "the absolute loss of our political existence as a republic." [14]

The juridical arguments Rejon advanced were that the treaty violated Mexican laws because it had been drafted clandestinely without input from Congress or the states. There had been no open discussion of the treaty prior to the debates over ratification. The treaty had not been published, and the signing of the treaty violated the constitution. In a word, Rejon argued that the government had exceeded its authority in agreeing to alienate its national territory. The Mexican government also had violated international law and precedent. [15] Although the government had argued that the territory being ceded was worthless, Rejon placed a high value on the lands, especially California. In his argument he called California "our priceless flower" and "our inestimable jewel." [16] By coincidence gold had been discovered a few weeks before Rejon wrote these words, but neither he nor the rest of the world would learn of it until the midsummer of 1848. [17]

In response to Rejon's arguments, Bernardo Couto, one of the original commissioners, published the commissioners' arguments in favor of the treaty. The recurring theme in the writings of treaty advocates was that, by ending the war, the treaty had saved Mexico from possible obliteration as a nation. If the war had continued, they argued, all of Mexico probably would have been annexed by the United States. The negotiations wrote: "The treaty not only prevents any increase of our losses by a continuation of the war, but recovers the greater part of that which was subjected to the arms of the conquerors; it may be more properly called a treaty of recovery rather than one of alienation."[18]

Regarding the territory and people being lost, the commissioners adopted a stoic attitude: "It can hardly be said that we lose any power, since that which we cede is almost all uninhabited and uncultivated.... We lose in our rich hopes for the future, but if we know how to cultivate and defend the territory that the treaty preserves or has rescued for us, we shall find it sufficient to console us for our past misfortunes."[19]

Couto naively argued that the rights of the former Mexican citizens would be protected because, in American law, "every treaty has a superiority and preference under civil legislation." The proponents asserted that the treaty provisions for citizenship and property rights in Articles VIII and IX would be sufficient to protect the former Mexican citizens. They were wrong: American local, state, and national courts later ruled that the provisions of the treaty could be superseded by local laws.[20]

Manuel de la Pena y Pena also published his arguments in favor of the treaty. He emphasized the extraordinary concern he and his fellow commissioners had felt for their abandoned Mexican populations. "If it had been possible," he wrote, "I would have enlarged the territorial cession with the condition of freeing the Mexican population living there." To resume the war, he continued would endanger their safety and condition; terrible sacrifices were necessary to end the war. [21]

On May 7, 1847, the Mexican Congress opened its debates on the treaty. At that time Pena y Pena, another commissioner, was acting president. His support for ratification was important, especially because he addressed freshman deputies and senators whose future political life might depend on their alliance with the president.

In considering the treaty, the Congress heard a report from

Minister of War Anaya outlining the military situation. They then listened to a detailed report from Luis de la Rosa, minister of the treasury, outlining financial justifications for a treaty. Finally, the Chamber heard a report from the commissioners explaining the provisions of the treaty. [22]

The military situation was not good. Besides the American occupation, factions opposing the treaty had made sporadic attempts at rebellion against the federal government. In Aguascalientes, General Paredes y Arrillaga pronounced against the government and captured Guanajuato for a few months until the city was recaptured by federal troops. [23] In early May 1848 the governments of Coahuila and Tamaulipas declared that they would not recognize the treaty of Guadalupe if it were ratified.[24] Benito Juarez, then governor of Oaxaca, formally announced that his state would oppose the treaty and keep fighting. [25] In addition protests against the treaty came from the state governments of Chihuahua, Zacatecas, Jalisco, and Mexico. As if this were not sufficient, several potentially dangerous Indian rebellions called for immediate action; in San Luis Potosi the Xichu Indians razed missions and buildings throughout a hundred-square mile area.

Opposition to the treaty was strongest in the Chamber of Deputies. Jose Maria Cuevas, brother of the Luis Cuevas who had signed the treaty, spoke eloquently in opposition, moving the delegates to a standing ovation and lengthy demonstration.[26] The published arguments of Senators Mariano Otero and Manuel Crescencio Rejon against the treaty were influential. Oral arguments in favor of ratification came from the minister of foreign relations, Luis de la Rosa, the minister of war, Pedro Anaya; and the president of the Chamber, Francisco Elorriaga. [27] Finally, on May 19, the deputies met and voted 51 to 35 for ratification. Then the Senate took up the debate. There was less intense opposition in this body, the principal leader being Mariano Otero. After three days of discussion, the modified treaty passed by a vote of 33 to 4. [28]

In ratifying the Treaty of Guadalupe Hidalgo, the majority of the Mexican Congress chose the lesser of two evils. Not to ratify the document would have meant continued American military occupation, a prolonged financial disaster for the Mexican government, and the probable loss of additional territory. In accepting the treaty, the politicians admitted that the loss of territory was inevitable and that a treaty would liberate Mexico from foreign domination while preventing further erosion of national territory. Most of the delegates probably accepted Pena y Pena's characterization: It was a treaty of recovery rather than of cession. [29]

PROTOCOL OF QUERETARO

Prior to the exchange of ratifications, Luis de la Rosa, the minister of foreign relations, requested a meeting with the American commissioners Clifford and Sevier to draft a protocol that would clearly explain what was intended by the U.S. Senate modification of the original treaty. Also attending the meeting were two former signatories of the treaty, Bernardo Couto and Luis Cuevas. The result of these conversations was the drafting of the Protocol of Queretaro (see Appendix). This document sought to clarify the intentions of the American government in modifying Article IX and deleting Article X. [30] The first part of the protocol stated that the changes in Article IX (dealing with citizenship rights) "did not intend to diminish in any way what was agreed upon by the aforesaid [original] article." [31] The second part of the protocol affirmed that in deleting Article X (land grants), the U.S. government "did not in any way intend to annul grants of land made by Mexico in the ceded territories." [32]

Later this protocol became a source of political controversy within the United States and cause for further disagreement with Mexico. The protocol was not included with the treaty papers sent to the Congress when the president proclaimed the ratification process complete on July 4, 1848. Six months later, Whig Congressmen embarrassed the administration by raising the issue of the secrecy and meaning of the Protocol of Queretaro. Congress debated it, the Whigs arguing that the protocol language restored guarantees respecting Texas land grants, and the Democrats arguing that the protocol did not enlarge on the meaning of the treaty. The intensity of the debate suggested the importance of the treaty's relationship to incomplete titles in the new territories. Luis de la Rosa, the Mexican envoy to the United States, enlarged the discussion on February 10, 1849, by objecting to Buchanan's assertion that the protocol had "no value" and that the document was merely a record of conversations, having no legal force. Later, the new secretary of state, John Clayton, reaffirmed this view to de la Rosa, saying that the U.S. government "at no time regarded the Protocol as obligatory." [33] In Mexico City, Nathan Clifford met with the minister of foreign relations, Jose Maria de Lacunza, and agreed to a three-point interpretation: (1) the protocol was not an addition to the treaty; (2) it did not change any of its provisions; and (3) it was a correct interpretation of the treaty. In a short time the State Department vociferously objected to this last point. The difference of opinion between Mexico City and Washington, D.C., remains to this day. [34]

BOUNDARY DISPUTES

The final ratified version of the Treaty of Guadalupe Hidalgo (see Appendix) substantially resolved the issue of the status of the Rio Grande as the southern border between Texas and Mexico, but it also created a new boundary dispute in its designation of the southern border between the territory of New Mexico (including Arizona) Sonora and Chihuahua. Article V in the treaty specified that the new dividing line for this region would proceed up the Rio Grande "to the point where it strikes the southern boundary of New Mexico; thence, westward along the whole southern boundary of New Mexico (which runs north of the town called Paso) to its western termination; thence northward along the western line of New Mexico until it intersects the first branch of the River Gila," and down the Gila to the Colorado. [35] The boundary in California would be a line drawn eastward starting one marine league south of the bay of San Diego.

In July 1849 the commissioners from each country met in San Diego to begin the task of surveying and marking the new international boundary. A year later they finished tracing and marking the line between the two Californias. But when the commissioners met in El Paso in December 1850 to begin surveying the boundary between the New Mexico territory and Chihuahua and Sonora they discovered that there were serious geographical errors in Disturnell's 1847 Map of Mexico which was cited in the Treaty of Guadalupe Hidalgo. The map placed El Paso half a degree too far north and the Rio Grande two degrees too far east. If the map were followed literally, the rich Mesilla Valley and the Santa Rita de Cobre mines would remain in Mexican territory. Thus, the boundary commissioners charged with surveying the line were confronted with a dilemma: Should they follow the latitudes of the boundary as marked on the map, or should they, using the relationship of the line to the town of El Paso shown on the map, mark the boundary eight miles north of the town? The difference between the two methods for determining the southern line between New Mexico and Chihuahua would mean a loss or gain of about six thousand square miles of territory along with about three thousand persons.

In 1851, when the commissioners met to discuss the problem, the Mexican representative, General Garcia Conde, argued to accept the northern latitude, and the U.S. representative, John R. Barlett, argued for a more southerly one. After four months of discussion they agreed to a compromise that set the New Mexican-Chihuahua border at 32 degrees, 22 minutes north latitude. [36]

Political pressured from American expansionists who wanted a more southerly line for a transcontinental railroad and land access to the Mesilla region's rich mines prevented acceptance of the Barlett-Conde agreement Southerners anxious to secure the route for their section voted to withhold further money for the survey unless a more southerly line were agreed upon.

In 1852 the situation in the Mesilla Strip became explosive as Mexican repatriates and Anglo-Texan and New Mexican cattle ranchers moved into the area. The governor of Chihuahua claimed jurisdiction and the governor of New Mexico threatened to occupy the area with force. [37] Further provocation came when American troops occupied the Mexican communities of Isleta, Socorro, and San Elizario claiming that the changes in the Rio Grande's water course now made them part of the United States. These three communities, which included almost six thousand people, had been on the Mexican side of the river in 1848. [38]

The U.S. government's rejection of the Barlett-Conde agreement was not the only source of conflict between the two countries. Under Article XI of the Treaty of Guadalupe Hidalgo, the United States was bound to prevent Indian raids into Mexico from the U.S. side of the border. This task turned out to be impossibly expensive. More than 160,000 Indians lived in the border region, and many of them, particularly the Apaches and Comanches, had a long history of raiding pueblos on the Mexican side. In an attempt to comply with its obligations, the United States stationed more than eight thousand troops along the border. The cost of keeping the peace turned out to be more than the cost of the original treaty. Between 1848 and 1853, military expenditures in New Mexico alone rose to 12 million dollars and the raids continued. [39] In 1868 the Mexican government presented claims for damages that amounted to more than 31 million dollars. [40] Needless to say, the U.S. government was anxious to be released from the provisions of Article XI.

THE GADSDEN TREATY

This volatile situation along the border, confusion over the international boundaries, U.S. desire for rights of transit across the Isthmus of Tehuantepec, and a release from the obligations of the Treaty of Guadalupe Hidalgo's Article XI, led to the U.S. dispatch of James Gadsden to Mexico. The Tehuantepec issue had increased in importance since the discovery of gold in California in 1848. Various U.S. investors had been granted concessions to construct a trans-isthmus railroad, but they were not willing to proceed until the United States and Mexico agreed to protect the project. After conversations with President Santa Anna and threats of military force, Mexico signed the Gadsden Treaty, or Tratado de Mesilla. As eventually modified by the American Congress, the United States agreed to pay 10 million dollars and Mexico ceded the territory the Americans wanted for a railroad while allowing the United States to abrogate Article XI in the Treaty of Guadalupe Hidalgo and granting the rights of transit across the Isthmus of Tehuantepec. The new treaty granted the United States an additional 29,142,000 acres of Mexican territory and released it from the obligation of policing the border Indians.

The Treaty of Guadalupe Hidalgo was imperfect, and it became a source of continuing ill will and misunderstanding on both sides of the border. The Gadsden Purchase did not end the boundary problems. In later years an International Boundary Commission would have to deal with unforeseen geographical and political issues. The problem of violence along the border did not disappear. Indian warfare, banditry, smuggling, and filibustering expeditions persisted. The last decades of the nineteenth century witnessed numerous occasions on which American troops pursued outlaw bands of Indians and Mexicans across the border. This chronic condition required additional negotiations between the two countries. In 1910 the Mexican revolution further destabilized conditions along the border. [41]

Thus the Treaty of Guadalupe Hidalgo solved some problems but created others that would become a source of continuing dialogue between the two nations. One of the most pressing issues created by the treaty was dealt with inadequately by both parties: the failure of the U.S. government to provide for the civil and property rights of the Mexican population in the newly annexed territory.

NOTES

1. David Pletcher, The Diplomacy of Annexation: Texas, Oregon, and the Mexican War (Columbia: University of Missouri Press, 1973), p. 558.

2. Senate Executive Documents No. 52, 30th Congress, 1st session, 4-5.

3. Ibid., 9.

4. Robert Selph Henry, The Story of the Mexican War (New York: Frederick Unger, 1950), pp. 386-388. The most complete documentary collection regarding the treaty and its ratification is assembled in David Hunter Miller, Treaties and Other International Acts of the United States of America, vol. 5, Mexico, 1848 (Washington, D.C.: Government Printing Office, 1937), pp. 207-428. The best account of the Senate's ratification debates is Ralph A. Rowley, "Precedents and Influences Affecting the Treaty of Guadalupe-Hidalgo," (Master's thesis, University of New Mexico, 1970), pp. 78-96.

5. Miller, 5 : 241.

6. Matt S. Meier and Feliciano Rivera, Dictionary of Mexican American History (Westport, Conn.: Greenwood Press, 1979), p. 409.

7. Miller, 5 : 255.

8. See Francois Xavier Martin, The History of Louisiana From the Earliest Periods, (New Orleans: James A. Gresham, 1882), pp. 322-323.

9. Miller, 5 : 242.

10. Conditions required by the federal government usually included five actions: (1) presentation of a petition describing the parcel along with a map (diseno) to the local government official; (2) examination of the land to ascertain its availability and the filing of a report (informe); (3) the issuance of formal grant by the local government (expediente); (4) approval of the grant by the territorial or state Assembly or Deputation; and (5) approval by the central government. See William W. Robinson, Land in California, (Berkeley: University of California Press, 1948).

11. Miller, 5 : 255.

12. Later these broadsides were published as Pensamiento Politico (Mexico, D.F.: UNAM, 1968). See "Observations on the Treaty of Guadalupe Hidalgo," in that work, pp. 93-145.

13. Ibid., pp. 119-20.

14. Ibid., pp. 122, 123.

15. Ibid., pp. 127-33.

16. Ibid., pp. 127-133.

17. The news of the discovery of gold in Alta California did not reach Mexico City until after the ratification of the treaty. Although gold was discovered on January 24, 1848, John Marshall and John Sutter tried to keep the discovery a secret. It was not until the middle of May that news reached San Francisco. See J.S. Holliday, The World Rushed In: The California Gold Rush Experience (New York: Simon & Schuster, 1981).

18. Siglo XIX, June 2, 1848, 3 : 2.

19. Ibid., June 7, 1848, 3 : 4.

20. Ibid., June 10, 1848, 3 : 3.

21. Ibid., June 2, 1848, 1 : 5.

22. Jose Maria Roa Barcena, Recuerdos de la invasion norteamericana (1846-1848), vol. 3 (1883; Reprint, Mexico, D.F.: Editorial Porrua, 1947), 3 : 323.

23. Francisco de Paula de Arrangoiz, Mexico desde 1808 hasta 1867 (1872; Reprint, Mexico, D.F.: Editorial Porrua, 1969), p. 401.

24. Siglo XIX, May 19, 1848, 3 : 6.

25. Algunos documentos sobre el tratado de Guadalupe y la situacion de Mexico durante la invasion Americana, (Mexico, D.F.: Editorial Porrua, 1970), p. 380.

26. Roa Barcena, p. 304.

27. Algunos documentos, pp. 51-65, 168-92.

28. Dennis E. Berge, "Mexican Response to United States Expansionism, 1841-1848" (Ph.D. diss., Berkeley, 1965), pp. 304-306.

29. Siglo XIX, June 2, 1848, 3 : 2.

30. The Protocol of Queretaro also dealt with the modified Article XII, which did not specify the timing of the final 12 million dollar U.S. payment to Mexico.

31. Miller, 5 : 381.

32. Geofry Mawn, "A Land Grant-Guarantee: The Treaty of Guadalupe Hidalgo or the Protocol of Queretaro?" Journal of the West, vol. 14, no. 4 (October 1975) : 57-58. This article is a detailed study of the protocol issue.

33. Mawn, p. 59.

34. Mawn (p.61) believes that the protocol did not guarantee land grants any more than the treaty.

35. Meier and Rivera, p. 403.

36. For the primary reports of the boundary survey from the American point of view, see John Russell Bartlett, "Report on the United States and Mexican Boundary Commission," House Executive Documents, 34th Cong., 1 st sess. (Serial no. 861). Recent researchers using the Mexican Archives, have begun to tell the Mexican side of the story. See Joseph Richard Werne, "Mexico's Interpretation of the Guadalupe Hidalgo Line," (a paper presented for the American Historical Association, Washington, D.C., 1987); and Harry P. Hewitt, "The Treaty of Guadalupe Hidalgo Revisited: Myths and Realities of the Mexican Boundary Survey,")paper presented for the American Historical Association, Washington, D.C., 1987).

37. Luis Zorrilla, Historia de las relaciones entre Mexico y los Estados Unidos de America, 1800-1958, vol. 1 (Mexico, D.F.: Editorial Porrua, 1977), pp. 338-339.

38. Angela Moyano Pahissa, Mexico y Estados Unidos: Origenes de una relacion, 1819-1861 (Mexico, D.F.: Secretaria de Educacion Publica, 1985), pp. 175-177. Pahissa believes that the transfer of these three communities after 1848 was a violation of Article V of the treaty specifying boundaries.

39. Paul Garber, The Gadsden Treaty (Gloucester, Mass.: Peter Smith, 1959), pp. 29-30. This is the best study of the origins of this treaty.

40. For the best detailed study of the complicated boundary disputes arising between 1848 and 1853, see W.H. Goetzmann, "The United States – Mexico Boundary Survey, 1848-1853," Southwestern Historical Quarterly, vol. 62, no. 2 (October 1958) : 164-190. See also Jack D. Rittenhouse, The Story of Disturnell's Treaty Map (Santa Fe: Stage Coach Press, 1965).

41. See Robert D. Gregg, The Influence of Border Troubles on Relations Between the United States and Mexico, 1876-1910, (Baltimore: John Hopkins Press, 1937).

Citizenship and Property Rights: American Interpretations of the Treaty

Richard Griswold del Castillo

Articles VIII and IX of the Treaty of Guadalupe Hidalgo had set forth the terms by which the former Mexican citizens and their property would be incorporated politically into the United States. These articles in the treaty affected some 100,000 Mexicans in the newly acquired territories, including a large number of Hispanicized as well as nomadic Indians in New Mexico and California.[1] As provided by Article VIII, a person had one year to "elect" his or her preference for Mexican citizenship. If this were not done, it was stipulated that they had elected to become United States citizens and that they would be granted citizenship by Congress at some future time. The two articles also treated the property rights of the conquered people. Absentee Mexican landholders would have their property "inviolably respected," and others would "be maintained and protected in the free enjoyment of their liberty and property." In the six decades following the ratification of the treaty, its deceptively clear provisions regarding citizenship and property were complicated by legislative and judicial interpretations. This chapter surveys the ways in which the American institutions interpreted the Treaty of Guadalupe Hidalgo in the crucial period following its promulgation. In the end the application of the treaty to the realities of life in the Southwest violated its spirit.

Mexican Citizenship and Repatriation

A number of persons living in the territories ceded to the United States chose to remain Mexican citizens, either by announcing their intent before judicial officials or by returning to Mexico. No one knows their exact number, but probably they were few by comparison with the total population in the Southwestern states and territories. The Mexican government was anxious to encourage its nationals to return to Mexico, to populate the sparsely settled northern frontier regions. Since colonial times, Mexican governmental officials had looked toward their far northern frontier with apprehension and had tried to populate it with hardy settlers. The idea of the northern frontier as a buffer zone protecting the more civilized and wealthy settlements to the south emerged time and again in imperial planning. During the negotiation of the Treaty of Guadalupe Hidalgo, General Santa Anna proposed the creation of a buffer zone separating the two republics. Eighteen forty eight presented the Mexican administration with an opportunity to reorganize frontier defenses. The Mexican government hoped that new colonists migrating from the American Southwest would defend their frontier from Indian attacks as well as from U.S. incursions.

In the governmental decrees of July, and of August 19, 1848, Herrera's administration drew up detailed plans to establish military colonies along the U.S. Mexico border. These settlements were to be populated with repatriated Mexican citizens.[2] The plans were to set up eighteen settlements spanning the two-thousand-mile zone. The Southwest was to be divided into three sectors of colonization. Families from New Mexico would have lands reserved for them in Chihuahua; those from Texas would settle in Tamaulipas and Nuevo Leon; and those from California, in Baja California or Sonora. As an incentive to repatriate, each settler over the age of 14 would be given 25 pesos and his children 12 pesos each. Land, transportation and initial living expenses were to be paid from a fund of 200,000 dollars coming from the U. S. payments provided for under the treaty.[3]

To implement this ambitious plan, beginning in 1849, the Mexican government sent three commissioners who would receive, besides expense money, a bounty of one peso for each settler they encouraged to move. In California several repatriation expeditions were organized but the numbers who actually left were few.[4] The Californios were unwilling to give up their mild climate for the barren deserts of Baja California or Sonora. Besides the gold rush was a powerful reason to remain. The two commissioners to the more populous province of New Mexico, Padre Ramon Ortiz and Manuel Armendarias, met with somewhat more success. After a few months of activity, between fifteen hundred and two thousand New Mexicans reportedly left the territory taking with them their slaves and property. According to Ortiz's report, there was a great interest in repatriation; he estimated that up to eighty thousand might be induced to leave. Without doubt this number was exaggerated but it indicated that there was widespread dissatisfaction with the American administration of the territory. The military governor of New Mexico, fearful that the Mexican commissioners might instigate a rebellion, refused to allow them to visit other New Mexico counties.[5] Repatriation efforts from New Mexico continued sporadically into the next decade, with the Mexican government making occasional protests regarding the American government's lack of cooperation in the project. Nevertheless a number of frontier towns were founded by the New Mexicans who returned to Mexico: Guadalupe, La Mesilla, Santo Tomas and Refugio.[6]

In Texas the repatriation program was a qualified success. At least 150 families left that state before the ratification of the treaty, settling on lands set aside by the government. On June 22, 1850, Commissioner Antonio Menchaca brought 618 people and more than 100 families from Nacogdoches to Coahuila and requested 20,602 pesos in expenses. Other groups from Texas moved to establish new border towns or settled in existing ones on the south bank of the Rio Grande. In this way the Mexican border towns of Guerrero, Mier, Camargo, Reynosa, and Matamoros grew in size, and new towns of Nuevo Laredo, Guadalupe, and Ascensión were founded.[7]

Under the provisions of the treaty, the conquered peoples of the new territories could "elect," besides repatriation, to remain Mexican citizens and continue to reside in the U.S. territories. In New Mexico "a large number" chose to appear before the local county official as provided for by the governor to announce their continued Mexican citizenship. This was despite the very short interval allowed for them to declare their intention of remaining Mexican citizens (between April 21, 1849 and May 30, 1849). Their names were published and circulated among the county officials to prevent future voter frauds. There were however a number of problems that arose when those who declared their Mexican citizenship changed their mind later on and petitioned to become U.S. citizens without success. Approximately 2000 New Mexicans declared to retain their Mexican citizenship. There is no record that other Mexicans in California or Texas chose to remain Mexican citizens.[8]

United States Citizenship

Articles VIII and IX provided that those who did not choose to remain Mexican citizens would be considered "to have elected" to become U.S. citizens. As early as 1849 the nature of the citizenship rights of these Mexicans became the subject of controversy. In California the delegates to the state constitutional convention wrestled with the problems of race, rights of citizenship, and the Treaty of Guadalupe Hidalgo. Six of the delegates were native Californios who were aware that Mexicans who looked like Indians faced the prospect of racial discrimination. Ultimately they argued for the protection of their class even if it meant endorsing the racist views of their Anglo colleagues towards Indians and blacks. Mexico had granted citizenship to "civilized" Indians and to Blacks, yet the Treaty of Guadalupe Hidalgo clearly stated that former Mexican citizens would be given the opportunity to become citizens of the United States. Following the biases of their age, the framers of the state constitution sought wording that would exclude Blacks and Indians while including Mexicans. A Mr. Gilbert introduced a proposal that would eventually become the first section of the state constitution defining suffrage. It extended the vote to "every white, male citizen of Mexico who shall have elected to become a citizen of the United States." The convention agreed that Indians and Blacks might at some future date be given the franchise but that because voting was not an absolute right of citizenship, they could be excluded. There was some concern over whether in fact the Mexicans remaining were citizens of the United States. Ultimately the delegates agreed that "it would seem that they are not in fact American citizens, but require some further action of Congress to make them citizens of the United States." [9] California's admission as a state presumably would be that conferring act. (Later court cases, however, would challenge this assumption.) The ambiguous citizenship of the Californios meant that they could not expect the full protection of the laws during a stressful and violent period in California's history.

The discovery of gold in 1848 created a situation in which thousands of Yankee immigrants were competing with native-born Californio miners in the gold fields. One estimate is that about thirteen hundred native Californios (former Mexican citizens) were in the gold regions in 1848 and that probably an equal number returned in 1849.[10] Xenophobia, nativism, residual of war-time patriotism, and racism resulted in violent confrontations between English-speaking immigrants and other residents. Eventually most of the latter were driven from the most profitable gold fields. As a consequence of vigilantism and its attendant lynchings, harassment, and abuse of "foreigners," several countries lodged diplomatic protests and financial claims against the U. S. government. The Mexican government was active in lodging formal complaints in Washington D.C. even though many of them lacked specificity. As late as 1853 the Mexican Ambassador in Washington, Larráinzar, protested the treatment of Mexican miners in California invoking the protections of the Treaty of Guadalupe Hidalgo. The American Secretary of State responded that it was not clear that the treaty was being violated since there was a legal distinction between the Mexicans who had migrated to California after 1848 and those who were there before the gold rush.[11] Generally the Mexican government failed to present clear evidence that native Californios were being deprived of their property and civil rights in violation of the treaty.

There was evidence to substantiate the charges. In 1849 the military governor of California, General Percifor Smith, responding to nativist fears that foreigners were taking all the gold out of the mining regions, announced his "trespass" orders prohibiting non-citizens to mine gold on public property. He appealed to Americans to help him enforce his policy and under the protection of the military Anglo-American miners robbed and harassed foreigners. In his reminiscences, Antonio Coronel, a native Californio resident of Los Angeles, vividly described stabbings, extortions and lynchings as commonplace Yankee reactions to native Californios, whom they regarded as interlopers. Some Spanish-speaking natives even were issued passes, supposed proof of their new status as citizens of the United States, but this had little effect on the hordes of Yankees crowding into the mining district. Because neither the mass of Americans nor the Mexican government considered the Californios citizens, they were without the juridical protection of either nation.

The violations of their rights under the Treaty of Guadalupe Hidalgo were finally tested in the U.S. courts. In the California Supreme Court case of People v. Naglee (1851), the issue was whether or not a newly enacted Foreign Miner's Tax Law violated the U.S. Constitution, the Treaty of Guadalupe Hidalgo or the California State Constitution.[12] The defense argued, "It does not appear that this act [the Foreign Miner's Tax Law] has ever been enforced against any person entitled to the benefit of this treaty or even against any citizen of Mexico." The Foreign Miner's Tax Law specifically exempted Mexicans who had become U.S. citizens under the treaty. In the Naglee case the defense did not introduce evidence of the violation of treaty rights.[13] The prosecution, on the other hand, argued that the law should apply to Mexican Americans because they were not yet officially U.S. citizens. This view was rejected by the court but it reemerged twenty years later in the case of People v. de la Guerra (1870).

In People v. de la Guerra, the status of the former Mexican citizens finally was resolved. Pablo de la Guerra, a venerable Californio landholder who signed the California Constitution, ran for district judge in 1869. His political opponents in that election challenged his right to office based on the argument that he, along with thousands of other Californios, had only "elected" to become a citizen of the United States under the provisions in the treaty. In fact, none of these people were yet citizens because Congress had not yet formally given them citizenship. The California Supreme Court ruled against this view and in de la Guerra's favor, stating that the admission of California as a state constituted the positive act conferring citizenship on former Mexican nationals.[14] *Article 9 — becomes a State — Citizen*

The fate of the California Indians is further evidence of the violation of the spirit of the treaty. Under the Mexican Constitution of 1824, Indians were considered full Mexican citizens. Upon the transfer of territory to the U. S. government, however, these Mexican citizens received neither U.S. citizenship nor the protections of the treaty as specified in Article VIII. The California state constitutional convention recoiled from the idea of granting Indians full citizenship. In violation of the treaty, the California Indian tribes were deprived of the protections specified in the treaty. Consequently they became the victims of murder, slavery, land theft, and starvation. The Indian population within the state declined by more than 100,000 in two decades. Whites overran tribal lands and people were exterminated. Genocide is not too strong a word to use in describing what happened to the California Indians in this period.[15]

In New Mexico, where the largest Hispanicized Indian population lived, there was little debate about the citizenship rights of these people. In the territorial framework the franchise was limited to whites only. On September 24, 1849, a convention met to draw up an organic act to govern the territory during its wait for statehood. A majority of the delegates were from old line Hispano families. They declared that the rights of citizenship would be restricted to "free white male inhabitants residing within the limits of the United States, but who [were residents] on the 2nd day of February, 1848 . . ."[16] They specified that former Mexican citizens would have to take an oath of affirmation before a territorial or federal court renouncing allegiance to the Mexican Republic before they would be considered citizens of the territory. This stipulation was approved with no debate and approved by Congress the next year.[17]

Because New Mexico became a territory rather than a state, the civil rights of its inhabitants were less than those in California. Following the pattern established under the Northwest Ordinances

(1787) and the Wisconsin Organic Act of 1836, the people resident in the territories were conceived of as a dependent people who were not entitled to full participation in the national body politic. The laws and administration of the territory were subject to controls of Congress. The citizens of the New Mexico Territory (which, until 1863, included Arizona) did not have full civil rights: they were not allowed to vote for their governor or for the President of the United States; the decisions of their elected representatives were subject to federal approval; and they did not have an independent judiciary. During the period 1901-1922 in the Insular Cases the Supreme Court began to articulate the rights of the residents in the territories of the United States. The high court determined that the Constitution did not necessarily apply with full force to the residents in the U. S. territories. As Secretary of War Elihu Root put it, "[T]he Constitution follows the flag- but doesn't quite catch up with it." [18]

The Hispanos of New Mexico did not obtain all the rights of U.S. citizens under the terms of the Treaty of Guadalupe Hidalgo until statehood in 1912. Until then they remained dependent politically as the residents of a territory. For them the key phrase in the treaty was contained in Article IX: "and in the meantime [they shall] be maintained and protected in the free enjoyment of their liberty and property, and secured in the free exercise of their religion." Essentially these "citizens in waiting" had their rights guaranteed by the treaty until they gained full citizenship status.

As in California, the most obvious victims of the transfer of sovereignty in New Mexico were the Indian peoples. Approximately eight thousand Pueblo Indians who had been Mexican citizens in 1848 were disenfranchised thereafter. Initially in 1849 several pueblo villagers had participated in local elections under the assumption that they were citizens. The American officials however believed that the Indian vote was too easily manipulated by various factions and moved to convince the 19 Pueblo villages that it would be in their interest to reject full citizenship and to accept a ward status under the existing 1834 Indian Intercourse Act. Accordingly in 1849 the presidentially appointed Indian Agent at Santa Fe, James

S. Calhoun, traveled to visit all the pueblo villages to convince them to accept federal protection under the Intercourse Act. In 1851, as a result of Calhoun's labors, representatives of several tribes met and voted not to participate in New Mexican politics, apparently rejecting their rights under the Treaty of Guadalupe Hidalgo. In 1854 the legislature passed a law prohibiting the Pueblo tribes from voting except in the election of local water officials.

Despite this early history of disenfranchisement, some of it voluntary on the part of the Indians, the New Mexico Territorial Courts later decided cases which confirmed the citizenship of the Pueblo Indians. The Lucero case in 1869, the Santistevan case in 1874, the Joseph case in 1876, the Delinquent Taxpayers case in 1904, and the Mares case in 1907 all were decisions of the Territorial Supreme Court that confirmed the citizenship rights of the Pueblos. This judicial tradition, however, had little effect on the ward-like status of the Pueblos. A U.S. Supreme Court decision in 1913, United States v. Sandoval 231 U.S. 28 (1913), found that the Pueblos were entitled to Federal protection and that their citizenship status was not clear. When New Mexico was admitted as a state in 1912, its constitution contained a provision denying voting rights to "Indians not taxed", which included the Pueblo tribes. It was not until 1948 that this provision was declared unconstitutional and not until 1953 that the New Mexican Constitution was changed to allow Pueblo Indians the vote.[19]

As for the citizenship status of the other Indian groups in New Mexico, there was little argument. The Apaches and Navajos, who had fought so long to escape Hispanicization, remained the traditional enemies of the whites well into the 1870s and 1880s. Eventually, though, they were defeated in battle, placed on reservations and treated as conquered nations with separate peace treaties. They were eventually given citizenship at the same time as the Pueblo tribes.

Land

Admittedly the rights and benefits of U.S. citizenship were somewhat abstract blessings for Mexican Americans considering that for so long the Anglo Americans treated them all as foreigners.

A more tangible promise offered by the Treaty, included in Articles VIII and IX and the Protocol of Queretaro, was the promise of protection for private property. It was in the realm of property rights that the greatest controversies erupted.

In California thousands of gold-rush migrants encroached on the Californio land grants and demanded that something be done to "liberate" the land. The result was the passage in Congress of the Land Act of 1851. This law set up a Board of Land Commissioners whose job would be to adjudicate the validity of Mexican land grants in California. Every grantee was required to present evidence supporting title within two years. Those failing to do so would have their property pass to the public domain. The land commissioners were instructed by law to govern their decisions according to the Treaty of Guadalupe Hidalgo, the law of nations, Spanish and Mexican laws, and previous decisions of the Supreme Court.

A basic principle underlying the establishment of the Board of Land Claims and of land-confirmation processes in New Mexico and Texas, was that the vast majority of Mexican land grants in the ceded territory were "imperfect," meaning that the claimants had not fulfilled Mexican regulations for legal land ownership. In years subsequent to the treaty, American courts ruled that the U.S. government had inherited the Mexican government's sovereignty and thereby the right to complete the processes of land confirmation.[20]

Under this assumption the Board of Land Claims in California examined 813 claims and eventually confirmed 604 of them involving approximately nine million acres. This, however, did not mean that the majority of Mexican land holders were ultimately protected by the courts. On the contrary, most Californio land holders lost their lands because of the tremendous expense of litigation and legal fees. To pay for the legal defense of their lands, the Californios were forced to mortgage their ranchos. Falling cattle prices and usurious rates of interest conspired to wipe them out as a land holding class. Pablo de la Guerra summarized the dilemma for the California legislature:

"Sir, if he gained his suit if his title was confirmed, the expenses of the suit would confiscate his property, and millions have already been spent in carrying up cases that have been confirmed by the (Land Commission), and land owners in California have been obligated to dispose of their property at half its value, in order to pay for the expenses of the suit."[21]

Even if some landholders were able to fulfill the terms of the 1851 land law, they soon encountered tremendous pressure from Anglo American squatters to vacate their rights. Perhaps one of the most celebrated and controversial cases was that of Joseph Yves Limantour. Limantour was a Frenchman whose son later became the famous Secretary of Treasury under President Porfirio Diaz. In 1843 the governor of California, Manuel Micheltorrena, gave Limantour a grant of four square leagues comprising about half of the unpopulated area known as Yerba Buena, land that later was part of the city of San Francisco. When gold was discovered in northern California in 1848, thousands of immigrants flooded San Francisco settling on lots carved from Limantour's grant. To protect his rights Limantour presented his case before the Land Commission and in 1856 that body confirmed his title. Limantour was an absentee landholder whose rights were ostensibly protected under Article VIII of the treaty, as well as under Mexican law. Because he did not intend to reside in California Limantour offered to sell his land rights to settlers at 10 percent of their true market value. A number of squatters settled along these lines but a majority formed an Anti-Limantour party to challenge his ownership. The political pressure of the squatters, many of them wealthy and influential San Franciscans, resulted in accusations of fraud. After presenting witnesses who had changed their testimony, Limantour was jailed by a Grand Jury on charges of fraud and perjury in 1857. Released on bond after a few months he returned to Mexico to gather evidence to substantiate his case. He returned in 1858 for the trial with new documents and witnesses. Nevertheless the court decided against him and he lost his land.[22]

Other individuals who held perfect titles to their land under the

Mexican government and who were able to survive economically, lost their holdings because they had not fulfilled the terms of the 1851 land law. A number of court cases in this regard involving Mexican and Spanish grants emerged, but the most famous one pertaining to the Treaty of Guadalupe Hidalgo was Botiller et al. v. Dominguez (1883).[23]

In 1848, Dominga Dominguez, owner of Rancho Los Virgenes, just east of Mission San Fernando in California, had a "perfect" title to her land, a grant from the government of Mexico dated August 28, 1835. Her ancestors had taken all the steps required to legalize this claim. For some reason she and her relatives neglected to bring their papers before the Court of Land Claims within the specified time provided for in the 1851 law. For the next thirty years a number of Mexican-American and European immigrant families settled on the rancho assuming that the land was part of the public domain and that it had been opened for homesteading. Finally, in 1883, Brigido Botiller, a French born Mexican citizen headed a group of squatters to oust Dominguez from her land, claiming that by the 1851 law she had no legal title to it.[24] Dominga then sued Botiller and the other squatters for reclamation of her land and back rents. In the 1880s both the District Court and the California State Supreme Court ruled in her favor. Both courts were convinced that her title was legitimate because the provisions in the Treaty of Guadalupe Hidalgo meant that the Dominguez family was "not compelled to submit the same for confirmation. . . nor did the grantee Nemecio Dominguez forfeit the land described."[25] Botiller and the squatters appealed their case to the U.S. Supreme Court, where, in a decision issued on April 1, 1889, the court reversed the California Supreme Court decision ruling that, despite the Treaty of Guadalupe Hidalgo guarantees, Dominguez did not have legal title. The court reasoned that by admitting the legality of this title under this treaty, the government would open the floodgates to others who had perfect titles but had not presented them to the Court of Land Claims. The result would be to wreak havoc on California land ownership. Further, the justices argued that the Supreme Court had no power to enforce the Treaty of Guadalupe Hidalgo and that matters of treaty violation were subject to international negotiation and more treaties. Specifically, they stated, "This court has no power to set itself up as the instrumentality for enforcing provisions of a treaty with a foreign nation." They held that the Land Law of 1851 did not violate the due process provision of the Constitution because property holders were "at all times liable to be called into a court of justice to contest [their] title to it." Congress, the court ruled, had the power to require land holders to verify their claims and to fix penalties for failing to follow the law.[26]

In Botiller et al. v. Dominguez the Supreme Court held that the sovereign laws of the U.S. took precedence over international treaties. This appeared to contradict the Constitution, which (in Article VI, Section 2, and Article III, Section 2, Clause 1) gave treaties the same status as the Constitution. The ruling thus sparked learned debate. John Currey, a San Francisco attorney, published a booklet challenging the court's logic.[27] The Supreme Court's decision, he argued, sanctioned the confiscation of property and violated the due-process provision of the Constitution: "The fact of the existence of a title in fee simple to land cannot be destroyed by a sweep of the pen, nor by the obiter dictum of a learned judge."[28] Botiller et al. v. Dominguez was an important precedent, guiding the court in its future interpretation of conflicts between treaty obligations and domestic laws. In this case the protection of private property ostensibly guaranteed by the Treaty of Guadalupe Hidalgo was essentially invalidated.

New Mexico

The Compromise of 1850 made New Mexico a territory while California entered the Union as a state. This difference in political status would produce different resolutions of land-tenure problems. In California a state judiciary functioned to render relatively swift interpretations of the Treaty of Guadalupe Hidalgo; in New Mexico federally appointed officials had to have their decisions approved by Congress, a lengthy and often politicized process. Ironically, New Mexico's more direct link to the national government meant that the property-rights guarantees under the Treaty of Guadalupe Hidalgo would be even less importance than in California.

In 1848 private and communal land grants in New Mexico covered about fifteen million square miles. In order to determine the federal domain, Congress established the office of Surveyor General, who was given broad powers to "issue notices, summon witnesses, administer oaths, etc.," and to report to the Secretary of Interior and, ultimately, Congress regarding the status of New Mexico land grants. Until Congress acted to confirm the findings of the Surveyor General, all lands were to be withheld from sale.

In August of 1854 Congress appointed William Pelham to the office. Once in New Mexico, he had considerable trouble getting the Hispano land-grant owners to file their claims with his office; as a result, by 1863, only 25 town and private claims and 17 Pueblo Indian grants had been confirmed by Congress. By 1880, 1000 claims had been filed by the Surveyor General but only 150 had been acted upon by the federal government.[29] As the number of unconfirmed grants in litigation before the Surveyor General and the Congress lengthened, so too did the legal expenses incurred by the Hispano pueblos and ranchers. Such lawyers and politicians as Stephen Benson Elkins and Thomas Benton Catron formed the nucleus of the Santa Fe Ring, a confederation of opportunists who used the long legal battles over land grants to acquire empires extending over millions of acres. The most famous example of the land grabbing activities of the Ring was the creation of the Maxwell Land Grant, a Spanish claim of 97,000 acres that became inflated through the actions of the Ring to a final patent of 1,714,074 acres.[30]

Besides losing their lands to rapacious lawyers and politicians, the Hispanos suffered the changing whims of national politics. In 1885 the newly elected Democratic president, Grover Cleveland, removed the Republican Surveyor General of New Mexico and replaced him with his own man, William Andrew Sparks, an individual whom historian Ralph Emerson Twitchell described as "steeped in prejudice against New Mexico, its people and their property rights."[31] The new Surveyor General decided that his predecessor had been corrupt and had given away far too much federal land and that his decisions and those of the Congress regarding land should be reviewed. In the name of reform the new Surveyor General revoked the approval of twenty three grants. The process of reviewing the New Mexico claims gave no assurance that the Treaty of Guadalupe Hidalgo, or indeed the rule of law, outweigh the political influence of those behind the scenes.

When Benjamin Harrison became president in 1889, the federal land policies in New Mexico would again change. Under pressure from developers and New Mexico Hispanos, Congress in 1890 began to consider legislation that would settle the outstanding land claims. Railroad interests wanted to have the public domain so they established, so that they could get federal grants. Hispano land holders in New Mexico sought to speed up the land-confirmation process or to reverse previously adverse rulings. Writing to Matias Romero, the Mexican Minister Plenipotentiary to the U.S. in 1890, the predominantly Hispano Commercial Club of Las Vegas, New Mexico, laid out their complaints. They urged Minister Romero to use his influence to secure passage of a new land law:

"The American government has thus far, though over 40 years have elapsed, neglected to provide a competent court to pass on the validity of the claims of those who were once Mexican citizens. . . . We, with great respect petition you to champion the cause of our people and again represent to the State Department at Washington evil inflicted on us by the failure of the U.S. government to fulfill in this respect its obligations incurred by the Treaty of Guadalupe Hidalgo.[32]

For its part, the Mexican government followed the proposed legislation with interest but was unable, for diplomatic reasons, to advocate the Hispanos' cause in Congress. The Mexican government did instruct Romero to react to court cases when it appeared that there was prejudice against former Mexican citizens in the application of the law once it passed Congress. Romero, for his part, suggested that his government publicize its concern for its former citizens so that they would be better able to oppose unjust actions taken against them in violation of the Treaty of Guadalupe Hidalgo.[33]

On March 3, 1891, the president signed into law a bill to establish a Court of Private Land Claims. The Treaty of Guadalupe Hidalgo was specifically invoked as a guiding document for this court, although wording in the act provided that it would apply only to "persons who became citizens by reason of the Treaty of Guadalupe Hidalgo and who have been in the actual adverse possession of tracts not to exceed 160 acres."[34] The court was made up of five judges plus an attorney representing the interests of the U.S. government. Unlike the California Land Commission, the New Mexico Court of Land Claims did not require those holding perfect titles to apply to the court for confirmation only those who had not fulfilled all the regulations of the Spanish and Mexican laws. Those not presenting their claims within two years would be considered to have abandoned their grant. The law also restricted to eleven square leagues (about thirty six square miles) the amount of land that would allowed for a communal or town grant and stipulated that errors in previous decisions by Congress would be indemnified at not more than $1.25 per acre.

Meeting in Denver, Colorado and Santa Fe, New Mexico between 1891 and 1904, the New Mexico Court operated by the strict rule that confirmation of a land grant required proof that the Spanish or Mexican granting official had legal authority. There had been a good deal of confusion in Mexico's political history; therefore, many New Mexican grants were held not to be legitimate because of the "illegitimacy" of the Mexican governing bodies.[35] The court also was very strict regarding what it considered a proper survey, documentation, and full compliance with every Mexican law regarding land tenure. As a result of this less-than-liberal interpretation of Spanish and Mexican laws, the New Mexico court rejected two-thirds of the claims presented before it. Ultimately only eighty two grants received congressional confirmation. This represented only 6 percent of the total area sought by land claimants. Thus, using the Court of Private Land Claims, the U.S. government enlarged the national domain at the expense of hundreds of Hispano villages, leaving a bitter legacy that would fester through the next century.[36]

Texas

In 1856 the U.S. Supreme Court ruled that the Treaty of Guadalupe Hidalgo did not apply to Texas. In McKinney v. Saviego the justices ruled that Articles VIII and IX of the treaty referring to property rights and citizenship,

> did not refer to any portion of the acknowledged limits of Texas. The territories alluded to (in Articles VIII and IX of the treaty) are those which previous to the treaty had belonged to Mexico. . . . The Republic of Texas had been many years before acknowledged by the United States as existing separately and independently of Mexico.[37]

This decision seemed to invalidate the meaning of the Protocol of Queretaro, which specifically identified Texas land grants as being protected. Under this agreement grants made prior to March 2, 1836 (the date of Texas' self-proclaimed independence from Mexico) would remain as legal land grants.[38] Thus, according to the Supreme Court, Texas was not to be considered part of the Mexican Cession. Congress had admitted Texas into the Union in 1845, and that state's constitution ran counter to the Treaty of Guadalupe Hidalgo (Article VIII) in forbidding aliens from holding property. (The Texas government had already declared as aliens those Tejanos who had left the Republic during the Texas Rebellion.)

The Mexican government took exception to this interpretation. In 1895, R. S. Sanchez, a legal consultant to the Secretaria de Relaciones Exteriores published his views, arguing that U.S. courts were in violation of the Treaty of Guadalupe Hidalgo because Mexico had never recognized the independence of Texas and the treaty specifically and formally recognized Texas as part of the U.S. by the delineation of the boundary (in Article IV).[39]

The issue of Texas and the treaty remained a point of contention well into the twentieth century. U.S. courts discounted arguments that cited the treaty when arguing for Texas land claims. In 1911, in State v. Gallardo et al., a Texas Civil Appeals Court reaffirmed the Supreme Court view that "the validity of the title under consideration should be determined without reference to any provision of the treaty," but, at the same time, recognized that prior decisions of the local courts in Texas had upheld grants of land based, in part, on interpretations of the Treaty of Guadalupe Hidalgo and the Protocol.[40]

During the Bucareli Conferences held in 1923 between the U.S. and Mexico, the issue of the status of the Texas land grants and the applicability of the Treaty of Guadalupe Hidalgo resurfaced. This conference was convened to settle the outstanding claims of both countries and to pave the way for U.S. diplomatic recognition of Mexico's revolutionary government. To counter U.S. claims for damages suffered by Americans during the revolution of 1910, the Mexican government decided to present the claims of its former citizens in the Southwest. Initially they presented 836 claims amounting to 245 million dollars. Almost 193 million of this amount was for Texas land claims invalidated in violation of the Treaty of Guadalupe Hidalgo.[41] The Mexican government, through its consulate in Texas, actively solicited land claims from heirs of the original land grant owners who had been dispossessed of their lands after 1848. Increased Anglo American migration into south Texas after 1848 was the origin of a large number of these claims. This was the area of Texas in which the first battles of the Mexican War had occurred and where there had been so much diplomatic disagreement prior to the signing of the Treaty of Guadalupe Hidalgo. Many Tejano grants in this region were perfected Spanish claims that had been recognized by the Mexican government.[42]

Unlike New Mexico or California, Texas had been admitted to the Union with full control over its public lands. Instead of federal laws guiding the settlement of land disputes, state laws and courts played a dominant role. It is difficult to generalize about the Texas claims because of the decades of litigation surrounding them. Two Texas historians, De Leon and Stewart, concluded that most Tejanos lost portions of their patrimony or all of it through "a combination of methods including, litigation, chicanery, robbery, fraud, and threat."[43]   As early as 1847 the citizens of Laredo, Texas, fearing how they would fare under the Texas administration, requested assurances from the state government that their property rights would be protected. Receiving no reply, they petitioned to be allowed to remain part of Mexico.[44] Many violent episodes marked the struggle between Tejanos and Ango Texans for control of the land. The Cortina Rebellion, in the Brownsville Matamoros area in the 1850s and 1860s and the El Paso Salt War, in the 1870s, had pitted entire communities against the Texas Rangers in a struggle for the land. Hundreds of lesser struggles that resulted in lynchings, beatings, and riots that also had their origin in conflicts over the land.[45] Tejanos had good reason to distrust the Texas government in its implementation of laws.

Tejano families found their lands in jeopardy because they had been forced to flee Texas during the Mexican war. The Las Mestenas grant, near Reynosa, is one example. The original heirs vacated their lands between 1846 and 1848. Their decision to reoccupy the grant in 1848 was an expensive one for it meant selling their lands to pay back taxes and paying the expense of rounding up stolen or stray cattle. The large families and the Hispanic tradition of equal inheritance worked against continuing land ownership. There were numerous heirs, some of whom had never seen the grant. American speculators bought up interests from these absentee owners, made high-interest loans, assumed mortgages on portions of the rancho, and purchased sections at tax sales. Tejano sued Tejano and Anglo Texan sued Tejano over conflicting claims until 1915, when a million-dollar law suit finally cleared title with few of the original claimants retaining an interest.[46]

Other Tejano grantees lost their lands because they had left Texas during the Texas rebellion in 1836. The Republic declared their lands vacant and issued certificates of land ownership to individuals who had fought in the Texan army. Litigation between these certificate holders and recipients of older Mexican and Spanish grants resulted in further violations of the Treaty of Guadalupe Hidalgo. Andrew A. Tijerina, who studied the process up to 1850, concluded, "Across the state, Tejano emigres lost their lands to 'fictitious law suits,' sheriff's auctions, and dubious transfer of titles."[47]

David Montejano who has also studied the loss of Tejano

lands concluded that the process was a complex one involving fraud, confiscation and the operation of the mechanisms of market competition. In the late nineteenth century the Tejanos did not have access to the capital to develop their lands so that they could remain solvent during the changes in the ranching industries. They also had inherited non-capitalist traditional view of the use of their lands. The death of a patriarch often meant the dismemberment of the ranch as it was sold for back taxes and old debts. A large portion of the famous King ranch in south Texas was pieced together during the forced sale of Tejano ranches during unfavorable market conditions in the period 1886-1889.[48]

The conflicts between Spanish and Mexican claims and those granted by the Republic and State of Texas resulted in various legislative attempts to clear titles. In 1850, Governor P. H. Bell appointed a commission to investigate land claims arising from the Treaty of Guadalupe Hidalgo in South Texas.[49] The Bourland Miller Commission, created by the legislature, gathered abstracts of titles and made recommendations to the Texas legislature. More than 135 claims were reviewed and presented to the legislature for confirmation. In 1854, 1861, 1866, 1870, 1881, and 1901, the Texas legislature passed laws providing mechanisms for the examination and confirmation of Spanish and Mexican grants. A number of claims rejected by the Texas legislature became issues for further litigation.

In the nineteenth century, Texas courts regularly considered the Treaty of Guadalupe Hidalgo as it applied to Spanish and Mexican grants made before March 2, 1836. In Texas v Gallardo et al. (1911), the Texas Supreme Court ruled that the validation acts passed in earlier decades should not apply to titles that were valid under the Treaty of Guadalupe Hidalgo--meaning those that were legitimate prior to March 2, 1836. The court ruled that "a title to lands within the original Mexican states of Tamaulipas and the present boundaries of Texas . . . is within the protection of the Treaty and entitled to recognition in the Supreme Courts." Subsequent court decisions affirmed the point of view that the treaty took precedence over state legislation, but many Tejanos became landless because they could not afford lengthy legal appeals.[50]

Whether by laws, force, foreclosure, or litigation, many Tejanos lost title to their ancestral lands in the period 1848 1923. Many had their cases presented on their behalf by the Mexican government during the Bucareli negotiations. On September 8, 1923 the United States and Mexico agreed to establish a commission to review the Texas land grants. Eventually 433 cases, valued at 121 million dollars, were presented on behalf of the heirs. In 1941, after much delay, the Texas land claims were settled on the international level with the Mexican government assuming the obligation of compensating the Texas heirs. The issue, however, was not resolved, for while both the United States and Mexico recognized the legitimacy of the Texas claims under the Treaty of Guadalupe Hidalgo, the Mexican government refused to carry out its financial obligations this despite constant pressure from the Tejano land-grant heirs.[51]

In the first half century after ratification of the Treaty of Guadalupe Hidalgo, hundreds of state, territorial, and federal legal bodies produced a complex tapestry of conflicting opinions and decisions. The citizenship rights seemingly guaranteed in Articles VIII and IX were not all they seemed. The property rights for former Mexican citizens in California, New Mexico, and Texas proved to be fragile. Within a generation the Mexican Americans who had been under the ostensible protections of the treaty became a disenfranchised, poverty stricken minority. The promises of the treaty remained just that.

Notes

1. Oscar Martinez, "On the Size of the Chicano Population" Aztlan, 4, no.1 (Spring 1975) : 43-67.

2. Francisco F. de la Maza, ed., Codigo de Colonizacion y Terrenos Baldios de la Republica Mexicana (Mexico, D.F.: Secretaria de Fomento, 1873), pp.402-427.

3. Hubert Howe Bancroft, History of Arizona and New Mexico (San Francisco: The History Book Co., 1889), p. 473. The Mexican government made only 25,000 dollars available for the recruitment drive; the funds were to be drawn from those paid by the United States under the terms of the Treaty og Guadalupe Hidalgo. By 1851 eighteen frontier outposts were established, with 1,093 Mexican soldiers including people from the northern provinces and repatriated Mexicans from the United States. The Mexican government also recruited Seminole and Muskogee Indians to establish settlements. See Angela Moyano Pahissa, Mexico y Estados Unidos: Origenes de una relacion, 1819-1861 (Mexico, D.F.: Secretaria de Educacion Publica, 1985), pp. 206-207.

4. Richard Griswold del Castillo, The Los Angeles Barrio: 1850-1890: A Social History (Los Angeles: University of California Press, 1980), pp. 123-124.

5. Bancroft, p. 472; Ralph Emerson Twitchell, The Leading Facts of New Mexican History, vol. 1, (1911-1912; Reprint, Albuquerque: Horn and Wallace, 1963), p. 102.

6. The most detailed account of the activities of the commissioners in New Mexico is Mary Childers Mangusso, "A Study of the Citizenship Provisions of the Treaty of Guadalupe Hidalgo," (Masters thesis, University of New Mexico, 1966). For later protests see Manuel Marrimar to the Minister of Relaciones Exteriores, June 2, 1852, Archivo de la Secretaria de Relaciones Exteriores (ASRE), Mexico City, no. 2-12-2904. See Also Angela Moyano Pahissa, Mexico y Estados Unidos: Origenes de una relacion, 1819-1861 (Mexico, D.F.: Secretaria de Educacion Publica, 1985) pp. 182-184

7. Offical correspondence, ASRE, nos. 2-13-2976 and 2-13-2975.

8. Twitchell, p. 241. Later problems with non-citizens serving on juries in New Mexico led the territorial legislature to pass a law to allow persons who had declared their intention of becoming naturalized citizens to serve; see Mangusso, pp. 67-68.

9. J. Ross Browne, ed. Report of the Debates on the Convention of California on the Formation of the State Constitution in September and October 1849 (Washington, D.C.: John Towers, 1850), p. 62.

10. Leonard Pitt, Decline of the Californios: A Social History of the Spanish-Speaking Californians, 1846-1890 (Berkeley: University of California Press, 1970), p. 50.

11. The history of the Mexican government's protests regarding the

treatment of Mexicans in the United States in the period immediately after the Mexican war can be found in a number of published works: William R. Manning, ed., Diplomatic Correspondence of the United States, Interamerican Affairs, vol. 9 (Washington, D.C., 1937), pp. 129-130, 133-134, 568-570; Maria de Los Angeles, "La anexacion de Texas a los Estados Unidos," (Thesis, U.N.A.M, 1959), pp. 192-195; and Toribio Esquivel Obregon, Apuntes para la historia del derecho en Mexico, 4 vols. (Mexico, D.F.: Porrua e hijos, 1948), 3:426-427.

12. I Cal 232; Cal Stats 1850, Ch. 97; Pitt, pp. 66-67. The legal history of the Foreign Miner's Tax Law is given in Carl I. Wheat, ed., "California's Bantam Cock: The Journals of Charles E. De Long, 1854-1863," California Historical Quartely 8 (1929): 353-355.

13. Pitt, pp. 48-57.

14. The argument against de la Guerra's full citizenship is a revealing comment on the status of Mexican Americans after 1848. "In conclusion we insist that the respondent was an alien enemy up to the ratification of the Treaty of Guadalupe Hidalgo; that between that time and the date of the admission of California into the Union, he joined, by virtue of his silence, that class of Mexicans who are deemed to have elected to become citizens of the Unites States, but he is not and never was a citizen." People v. de la Guerra 40 Cal 311 (1870).

15. Van Hastings Garner, "The Treaty of Guadalupe Hidalgo and the California Indians," The Indian Historian 9, no. 1 (Winter, 1976): 10-13.

16. Robert W. Larson, New Mexico's Quest for Statehood, 1846-1912 (Albuquerque: University of New Mexico Press, 1968), p. 19.

17. See U.S. Congress, House of Representatives, New Mexico Convention of Delegates: Journal and Proceedings, 31st Cong. 1st sess., 1850, House Misc. Doc. 39, pp. 1-13.

18. Quoted in Walter La Feber, "The Constitutions and United States Foreign Policy: An Interpretation," Journal of American History, vol. 74, no. 3 (December 1987): 705. See Downs v. Bidwell, 182 US 244 and Balzac v. Puerto Rico 258 US 309; Also Whitney Perkins, Denial of Empire: the United States and Its Dependencies (The Netherlands: A.W. Sythoff-Lyden, 1962), pp. 13, 28. The question of citizenship for residents of the territories was a thorny one for jurists. The net effect of the Spanish- American War was to restrict the rights of citizenship to those residing within the borders of continental United States. By 1901 the people of Puerto Rico and the Philippines were made citizens of those places, not of the United States.

19. U.S. v. Lucero 1 NM 422 (1869); U.S. v Santistevan 1 N.M. 583 (1874).

20. For a complete discussion of Pueblo Indian citizenship after 1848 see Mary Childers Mangusso, "A Study of the Citizenship Provisions of the Treaty

of Guadalupe Hidalgo," (Master's thesis, University of New Mexico, 1966), pp. 77-99. Ralph Rowley, "The Acquisition of the Spanish Borderlands: Problems and Legacy" (Ph.D. diss., University of New Mexico, 1975), p. 168.

21. See Teschmacher v. Thompson 8 Cal 23.

22. See Griswold del Castillo, pp. 41-49; "Speech of Hon. Pablo de la Guerra of Santa Barbara," April 17, 1855 (Sacramento: State Tribune Office, 1855), p. 7.

23. Jan Bazant, "Joseph Yves Limantour (1812-1885) y su Aventura californiana-I," Historia Mexicana, 28, no. 1 (julio-septiembre, 1978): 1-23; "Joseph Yves Limantour (1812-1885)) y su aventura californiana-II," Historia Mexicana, 29, no. 3 (enero-marzo, 1980): 353-374. Bazant uncovered new evidence at the University of Texas archives that seems to support Limantour's case.

24. 130 U.S. 238 (1889); for a citation of cases that challenged the 1851 land law citing the Treaty of Guadalupe Hidalgo see Mintern v. Brower 24 Cal 644 (1864). An excellent discussion of the court cases affecting Mexican land grants is Richard Powell, Compromises of Conflicting Claims: A Century of California Law, 1760 to 1860 (Dobbs Ferry, New York: Oceana Publications, 1977), pp. 170-171.

25. U.S. Supreme Court, Brigido Botiller et al. v. Dominga Dominguez, File Copies of the Briefs, October Term, 1888, vol. 15, pp. 1-23; others who opposed Domingas's claim were Pedro Sepulveda, Manuel Felix, Manuel Sanchez, Pablo Bojorquez, Gregorio Tapia, and Ramon Tapia.

26. Willard B. Cowles, Treaties and Constitutional Law: Property Interferences and Due Process of Law (Washington, D.C.: American Council of Public Affairs, 1941), p. 240. 74 Cal 457 (1887).

27. 130 US 238; 9 S,Ct. 525, 527.

28. John Currey, The Treaty of Guadalupe Hidalgo and Private Land Claims and Titles Existing in California at the Date of the Treaty (San Francisco: Bancroft Whitney, 1891), p. 22.

29. Ralph Emerson Twitchell, The Leading Facts of New Mexico's History (Albuquerque: Horn and Wallace, 1963), 2: 458. New Mexican land-grant litigation, a complex subject, can be treated only superficially in a survey such as this. For a more detailed analysis of the legal and historical aspects involved, see: Victor Westphall, The Public Domain in New Mexico: 1854-1891 (Albuquerque: Univeristy of New Mexico Press, 1965); and J.J. Bowden, Spanish and Mexican Land Grants in the Chihuahuan Acquisition (El Paso: Texas Westernlore Press, 1971).

30. Howard Robert Lamar, The Far Southwest, 1846-1912: A Territorial History (New York: W.W. Norton, 1966), pp. 141-146.

31. Twitchell, 2 : 462.

32. Commercial Club of Las Vegas, New Mexico to Matias Romero,

Minister Plenipotentiary, December 27, 1890, ASRE, no. 11-5-1.

33. Matias Romero to Secretaria de Relaciones Exteriores, April 20, 1891, ASRE, no. 11-5-1.

34. Analysis of the Act to Establish a Court of Private Land Claims, ASRE, no. 11-5-1, p. 309.

35. Rowley, p. 210.

36. Ibid., pp. 213-214.

37. McKinney v. Saviego, S.C. 18 Howard 235.

38. Miller, Doc. 129, p. 381.

39. R.S. Sanchez to the Secretaria de Relaciones Exteriores, June 10, 1895, Boletin Oficial, tomo I, num. 1 (1895), p. 135. This volume also contains correspondence regarding the applicability of the treaty to Texas.

40. State v. Gallardo et al, 135 S.W. 664; "Juridical Decisions Involving Questions of International Law," American Journal of International Law, vol. 6 (1912), p. 227.

41. Rudolfo O. de la Garza, and Karl Schmitt, "Texas Land Grants and Chicano-Mexican Relations: A Case Study," Latin American Research Review 21, No. 1 (1986): 123-138.

42. Florence Johnson Scott, Royal Land Grants North of the Rio Grande, 1171-1821 (Rio Grande City: La Retama Press, 1969). This book studies the histories of the grants in the area of Reynosa, Texas: Llano Grande, La Feria, Las Mestenas, San Salvador de Tule, Santa Anita, and Padre Island.

43. Arnoldo de Leon and Kenneth L. Stewart, "Lost Dreams and Found Fortunes: Mexican and Anglo Immigrants into South Texas, 1850-1900," Western Historical Quarterly, vol. 14, no. 3 (July 1983): 296.

44. Gilberto Miguel Hinojosa, A Borderlands Town in Transition: Laredo, 1775-1850 (College Station: Texas A & M University Press, 1983), pp. 58-59.

45. Arnoldo de Leon, They Called Them Greasers (Austin: University of Texas Press, 1983).

46. Scott, p. 38.

47. Andrew A. Tijerina, "Tejanos and Texans: The Native Mexicans of Texas, 1820-1850" (Ph.D. diss., University of Texas Austin, 1977), pp. 319-320.

48. David Montejano, Anglos and Mexicans in the Making of Texas, 1836-1986 (Austin: University of Texas Press, 1987), pp. 63-70. This discussion of the Tejano lands is the best summary of a complex process.

49. Message of the Governor Transmitting the Report of the Commissioners to Investigate Land Titles West of the Nueces (Austin: Cushney and Hampton, 1851). The commissioners reported on Webb, Kinney, and Cameron counties, recommending the vast majority of the land grants; See Scott, pp. 105-106.

50. State of Texas v. Gallardo et al., 135 SW 664 (1911); State of Texas v. Bali, 173 SW 2nd 522.

51. Robert Salazar, "Texas Land Grant Heirs Seek Compensation," Ajenda: A Journal of Hispanic Issues, vol. 9, no. 2 (March/April, 1979): pp. 14-16. Asociacion de reclamantes et al. v. The United Mexican States, no. 81-2299, U.S. Court of Appeals for the District of Columbia Circuit, 561 F. 2d. 1190 (June 20, 1983); Asociacion de reclamantes et al. v. The United Mexican States, no. 83-1596, U.S. Court of Appeals for the District of Columbia Circuit, 735 F. 2d. 1517 (June 5, 1984).

5

Juan N. Cortina

Rodolfo Jacobo & Carlos M. Larralde

The era following the United States-Mexican War (1846-1848) was characterized by an ever growing yet changing kaleidoscope of violence and injustice against the Mexican population. This socio-economic and political environment was the product of Manifest Destiny and its explicit premise of Anglo political, racial and moral superiority, a premise which had led directly to the military confrontation. Throughout the Southwest there occurred gross violations of basic human rights as well as rights guaranteed by international treaty. The Mexican government, concerned about the future of the Mexicans who would remain in the ceded territories after the war, and about the protection of their rights and property, had secured Articles VIII, IX, and X in the Treaty of Guadalupe Hidalgo. These articles dealt specifically with the civil and property rights of Mexicans now under American rule. The treaty, designed to end the calamities of war and establish the guarantees of the former Mexican citizens was, however, largely ignored. Indeed, violations of the Treaty of Guadalupe Hidalgo took place in every corner of the former Mexican territory.

For example, in California, the Gold Rush attracted a wave of immigrants, many of whom were from Sonora, Mexico, a region with a rich mining tradition. Economic competition and the sentiments associated with Manifest Destiny immediately led to an anti-Mexican, nativist attitude among the Anglo population. Moreover, little was done to distinguish among the newcomers and legal residents and citizens of Mexican descent. In the absence of a well-structured and impartial legal institution, Mexicanos suffered the repercussions. Repression came in the form of direct violence at the hands of the citizenry or in the form of institutional litigation such as the Foreign Miners' Act of 1850. Clashes occurred over the rights of the former Mexican citizens, many of whom had become United States citizens by rights established under the Treaty of Guadalupe Hidalgo, as well as over the validity of their land grants.

Throughout the former Mexican territories, land disputes were at the center of almost all clashes, and ill feelings emerged between Americans and Mexicans because the property rights of Mexicanos were ignored by United States government authorities and laypersons alike. A complicated and totally alien legal system (English Precedent Law vs. Hispanic Code Law) often led to costly cases in which the Mexican land owners lost the very land they were trying to retain. In short, the decades following the United States-Mexican War, were ones in which the Mexican community experienced displacement and injustice in the new social order. Not surprisingly there was resistance to such conditions. There were numerous groups and individuals who confronted the American occupation of their soil. One of the most renowned and successful resistors to the new American socio-political structure was Juan Nepomuceno Cortina.

Cortina was born on May 16, 1824, in the border town of Camargo on the Mexican side of the Rio Grande. This spacious terrain is on the western edges of an alluvial delta. This coastal plain embraces some of the richest soil in the world, including immense cotton fields. Here, Juan Cortina's family owned livestock and over a thousand acres of land. His father, Trinidad, a shrewd, hard-working attorney, died when Cortina was a young man. Young Cortina was raised by his mother Estefana Cavazos, a strong and fearless woman who possessed a keen interest and great acumen in business and politics. In time, Juan Cortina would become an aristocratic rancher and family man in this region of violent hurricanes, bitter winter "northers", and suffocating humid summers.

Throughout his life, Cortina exhibited leadership values which were more instinctive rather than the product of any formal training. Noted scholar, Walter Prescott Webb, wrote that Cortina's qualities combined with a flair for leadership, "the disposition of a gambler, an eye for the main chance, and a keen intuitive insight into the character of the Mexicans, made him a man of destiny." [1] Cortina's upbringing and experience nourished his authority and persisted to provide his greatest strength. It was his love for the land and his charisma, however, which eventually gave him unparalleled fame and notoriety in the region both among his compatriots and his enemies.

Numerous documents attest to Cortina's charisma and leadership skills. Benjamin F. McIntyre, a soldier in the Union Army, wrote of Cortina in 1864, "In appearance he is of medium size, about 40 years of age... he is a genial companion but a man of a few word... he is a daring intrepid soldier and inspires those under him with confidence." [2] The Brownsville Herald echoed popular sentiment when it noted that Cortina "was a man of very few words, and the silence he maintained on any and all occasions led to the belief that he was a man of deep knowledge. There is no doubt but that he possessed a large amount of common sense, and he was also a good judge of men." [3]

Throughout his early life, then, Juan N. Cortina stood as a complex individual with an endless drive and energetic mind. Jose Tomas Canales stated it well when he wrote that Cortina, "disciplined himself to become a model of a good soldier, which enabled him to weather the hardships of military life. It made him a hardened man and a heroic figure to his people. He could be methodical, persistent, and clearheaded under intense pressure. Cortina had a skill that could almost remove himself from reality as if he was staring at himself." [4]

Not everyone, however, believed that Cortina was worthy of such glowing accolades. For many he was a thief and a merciless assassin. Texas Ranger N.A. Jennings wrote in 1899 that "About three thousand robbers were under him and he was virtually the ruler of the Mexican border." [5] An article in the Corpus Christi Ranchero stated that under Cortina, the area had been sacked for hundreds of miles and its inhabitants ruthlessly murdered." [6] But the answer to the enigma of Cortina's life lies in the study of the United States-Mexican War and in particular the post war period. The end of the United States - Mexican War did not bring an end to the ideologies and hostility which in part led to the conflict. Instead, the end of the war brought on a variety of new attacks on the Mexican community and gave rise to bitter resentment. In a climate of violence, flagrant prejudice and unrestrained abuses against Mexicans, the emergence of organized resistance was inevitable. The situation all along the Rio Grande was extremely volatile. The only real obstacle to the emergence of a movement of resistance and retribution was the rise of a charismatic leader. In fact, such resistance was already solidifying around a man named Juan N. Cortina whom the people in the lower Rio Grande called "Cheno."[7] This man, according to historian Jerry Thompson, became the leader to the poor vaqueros, campesinos, and the general illiterate persons of Mexican descent on both sides of the lower Rio Grande, who had nothing but poverty, exploitation, and suppression.[8]

Cortina believed fervently that he had a responsibility and a need to dedicate his life to the welfare of Mexicans whose lives were being destroyed by the post-war occupation, and much of the Mexican community in the region gave their support to Cortina as defender of Mexican rights, one who would free them from American control, amend grievances, and punish the enemy. The Texas Ranger John Ford said clearly that "to the poor who heard him, Cortina was a sign of hope in a land where hope heretofore had no meaning."[9] Ford further recounts:

> Sometimes Cortina would make a speech in the market place and the poor would listen intently to what he had to say. He would not harm the innocent, but would fight for the emancipation of the hungry peons along the border... After Cortina and his body guard rode away, the peons seething with hatred for the Americans, returned to their baked fields and mud huts to await his signal for them to follow.[10]

Congressional records from 1859-1860 document that Cortina was seen as a remarkable leader in south Texas as early as 1848. An 1860 affidavit states that "a certain movement ... in 1848 tended to impress the Mexicans on this [Texas] side of the river with the idea that Texas had no [legal] claims" to the territory. Juan Cortina was cited as one of the leaders of this movement advocating separate territory and full rights for Mexicans. Obviously, the idea, and its leader, worried American government officials because the affidavit describes Cortina as a man to be "feared ... on account of his political influence." [11] It would appear that authorities were well aware of the probability of resistance and violence against the new social order and that their fear of a charismatic leader fomenting a revolt was clearly justifiable.

On both sides of the Rio Grande (but especially in the north), Cortina became and remained a feared and disreputable rebel, a reputation fueled by racism, propaganda, and journalistic excess. All helped to promote an ever worsening picture of Cortina, as can be seen in early 1860, when Robert E. Lee, while trying to maintain peace in Texas, alluded to the conflicting ideas of "that myth, Cortina." [12] During the American Civil War, a California historian, Nicholas Herdeman, wrote, "a short ride from the Rio Grande brought them (Confederate soldiers) face to face with the greatest danger extant in that region. They suddenly found themselves surrounded by a fierce looking ring of bandits from the guerrilla gang of the notorious 'Red Robber of the Rio Grande,' Juan Cortina." [13]

A number of early contemporary references to "Cheno" depict him as a bandit. Writings of that period include such characterizations as: "the most daring as well as the most illusive Mexican bandit ... that ever wet his horse in the muddy waters of the Rio Grande;" "a notorious guerrilla;" and, "the scourge of the lower Rio Grande valley." [14] Nevertheless, in an otherwise dismal portrait of Juan Cortina, writer Lyman W. Woodman did make this concession: "For all of his rascally and evil ways, Cortina did retain one commendable trait; he had a deep love for his country and wanted to see it prosper under a fair and peaceful Mexican administration." [15]

More recent works on Cortina reflect a much more favorable view of the man. In 1980, Arnoldo de Leon wrote that "Cortina's movement, then . . . called attention to a government that had deviated from the democratic principles it espoused. In this respect, the rebellion was similar to Shay's rebellion, the Whiskey Rebellion, and the Texas Revolution."[16] Cortina was outraged upon observing the treatment Mexicans received at the hands of the Americans, realizing that he and his fellow countrymen were without civil rights under the new social order. Anglos controlled the police force and the courts and many considered the mistreatment or even the killing of Mexicans no crime.

Historian Pedro Castillo asserted:

"Cortina led and organized a revolt and was a man fulfilling what he felt was his duty ... both resisting the Anglo and standing up for the rights of his countrymen."[17] Cortina believed that under the American control of the region the Tejanos would not know peace, a fact recognized by the Corpus Christi Ranchero which reported in 1860 that Cortina had "sworn in his wrath, that since he cannot enhance the dominions of the serpent clutching eagle, by removing the boundaries of Mexico eastward, he will not allow Americans to enjoy any privileges in the valley of the Rio Grande. It is very easy for his guerrilla bands to carry his threats into execution."[18]

Still a majority of scholars have failed to recognize that Juan Cortina was only a symbol of political resistance. He personified the struggle against an injustice that was all too common. Cortina and his followers, as well as other groups and individuals, were in a struggle for justice, in a place where justice did not exist for most Mexicanos. Cortina simply took this struggle to a higher level. Indeed, his fame was such that he would be blamed or praised for the political deeds of Pedro Garcia, Apolinar Hernandez, Gregorio Villareal, Octavio Zapata, Adrian J. Vidal, and numerous others associated with Cortina who resisted and fought the oppression of the new social order. The most successful of these individuals was one of Cortina's followers on the Texas side, Carlos Esparza, who directed guerrilla warfare against the Texas Rangers.[19]

The Cortinista movement, as the struggle for justice led by Cortina became known, survived numerous attempts to destroy it, including attacks, bribes, and false promises, by powerful economic and political interests. The opposition, notwithstanding, underrated the personal power of Cortina and the strength and devotion of his followers."[20] In the end however, incumbent Mexican President Porfirio Diaz, fearful of Cortina's power, ordered Cortina arrested and brought to central Mexico in 1877 where he could be watched. Cortina was later imprisoned for suspicion of revolutionary activities and died in 1894 at the age of 70. He was buried with military veneration in the Panteon de Dolores near Mexico City.

What follows in the next article is a detailed account of the man, Juan Nepomuceno Cortina. But more than that, it is a study of the motives that led this highly respected man to take up arms against the American forces. We begin with the United States-Mexican War.

An Unjust War and The New Social Order

The life of Juan Nepomuceno Cortina can only be understood within the context of the events of his time - the Texas Rebellion in 1836 and the United States-Mexican War, 1846-1848. Having secured independence from Spain in 1821, the Mexican government viewed as vital the incorporation of the far northern territories. Mexican authorities believed that by increasing the population, the region would develop, thus securing it from foreign threats. Failing to attract its own citizens to the remote region, the government looked outward and passed a colonization act on August of 1824. The law offered land, exemption from taxes for four years, and security to foreign settlers. Ironically, the passage and success of this act all but guaranteed the loss of Mexico's northern territories to the United States. American immigrants failed to obey the conditions set by the Mexican government and, in turn, the Mexican government failed to consolidate its control over Texas. As early as 1826 a revolt took place in Texas by Anglo colonists who were critical of the Mexican government. While the Haden Edwards Revolt, as it is known, was short lived it was nevertheless a presage of things to come as the interests of the colonists and the Mexican government increasingly came into conflict.

Cultural collision and the beliefs associated with the doctrine of Manifest Destiny created an atmosphere of discord and violence that culminated with the declaration of Texas independence in 1836 and ultimately with a war between the United States and Mexico, the catalyst for which was the United States annexation of Texas in 1845. Mexican authorities had never recognized the independence of Texas and the annexation by the United States was seen as an absorption of Mexican territory. Moreover, the disputes over the exact boundaries of Texas brought the Mexican and American military into direct confrontation. This clash gave rise to President Polk's cry that American blood had been shed on American soil which led to formal declaration of war against Mexico on May 11, 1846.

While a number of North Americans were opposed to the war on the grounds that it was immoral and unjust, the American Congress, echoing popular sentiment, overwhelmingly voted in favor of a declaration of war. The conflict led to Mexico losing one half of her territory, including the land Mexican authorities had planned to incorporate into the nation state through the passage of the 1824 colonization law. That territory now composes the states of California, Arizona, New Mexico, Texas, Nevada, and Utah as well as parts of Wyoming and Colorado. The conflict and its repercussions have shaped bi-national politics for the past 150 years and continue to be a cause for resentment even today.

During the war, the United States soldiers-mainly from Texas-brutalized the Mexican population. The number and variety of these sources which document this experience are extensive. In 1846, a correspondent for the Charleston Mercury wrote that United States soldiers in Matamoros were responsible for "murder, robbery, and rape ... committed in the broad light of day."[21] Months later, the military correspondent of the New Orleans Picayune reported that Gen. Zachary Taylor's forces had "committed ... outrages against the [Mexican] citizens of the most disgraceful, and character-stealing... insulting women, breaking into houses."[22] One account in January 8, 1847, stated that in Camargo "assassinations, riots, robberies, etc., are so frequent that they do not excite much attention. Nine-tenths of the Americans here think it is a meritorious act to kill or rob a

Mexican."[23] The degree of violence even disturbed officers. In letters to Julia Dent, Lt. Ulysses S. Grant, described the great number of murders committed by volunteers and Texans. In one such letter Grant wrote, "I would not pretend to guess the number of murders that have been committed upon the persons of poor Mexicans ... but the number would startle you."[24]

The primary problem facing the officers was the lack of discipline of the military volunteers. General Zachary Taylor, for sample, had endless difficulties. In a letter to the War Department, on May 23, 1847, Taylor complained about the atrocities of the volunteers. "I have found it entirely impossible to enforce ... the repeated orders ... against marauding and other irregularities."[25] Later in a dispatch to the War Department on June 16, 1847, he remarked, "I deeply regret to report that many of the twelve month volunteers, in their route hence to the lower Rio Grande, have committed extensive depredations and outrages upon the peaceable inhabitants. There is scarcely a form of crime that has not been reported to me as committed by them."[26] George Gordon Meade, a Lieutenant under Taylor, complained that the volunteers were "always drunk ... and killed for their own amusement." He was "disgusted with Taylor's poor discipline."[27]

The abuses persisted and the depredations did not stop at the Rio Grande. "Between Matamoros and Monterrey," according to one report, "nearly all the ranches and towns are destroyed."[28] On May 11,1847, the Boston Times published a letter from General Taylor stating that, "under Col. Mitchell's command, the 1st Ohio along with some Texas Rangers, made prisoners of twenty-four Mexicans at Guellapea, gave them a mock trial by night, and then shot them through the head!"[29] From Monterrey, Irvin McDowell, a young army officer, wrote on February 27, 1848, that from Parras to the Rio Grande, "a band of American ... deserters ...were ravishing the women, and committing every species of atrocity on the defenseless inhabitants."[30]

In central Mexico too there were many atrocities and outrages committed by United States troops. General Antonio Lopez de Santa Anna in a letter to General Winfield Scott wrote:

"I have with pain and indignation, received communications from the cities and towns occupied by the army of your Excellency, upon the violations of temples consecrated to the worship of God; upon the robbery of the sacred vessels and profanation of the images, venerated by the Mexican people."[31] In 1848, Santa Anna also complained that American troops had looted several cities and abused women in violation of the armistice. Finally he noted, "I have guarded silence until now, for the purpose of not chilling a negotiation that gave hopes of terminating a scandalous war, which your Excellency has justly characterized as unnatural."[32] News of atrocities echoed throughout Mexico. The invaders it seemed were embarking in a racial and religious war where few rules applied. "Anti-Catholic sentiment was a particularly chronic tenet of Americans' faith in themselves, and in Mexico many officers and men got their first look at a Catholic country."[33]

In central Mexico, General Winfield Scott "inflicted punishment upon several Americans for outrages upon the unoffending inhabitants of the country."[34] Concerning treatment of the locals at the hands of the North Americans, journalist Loring Moody stated that "bitter experience has taught the poor Mexicans that it has been thus far no better than that afforded to sheep, by a pack of hungry wolves."[35] General Scott as well as other officers of the United States Army left damaging evidence of the brutalities committed against the Mexican population. Scott contended that his comrades had "committed atrocities to make Heaven weep and every American of Christian morals blush."[36] He claimed, "Murder, robbery, and the rapes of mothers and daughters in the presence of tied-up males of the families have been common all along the Rio Grande."[37] Testimony by Lieutenant George C. Meade, later of Civil War fame, corroborated Scott's claims; Meade referred to the volunteers as "a set of Goths and vandals without discipline" who turned his regiment into "a terror to innocent people."[38]

Sadly, the fate of the people mirrored the fate of the Mexican military. Despite fierce fighting the Mexican forces suffered horrible losses and devastating defeats. Ulysses S. Grant admitted: "I had a horror of the Mexican War ... only I had not moral courage enough to resign."[39] Grant wrote in 1847, "There is no force in Mexico that can resist this [American] army. The Mexicans ... if they were well drilled, well fed and well paid, no doubt...would fight ... they are put to the slaughter without avail."[40] He went on to state: "With an able general the Mexicans would make a good fight, for they are a courageous people."[41] The brutality of the war lasted until its conclusion in 1848 and in some areas well after, most particularly in the ceded territories where the carnage barely subsided with the conclusion of the war.

By many accounts the United States conquest of Mexico constituted no less than a brutal and indiscriminate attack upon the population. Scholar Jovita Gonzales wrote that the "Mexicans considered the Americans in Texas as intruders, vandals, [and] aggressors waiting for the opportunity to deprive them of their personal possessions, as they had denied the mother country a whole province."[42] These feelings added greatly to the postwar turmoil.

After the signing of the Treaty of Guadalupe Hidalgo in 1848, and the end of the declared war, Manuel Crecensio Rejon prophesied the future of the Mexican American:

> Our race, our unfortunate people will have to wander in search of hospitality in a strange land, only to be ejected later. Descendants of the Indians that we are, the North Americans hate us, their spokesmen depreciate us, even if they recognize the justice of our cause, and they consider us unworthy to form with them one nation and one society, they clearly manifest that their future expansion begins with the territory that they take from us and pushing (sic) aside our citizens who inhabit the land.[43]

By most accounts, Rejon would prove to be correct. The United States-Mexican War has been blotted out by a number of historians who apparently see it as part of a tragic event during the era of

Manifest Destiny. As Glenn W. Price explained, "Americans have found it rather more difficult than other people to deal rationally with their wars. We have thought of ourselves as unique, and of this society as specially planned and created to avoid the errors of all other nations."[44] Of the war, Carey McWilliams states "It should never be forgotten that, with the exception of the Indians, Mexicans are the only minority in the United States who were annexed by conquest; the only minority, Indians again excepted, whose rights were specifically safeguarded by treaty provision."[45]

In contrast to the United States, however, the war remains highly controversial in Mexico. Recently, in revised textbooks distributed by the government, a desire to placate the United States and encourage a free trade treaty agreement is evident. No longer is United States "imperialism blamed ... for the loss of Texas, California, Arizona and New Mexico."[46] The seizure of Mexico's land is blamed as much on Mexico's weakness and disorder as "on greedy imperialists to the north. These textbooks are part of a program to encourage a generation of school children to think of the United States as a friendly trading partner, "not an arrogant Goliath that swallowed up much of Mexico's richest land."[47]

The Legacy of a Treaty

On February 2, 1848, Mexico signed the Treaty of Guadalupe Hidalgo ending the United States-Mexican War. The agreement stipulated that the Rio Grande and Gila River were part of the new border between the two countries. By ratification, the United States acquired a territory two and a half times as large as France. The Mexican Cession included vast mineral resources in California, Nevada, New Mexico, and Colorado. Also zinc, copper, oil, and uranium were discovered in other parts of the Southwest. Parts of this area, including the central valley of California and the Mesilla Valley in southern New Mexico, contained rich farmland.

Articles VIII, IX and X of the treaty protected the rights of Mexicans who now found themselves in the American Southwest, and there was a particular emphasis on the protection of property rights. Judge Jeremiah S. Black stated, "The pledge was not only that the government itself would abstain from all disturbance of them but that every blow aimed at their rights, come from what quarter it might, should be caught upon the broad shield of our blessed government."[48] In reality, however, gross violations of the Treaty of Guadalupe Hidalgo took place and clashes over land were soon an all too common occurrence.

After 1848 violent episodes erupted between Tejanos and Anglo Texans all along the Rio Grande. According to historian Richard Griswold Del Castillo, "The Cortina Rebellion, in the Brownsville Matamoros area in the 1850s and 1860s and the El Paso Salt War in the 1870s pitted entire communities against the Texas Rangers in a struggle for the land." Griswold Del Castillo goes on to state that "hundreds of lesser struggles that resulted in lynching, beatings, and riots also had their origin in conflicts over the land."[49]

Tejano families found their lands threatened since many had been forced to flee Texas during the Mexican War. For most, the decision to reoccupy their land in 1848 was an expensive one. It meant selling some of their lands to pay back taxes and dealing with a foreign and hostile judicial system. From these absentee owners and other relatives, American speculators floated high-interest loans, assumed mortgages on portions of the ranch, or purchased sections at tax sales. Most of the time this was done through fraud, confiscation, or simply by murdering the owners.

Prominent scholar David Montejano wrote, "In the immediate postwar period ... the Rio Grande settlements attracted the worst elements among the Anglo pioneers."[50] A Brownsville priest, Abbe Emanuel Domenech, observed, "The Americans of the Texas frontiers are, for the most part, the very scum of society--bankrupts, escaped criminals, old volunteers, who, after the Treaty of Guadalupe Hidalgo, came into a country protected by nothing that could be called a judicial authority, to seek adventure and illicit gains."[51]

The despotism of the Anglos and their intense brutal subjugation of the Mexicans persisted. This oppression was not only a rational excuse to seek grazing land for settlements and farming, but it also demonstrated an intense phobia and hatred for Mexicans and Indians alike. They were perceived as skilled at committing the most barbarous deeds. Gripped both by deep-seated fears and an intense desire for retribution, Anglos responded with horrible atrocities and used rebellions such as Cortina's as a pretext for more violence.

Extreme racism also played a major role in the post war conflict. Major William H. Emory stated in a Report on the United States and Mexican Boundary Survey in 1859: The "white race" was "exterminating or crushing out the inferior race." Others echoed his remarks. A United States soldier in the same year noted that "the Mexican, like the poor Indian, is doomed to retire before the more enterprising Anglo Americans."[52] Frederick Olmsted noted that Mexicans were seen "not as heretics or heathens to be converted ... but rather as vermin, to be exterminated."[53] Mexicans were bitterly resented for their amalgamation or assimilation through miscegenation. Edward B. Foote wrote in his renowned, bulky medical reference book on the subject of marriage that the Mexican

"...population is divided between Mestizos, Mulattoes, and Zamboes, many of whom are but little above the savage, go naked, have no established forms of marriage ... Those who do not associate with and imitate the customs of the whites, are omnigamic, and governed by their impulses."[54]

These statements were often supported by distinguished scholars such as Joseph Simms, who compiled a massive, celebrated college textbook that went through ten editions. Those of Indian background, Simms wrote, had a face that "clearly betray a degenerate nature."[55] He stressed that "Dark races, like the Indian and Negro, are naturally revengeful, like the elephant; and black eyes evince more or less a revengeful disposition."[56] He concluded that dark people especially those of Indian blood had "a wide mouth, in a narrow face,[that] may safely be defined as indicative of animal imitation."[57] Since Mexicans were viewed as inferior, they were merely excluded from the human race. Their physical appearance and conduct made it possible to regard them as repulsive. In 1874 for example Edward King and J. Wells Champney noted how the Mexican in San Antonio could not be made to see that "his slow, primitive ways, his filth and lack of comfort, are not better than the frugal decency and careful home management of the Germans and Americans who surround him."[58] The violent treatment of Mexicans by Anglos in antebellum Texas was widespread. "Stories of Texas violence circulated throughout the United States, and even in England" adding to Texas' poor reputation."[59] In 1860, writer J.F.H. Claiborne asserted that "Civilized communities provide guardians for the helpless and imbecile, and defenses against the lunatic and the outlaw," and consequently it was the American duty to conquer and rule such a country as Mexico, "with or without her consent."[60] James Rawls wrote, "This sequence of events was hardly unique to the [Texas and] California frontier. Similar situations have existed elsewhere on Anglo-American frontiers and, for that matter, throughout human history. Fearing the savage without, if not within themselves, `civilized' men have destroyed `savages' with a special fury."[61]

Not surprisingly, with such views of the Mexican race, there was no law that truly protected the Mexican community. As early as 1850, Texas ignored the legal protections of the Treaty of Guadalupe Hidalgo. Seeing this, Governor P.H. Bell appointed a commission to investigate land claims in South Texas arising from the treaty. "The Bourland-Miller Commission, created by the legislature, gathered abstracts of titles and made recommendations to the Texas legislature. More than 135 claims were reviewed and presented to the legislature for confirmation."[62] Although most grants were confirmed, a number of claims rejected by the Texas legislature became issues of further litigation and later added fuel to what became the Cortinista struggle that would plunge most of south Texas into guerrilla war.

Las Mujeres Cortinistas

Women played an extremely important role in the Cortinista's struggle for justice and liberation in south Texas just as they would in the Mexican Revolution of 1910. It was Canales who discovered numerous women, later termed Aguilas Damas. They fought and spied for Cortina's army during and after the American Civil War, and in the early 1900s, Canales interviewed several of them. Beyond the few names and stories obtained through Canales' research,

139

however, we can only speculate as to the actual number, activities, motivations, and accomplishments of the Cortinista women.

From the interviews conducted by Canales, we may deduce that most of these women had either witnessed or been subjected to violence, including rape. Some had been forced into prostitution in order to survive. Rather than continue as passive victims, they chose to act by serving the Cortinista cause in the capacity of spies, smugglers, cooks, nurses, or messengers. Many even served as soldiers. Known as soldaderas, some of these courageous women dressed as men and engaged in battle, several of them dying in the conflict. Women also carried small kegs of whiskey to the front lines to comfort the injured and those suffering from shock. As stretcher bearers, they carried the wounded in wagons to the nursing camps. Moreover, they worked as scavengers, roaming the battlefields during the night, stripping the dead of their uniforms, caps and shoes. These uniforms were often dyed for Cortinista soldiers and civilians who needed them.[63]

Around the turn of the century, Canales had the opportunity to speak personally to two Aguilas Damas, both of whom were over the age of sixty at the time of the interview. They were now thin, hollow checked women with pale and strained faces. Yet Canales found a mystery about them:

These women retained an Aguilas dignity; a timeless nobility still clung about them ... They actually carried an undying bitterness, a bitterness too deep for words. Rarely would their soft-spoken words express the murder of their families and friends by the Gringo soldiers during the conflicts along the Rio Grande. [64]

According to the interviews, one well known Aguila was "Lora La Leona" (Lora the Lion). Initially a spy, she became an advisor to Cortina and eventually an administrator. She assisted in keeping operations running efficiently and discreetly. Her office was furnished with plush upholstered furniture, heavy velvet draperies and gilded French mirrors with elaborate frames. Because of her prominence, she was often identified incorrectly as Cortina's mistress.[65] General William Steele recorded in 1875, "It is a well-known fact that not only Cortina himself, but even his mistress, gives orders to judges as to their decisions in cases, either civil or criminal and such orders are obeyed."[66] The people whom Canales interviewed in 1905 remembered Lora warmly. One said, "She was extremely well-read, a quick and witty conversationalist; Lora loved politics."[67] Another Aguila Dama, Carmen Flores, helped secure funds for weapons and medicines at various locations throughout the region. She maintained a low profile, dressing like a witch in an aged, fading oversized black dress, beneath which she carried money or supplies sewn into her petticoats. According to accounts, "Like Lora, Carmen Flores had a sense for business, and both women had financial interests in several enterprises along the lower Rio Grande".[68] Their enterprises and talents served the Cortinista agenda.

An Aguila Dama remembered only as "Alma," discovered that a supposedly harmless and well-meaning local teacher named McMahan was actually supplying the Texas Rangers with information about the Cortinistas."After gathering enough evidence revealing McMahan as a spy and saboteur, Alma turned him in to other Aguilas."[69] In June of 1875, McMahan "was found horribly mutilated, the head, arms, and legs being severed from the body and scattered over the prairie."[70] Frank Pierce wrote, "these men tortured McMahan by cutting off his fingers, toes, wrists and ears. They finally severed his legs from his body and left him lifeless."[71] This atrocity was done under the command of aguja [the needle]. According to Canales, this degree of violence was not unusual: "Most Aguilas were equally brutalized by McNally's troops and McMahan was one of those who had tortured some Mexicans."[72]

It was later learned that McMahan "had been in fact a Brownsville policeman."[73] According to one of Canales interviews, "McNally's state troops,"[74] as W. Whipple referred to them, "had many clashes with the Cortinistas, in one of which Alma was killed."[75] The truth about her death, and that of most other Cortinistas, will never be fully known as the only records are the testimony of McNelly's men.

One entrepreneur in the Cortinista cause was Gregoria Herrera.

As a hotel keeper in Bagdad, she hid her political feelings so as to act as a spy for the Cortinista cause. She was always in close contact with two Aguilas, Antonio Villarreal and Manuel Luna, both of whom were stage drivers. Her hotel was a valuable spot from which to spy since the stage line stopped there. One account noted, "Saloons and hotels operated at full capacity. There were ten stagecoaches daily between Brownsville and Bagdad."[76] Cortina depended on her to keep records on the movement of Confederate, French and Union vessels and military officers. According to the research of Jose Canales, "Somehow she survived the sacking of Bagdad by numerous armies that almost destroyed the area."[77] The Aguila officers were now more or less acquainted with the tactics of their enemies, and responded accordingly. As the violence persisted, each side kept improving its army and new maneuvers had to be created. Both sides saw the lower Rio Grande turmoil as a long, bitter war, in which neither side dared to make a fatal mistake.

According to Canales, "It developed into a rigid, hard pounding conflict that was not fighting for peace, but to finally destroy the adversary once and for all. It brought bitter agony and endless sorrow to both sides."[78] Women were all but immune to the violence of the struggle. Most females who aided the Cortinista cause, suffered in deep silence. In winters, they lined their old dresses with rags or with bundles of newspapers to keep out the wind. They made shoes from carpets with soles of wood. These unknown, hard, bronze faced attendants molded bullets and provided military supplies.

They carried on with a dignity that Cortina greatly admired. They toiled long hours as cooks, burning blisters on their fingers. They prepared hundreds of daily meals which left them with endless greasy, dirty dishes to scrub. Even though their hands were swollen and bruised they diligently washed and mended the men's torn and smudged clothes. Always walking with their heads held high, these women never complained regardless of their trials or tribulations. With reddish and puffy eyes, they worked with an earnest and simple face. These women who were called burras, a term that does little justice to their contribution, were indifferent to their own hunger and remained serene regardless of aching muscles and tension."[79]

"Angels of Mercy"

A majority of these burras were Cortinista wives or widows. They served as nurses. Some of them were curanderas (healers). They needed nerves of steel to handle foul, naked men who bore terrible war injuries, such as gangrene, a broken jaw, a leg or an arm gone, missing fingers or blindness. These soldiers groaned from pain in the intense summer heat that added to their ailments. They fell victim to flies, mosquitoes and gnats that further tormented them. Like most other soldiers throughout the South, these men also suffered from typhoid fever, pneumonia, diphtheria and malaria."[80] Most soldiers were also victims of polluted water."[81]

The curanderas mission was noble and humanitarian. One surgeon noted that the soldiers would be "burning with fever, tormented with insatiable thirst, racked with pains, or wild with delirium; their parched lips, and teeth blackened with sores, the hot breath and sunken eyes, the sallow skin and trembling pulse, all telling of the violent workings of these diseases."[82] With personal intensity, these women treated Cortinista troops and even wounded or ill French soldiers in Matamoros. With Juan Cortina's encouragement, these Mexican nurses and curanderas also attended to the Union or the Confederate soldiers in Brownsville. A large, red brick house with green shutters and two story veranda that belonged to Judge Israel Bigelow became a hospital during the Civil War. Crippled and weary soldiers carved their names or symbols on the wooden floors and on the woodwork. Several of these men waited to suffer the knives of surgeons. Others lingered in agony to face amputations. They depended on the curanderas to get drugs to ease pains.

Canales recalled that "these aching, sweat-drenched burras were actually angels of mercy, working in the wee hours of the soft, warm night. Long torches burned serenely like altar candles. These women were gentle, cheerful and sympathetic, masking their indignation and despair. They walked around with iron stomachs to witness the endless misery and to weather the rotten odors that assaulted their nostrils, primarily when they had to clean maggots from festering flesh. If nothing else they had to wash their patients to get rid of the lice, bandage wounds or stumps."[83] Canales recounted meeting one of these ladies:

"Years later, I remembered talking to one of these burras. She had dark blazing, self-confident eyes set deep in a serene face. She triumphed over life with a dry humor even though she witnessed so much infirmity and grief. Like so many of these women, even in their youth, she appeared haggard and older than her years. Her eyes appeared deep. While looking into those eyes, my soul almost plunged into her spiritual self I sensed an everlasting tranquility."[84]

To these medical attendants, time stood still. These women had no past, no present, and no future. Not even nerve-shattering sounds could disrupt their composure.

They were immune to the daily agitations of life. They had seen everything and experienced just about everything; nothing appalled or unnerved them. Their large, dark eyes held the history of a people who for years witnessed all the tragedies that life had to offer. A variety of pre-Columbian drugs were used by these women and men who were healers of pain. Apparently, several American doctors were impressed with their work, particularly when a Mexican healer saved the life of General James Shields during the Mexican War. As Samuel Schmucker noted, "His case had been given over as hopeless by the regular surgeons of the army, when a Mexican doctor offered to save his life if he would permit him to operate. The permission was readily granted."[85] The officer recovered when the doctor (healer) used a fine silk handkerchief to remove blood from his lungs. Canales believed that the mysterious doctor actually used medical herbs. The curanderas treated soldiers suffering from burns or infections with nopal (cactus) juice and the juice of several other plants, together with honey and egg yolk. They also used jimson weed (datura) for burns and inflammations. Some of the seeds were used to induce visions and explore the inner mind for emotional problems. Although some thought they were witches, Cortina and his soldiers cherished these healers.

No one trusted the local doctors. As the Austrian Officer Ernst Pitner wrote in his diary, "Of all the four or five persons availing themselves of this title, not a single one is a real doctor. All in fact are nothing but quacks."[86]

Most physicians in the United States during the Civil War used the same treatments as the Mexican healers. Quinine, produced from the bark of the South American cinchona tree, was used with whiskey to treat headaches, toothaches, syphilis and fevers. Like the burras, these American physicians used opium and morphine to control diarrhea.[87] The curanderas knew about the concept of germs. They realized that scrubbing their hands and boiling instruments helped with their treatments, particularly when they had to remove bullets or perform operations. They saved soldiers' legs from amputation with their skillful treatment and herbs. According to Jose Canales,

> "These nurses would all dress alike in black garments. They appeared like nuns, and lapsed into silence when someone approached them. One could sense their nerve and cunning skills in handling the unexpected. They had a quick, penetrating look and could read one's face like an open book. No detail escaped their scrutiny."

People treated them with great respect since they were a critical part of the Cortinista survival.[88] The women who fought for, died for, and helped the Cortinista cause were an important reason for the survival of Tejano resistance along the Rio Grande. Their contributions were essential to the success of the rebellion. These courageous Tejanas were precursors of later soldaderas who would take part in the Mexican Revolution. While much remains to be written, some works already begin to shed light on the enormous contributions of Mexican American women in this period.

Notes

1. Walter Prescott Webb, The Texas Rangers: A Century of Frontier Defense (Austin: University of Texas Press, 1965), 177.

2. Nannie M. Tilley, ed. Federals on the Frontier: The Diary of Benjamin F. McIntyre, 1862-1864. (Austin, Texas: University of Texas Press, 1963), 293.

3. Brownsville Herald, March 10, 1894. See also David A. Williams, David C. Broderick: A political Portrait (San Marino: Huntington Library, 1969), 7. Like Cortina, he was "a quiet man: and had some familiar qualities."

4. Jose Tomas (J. T.) Canales Interview (with Larralde), April 6, 1964. See also the San Antonio Express, October 25,1878.

5. N.A. Jennings, A Texas Ranger (New York: Charles Scribner and Sons, 1899),139. 6.

6. Corpus Christi Ranchero, January 14, 1860.

7. "Cheno" is a term of endearment.

8. Jerry Thomson, Vaqueros in Blue & Gray (Austin: Presidial Press, 1976), 13.

9. Stephen B. Oates, ed., John Salmon Ford, Rip Ford's Texas, (Austin: University of Texas Press, 1963), 309.

10. Ibid., 308-309.

11. Affidavit of W.W. Nelson, Brownsville, January 17, 1860, U.S. Congress, House Executive Document, 36th Cong., 1st Sess., No.52, "Difficulties on the Southwestern Frontier," Vol.7, 1859-1860, Serial Number 1050 (Washington, D.C., Thomas H. Ford, Printer, 1860), 123.

12. This remark was made to his wife, Betsy, in Virginia. See Douglas Southall Freeman, R.E. Lee A Biography. (New York: Charles Scribner and Sons, 1936), 87. The remark is also quoted in Philip Van Doren Stem, Robert E. Lee: The Man and the Soldier, A Pictorial Biography (New York: Bonanza Books, 1963), 119. For most of Lee's letters relative to Juan Cortina see: John H. Jenkins, ed., Robert E. Lee on the Texas Border, 1860 (Austin: Jenkins Publishing Company, 1988). Also, J. Lee Stambaugh and Lillian J. Stanbaugh, Lower Rio Grande Valley of Texas (San Antonio: Naylor Company, 1954), 103-104. The Stambaughs also give an account of how writers have depicted Cortina. As an item of interest, see the biographical sketch of Cortina from 1859 to 1866 in the Matamoros Ranchero, May 18, 1866, 1.22 Mexcoehuani: Readings in Chicano and Border History

13. Nicholas Perkins Hardeman, Wilderness Calling; The Hardeman Family in the American Westward Movement, 1759-1900 (Knoxville: University of Tennessee Press, 1977), 253.

14. Canales Jose, Juan N. Cortina: Two Interpretations (New York: Amo Press, 1974), 4. Reprint of Juan N. Cortina 1824- 1892: A Re-appraisal, by C. W. Goldfinch, originally presented as authors thesis (M.A.), University of Chicago, 1950; of Juan N. Cortina presents his motion for a new trial, by J.T.

Canales, first published in 1951 in San Antonio.

15. Quoted in Ibid., 12.

16. Arnold De Leon, They Called Them Greasers: Anglo Attitudes toward Mexicans in Texas, 1821-1900 (Austin: University of Texas Press), 53. Shays Rebellion, which took place in Massachusetts in 1786 and 1787, was a revolt by debtor farmers against their creditors and especially against high taxes. Property owners and farmers faced imprisonment since they could not pay their debts.

17. Howard R. Lamar, ed., The Reader's Encyclopedia of the American West (New York: Thomas Y. Crowell Company, 1977), 264.

18. Corpus Christi Ranchero, May 26, 1860.

19. Canales Interview, April 10, 1964.

20. James R. Douglas, Juan Cortina: El Caudillo de La Frontera. M.A. Thesis, University of Texas, 1987, 109-110.

21. Loring Moody, Facts for the People. The Mexican War (Boston: Anti-Slavery Office, 1847), 109-110.

22. Ibid.

23. William Jay, A Review of the Causes and Consequences of the Mexican War Boston: American Peace Society, 1850), 230.

24. Ulysses S. Grant to Julia Dent; July25, 1846 in John Y. Simon, ed., The Papers of Ulysses S. Grant (Carbondale Southern Illinois University Press, 1967), 1:102.

25. Abriel Abbot Livermore, War With Mexico: Reviewed (Boston: American Peace Society, 1850), 148.

26. Ibid., 234. In 1849, Chañes T. Porter recalled that "the march of our army to the Rio Grande was a deliberate and intentional act of war against Mexico' See Porter's work, Review of the Mexican War (Auburn, New York Alden & Parsons, 1849), 79.

27. Nancy Scott Anderson and Dwight Anderson, The Generals: Ulysses S. Grant and Robert E. Lee (New York Alfred A. Knoll, 1988), 77.

28. Ibid., p.232. Also, Martha A. Sandweiss, Rick Stewart, and Ben W. Huseman, Eyewitness to War: Prints and Daguerreotypes of the Mexican War 1846-48 (Fort Worth, Texas: Amon Carter Museum, 1989), 103-120.

29. Moody Facts for the People, 134.

30. Livermore, The War With Mexico, 151.

31. Ibid.,155.

32. Ibid.

33. Anderson and Anderson, The Generals, 83.

34. Ibid., 135.

35. Ibid., 134.33 Section 1.

36. Carey McWilliams, North from Mexico (New York Gienwood Press, 1968), 102.

37. Ibid.

38. Bernal Devoto, The Year of Decision 1846, (Boston: Utile, Brown and Company, 1943), 103.

39. Grady McWhiney and Sue McWhiney, eds., To Mexico with Taylor and Scott. 1845-1847, (Waltham, Massachusetts: Praisdell Publishing Co., 1969), 3.

40. Grant to addressee unknown, (August 221847) in Papers to Ulysses S. Grant, 144.

41. John Russell Young, Around the World: General Grant (New York The American News Company, 1879), 2:162.

42. Jovita Gonzalez "Historical Background of the Lower Rio Grande Valle, LULAC News (September, 1932). In 1866, George Lunt wrote, "To be sure, by the treaty of Guadalupe Hidalgo, ratified at the termination of the war with Mexico, the Rio Grande was afterwards agreed upon as the future boundary between that country and the United States, ... Mr. Tyler, however, had seen fit to adopt that river as the boundary, without taking the trouble to seek any adjustment of preliminaries with Mexico George Lunt; The Origin of the Late War: Traced from the Beginning of the Constitution to the Revolt of the Southern States (New York D. Appleton and Co., 1866), 141-142.

43. Antonio de Peña y Reyes, Algunos Documentos Sobre el Tratado de Guadalupe Hidalgo (Mexico: Sec de Rd. Ext., 1930), 159, quoted in Feliciano Rivera, A Mexican American Source Book (Menlo Park Calif Educational Consulting Associates, 1970), 185.

44. Glenn W. Price, Origins of the War with Mexico: The Polk-Stockton Intrigue (Austin: University of Texas, 1967), 7.

45. Carey McWilliams, North From Mexico, 103.

46. See Gregory Katz, "Mexican Textbooks play down Revolution and play up U.S.," Long Beach Press-Telegram (Long Beach, California), September 10, 1992.

47. Ibid. In the past, Mexico's official history was written "by leftist historians with a negative view of the United States. Now that trend has been reversed." Adolfo Aguilar, an academic and writer, said that it is time for Mexico to drop the concept of an official history text once and for all. "Why don't we let historians write the story and let teachers and administrators choose?" he asked.

48. Chauncey F. Black, Essays and Speeches of Jeremiah S. Black (New York: D. Appleton and Co., 1885), 468. After the war Americans remained contemptuous of Mexico. To them it was a failed republic. They thought that Mexico, however, might be politically regenerated under the Anglo-Saxon conquerors. "Assuming that the United States was essentially Anglo-Saxon and that the Indian, Hispanic, and mestizo people of Mexico were inferior, these Americans explained Mexico's decline or could be made fit only by emulating Americans, who had a special cultural genius for republican liberty."

The Mexican War haunted Yankee politics for years, especially during the American Civil War. It reminded the United States that it might become as pitiable a failure as Americans held Mexico to be. Now the Confederacy and the United States would be in perpetual war, burdening the continent with " jarring, warring, fragmentary states," and conducting themselves as "a race of chieftains, who will rival the political bandits of South America and Mexico." Gen. William Sherman saw American politics as absurd and wanted the United States to avoid "the fate of Mexico, which is eternal war." To him the failure of Mexico was a fate which the United States could never be sure of escaping. See: Charles Royster, The Destructive War: William Tecumseh Sherman, Stonewall Jackson, and the Americans (New York: Alfred A Knopf, 1991), 125-126. One Civil War figure, Confederate General Gideon Johnson Pillow, was Gen. John B. Floyd's second in-command and was haunted by his mistakes during the Mexican War. In 1846, Pillow earned a reputation for incompetence while defending the village of Camargo on the lower Rio Grande. "He mistakenly ordered his men to build their breastworks on the wrong side of their trench leaving them exposed to the enemy." See David Nevin, The Civil War: The Road to Shiloh, Early Battles in the West (Alexandria: Time-Life, 1983, 87.

49. Richard Griswold Del Castillo, The Treaty of Guadalupe Hidalgo: A Legacy of Conflict (Norman: University of Oklahoma, 1990), 83.

50. David Montejano, Anglos and Mexicans in the Making of Texas, 1836-1996 28 (Austin: University of Texas Press), 31.

51. Quoted in Ibid., 32.

52. McWilliams, North from Mexico, 105. In California, the same thing happened to some Hispanics and the majority of Indians. The San 35 Section 1 Francisco Alta California, December 5, 1850, wrote that the Indians must fade away "like a dissipating mist before the morning sun from the presence of the Saxon." Then in the following year the Alta (March 17, 1851), forecast "certain doom" for the Indians. "They must fade away before the Saxon race as the cloud in the West before the light and heat of a greater power." See: James J. Rawls, Indians of California: The Changing Image (Berkeley: University of California Press, 1984). See his chapter "Extermination," 171-201. One could only speculate if Foote were alive today and saw American society and read Richard Rodriguez, "Perspective on the Americas: The Indian Doesn't Need Your Pity," Los Angeles Times, October 11, 1992, what the reaction would be. Rodriguez wrote that "The first Americans were not hapless victims; their descendants are refining and redefining the European legacy." Then he wrote that five hundred years after Christopher Columbus set foot in the Americas, "Indians are alive and growing in number from the tip of South America to the Arctic Circle. If you do not believe me, look at brown Mexico City." Also, Carlos Fuentes, "The Birth of the Hispano-Indian Civilizations of the New World, Los Angeles Times, October 11, 1992, wrote, "For the Indian cultures

of the Americas, if it did not prevail, it did not perish, either. Rather, it became a part of what one might term the counter-conquest, that is, the Indian response, to the purely European presence in the Americas."

53. Ibid., 32.

54. Ibid., 32.

55. Joseph Simms, Physiognomy Illustrated or Nature's Revelations of Character (New York: Murray Hill Publishing Company, 1891), 320. Originally written in 1872, Simms used three hundred elaborate engravings to support his data.

56. Ibid., 301.

57. Ibid., 126.

58. Edward King and J. Wells Champney, Texas 1874, An Eyewitness Account of Conditions in Post-Reconstruction Texas, Robert S. Gray (Houston: Cordovan Press, 1974), 108-111. For a comparison of how California treated its Indians, see: Rawls, Indians of California, 198.

59. Dickson D. Bruce, Violence and Culture in the Antebellum South (Austin: University of Texas Press), 103. Also, Mark F. Nackman, "Anglo-American Migrants to the West: Men of Broken Fortunes? The case of Texas, 1821-46," Western Historical, Quarterly No.5, (1974), 441-55.36 Mexcoehuani: Readings in Chicano and Border History

60. Ibid., 174.

61. Rawls, Indians in California, 180. Rawls California chapters, "The Varieties of Exploitation" and "Extermination," reveal a familiar pattern to most 19th century conflicts in the American Southwest, especially in the treatment of Indians and Mexicans in Texas. Recently Eduardo Garrigues, Spain's consul General in Los Angeles, wrote: "And, while some place responsibility for the decline in population of the California Indians on the Spanish colonization and the mission system, anthropologist Robert F. Heizer has show that the real tragedy for the Indians came between 1848 and 1870, after the Gold Rush." Although the Treaty of Guadalupe Hidalgo guaranteed Chicanos their old grants, according to research by Patricia Limerick, author of "The Legacy of Conquest," "80% of those lands eventually fell in to the hands of American lawyers and settlers. In 1850, the Foreign Miners' Tax drove the Hispanic out of their mines." See Garrigues, "The Pathology of Hero-Making," Los Angeles Times, October 12, 1992. As for hero-making in Texas history, the life of David Crockett has been so muddled in fantasy that it is difficult to separate fact from fiction. One scholar who studied this subject was Richard Boyd Hauck. See: Hauck, Crockett: A Bio-Bibliography (Westport: Greenwood Press, 1982). Some of the fantasy started with a purported journal kept by Crockett and published as Col. Crockett's Exploits and Adventures in Texas. The diary, it turns out, was written mostly by Richard Penn Smith, who plagiarized material from other books. American historians rarely used sources from the Mexican

point of view. Finally the long-ignored eyewitness accounts left by Santa Anna's soldiers came to light. One such source is the account of Jose Enrique de la Peña. De la Peña pointed out that "Crockett did not surrender willingly, but he did survive the massacre, and he was executed." It was not the glorious death in the Alamo generally associated with Crockett. De la Peña's diary was carefully translated by Carmen Perry and published in 1975. Dan Kilgore, a past president of the Texas State Historical Association, carefully examined and interpreted the translation. "Mr. Kilgore tells us that the Texas Press and other parties who did not want the legend of Davy Crockett sullied responded with vehement protest to the publication of Carmen Perry's translation and the subsequent dissemination of these facts. Such uproar is ludicrous but understandable."

62. Montejano, Anglos and Mexicans in the Making of Texas, 85.

63. This practice was also common during the American Civil War. About 1863, a Virginia soldier wrote in his diary that "all the Yank dead had been stripped of every rag of their clothing and looked like hogs that had been cleaned. It was an awful sight." William K. Goolrick, The Civil War: Rebels Resurgent, Fredericksburg to Chancellorsville (Alexandria: Time-Life, 1985), 88.

64. Canales Interview, August 12, 1964.

65. Ibid.

66. W.M. Steele to the Adjutant General, July 1, 1875, "Texas Frontier Troubles," 122.

67. Canales Interview, November 16, 1964. 6. Ibid.

68. Ibid.

69. Ibid.

70. Report of the Brownsville Committee, April 17, 1875, "Texas Frontier Troubles."

71. Pierce, A Brief History, 108.

72. Canales Interview, November 16, 1964.

73. Affidavit of Joseph O'Shaughnessy, June 16, 1875, "Texas Frontier Troubles," 82.

74. Whipple to the Adjutant General, November 20, 1875, in Ibid., 89.

75. Canales Interview, November 16, 1964.

76. Stambaugh, Lower Rio Grande Valley, 112. For more data on Gregoria Herrera see Raybum, Centuries of Conflict, 72-77.

77. Canales Interview, November 16, 1964.

78. Ibid

79. Ibid.

80. See George T. Stevens, Three Years in the Sixth Corps (Albany: S.R. Gray, Publishers, 1866), 10,114. He was a surgeon. Cholera also took its toll. See the San Antonio Herald, October 16,1866. In November 1, 1866,

the Herald reported that the cholera epidemic "can be partially traced to the Mexican population who cannot protect itself from the rains..." In September, 1866, 116 Mexicans died from diseases. Also yellow fever swept the border several times, particularly in 1882. See Pierce, 137.

81. Stevens, 114. Foul water remained a problem. The San Antonio Express, October 25, 1878, stated that Mexicans depended on "contaminated water for cooking, drinking, and other purposes."45 Section 1.

82. Stevens, 74.

83. Ibid. The house of Judge Israel Bigelow, the first elected chief justice of Cameron County, remained standing in Brownsville for years until it was razed recently. For a photo of the house see: Ruby A. Wooldridge and Robert B. Vezzetti, Brownsville: A Pictorial History (Norfolk: Donning Company, 1982), 59.

84. Ibid.

85. Samuel Schmucker, A History of the Civil War in the United States with a Preliminary View of its Causes, (Philadelphia: Bradley & Co., 1864), 316.

86. Pitner, 138.

87. David Nevin, The Civil War: Sherman's March: Atlanta to the Sea (Alexandria: Time-Life, 1986), 106-107.

88. Canales interview, November 16, 1964.

Background Issues II

Rodolfo Jacobo

Structural violence, Institutional racism, Lewis M. Terman, Edward B. Foote, Joseph Simms, eugenics, Mestizo, John Box, Repatriation, segregation, Melting Pot

Deep seeded prejudice has historically undermined the struggle for equality of the Mexican origin community in the United States. From the post U.S./Mexican War period to the present, there has existed a tendency in this country to ignore, discredit and criminalize the Mexican origin community. The social, economic and political structures in the United States have often been avenues disseminating this bias and perpetuating its prejudice and injustice. These structures after all, have historically reflected the nation's dominant society's view of itself as well as the invention and construction of 'the other". Historian Howard Zinn tells us that since the creation of the "American way of life" in the 18th century, the socio-political and cultural identification of an "American" was based on white, protestant, Northern European male privilege.

The inferior position of blacks, the exclusion of Indians from the new society, the establishment of supremacy for the rich and powerful in the new nation-all this was already settled in the colonies by the time of the revolution. (Zinn, 1980, p. 89)

As a result, there is a long and painful history of blatant violence and discrimination against those that did not fit that prototype and stereotype of being American, including the Mexican origin community. The annals of history are extensive and clear with ample evidence of structural violence and the falsehoods of the premise of universal equality embodied in the myth of the Melting Pot in the American experience. Nowhere is there a more supportive argument for the contradiction of integration models in the United States and institutional racism than in the racist writings of Lewis M. Terman (1916) when he wrote:

> Among laboring men and servant girls there are thousands like them....The tests have told the truth. These boys are uneducable beyond the merest rudiments of training. No amount of school instruction will ever make them intelligent voters or capable citizens....They represent the level of intelligence which is very, very common among Spanish-Indian and Mexican families of the Southwest and also among Negroes. Their dullness seems to be racial, or at least inherent in the family stocks from which they came. The fact that one meets this type with such extraordinary frequency among Indians, Mexicans, and Negroes suggests quite forcibly that the whole question of racial differences in mental traits will have to be taken up anew and by experimental methods. The writer predicts that when this is done there will be discovered enormously significant racial differences in general intelligence, differences which cannot be wiped out by any scheme of mental culture. Children of this group should be segregated in special classes and be given instruction, which is concrete and practical. They cannot master abstractions, but they can often be made efficient workers, able to look out for themselves. There is no possibility at present of convincing society that they should not be allowed to reproduce, although from a eugenic point of view they constitute a grave problem because of their unusually prolific breeding. (pp. 91-92)

Eugenics, a sort of pseudo-science, was used to rationalize and legalize social segregation in the United States in the early 20th century and confined people of color to an entrenched subordination in all sectors of civil life. This was especially true in schools where the arguments of deficit theory were cemented in racism. Much of the seed of racism against the Mexican origin community had been planted centuries earlier. Indeed, to locate the roots of anti-Mexican sentiment, which continue to plague society and its institutions, we must look deep into the past.

As we have seen in his work Origins of Anti Mexican Sentiment, Raymund A. Paredes traces the roots of the discrimination experienced by the community of Mexican ancestry in the United States. He proposes that the anti-Mexican sentiment had its roots in Europe as the product of political and religious conflict. From the conflict between Spain and England, and between the Protestant and Catholic Churches emerged powerful anti-Spanish sentiment and fear. From the pulpit and the podium, racist and anti-Catholic sentiments were spread giving rise to what historians have labeled Hispanophobia and the Black Legend (Paredes, as cited in Ornelas, 2000).

Hispanophobia and the Black Legend depicted a grotesque view of all things Spanish and Catholic. The Spaniards had also been placed at the bottom of the Elizabethan scale of beauty and worth because they were imagined as a product of Moorish miscegenation and morally corrupted by the Catholic Church and the Spanish Crown. Paredes, points out that this anti-Spanish sentiment was more pronounced in America, since the English colonies were established at a time when territorial rivalries in the Americas were well underway (Paredes, as cited in Ornelas, 2000).

This anti-Spanish and anti-Catholic sentiment transformed into an anti-Mexican sentiment which was used to rationalize horrible abuses including institutional racism and genocide as into the new world and the new American nations. The Mexican was thought to embody the worst elements of the Spaniard and the indigenous because of the stigmatization of racial miscegenation with indigenous peoples and the pronounced anti-Indian sentiment as competition for land and resources accelerated in the late 18th and early 19th centuries (Paredes, as cited in Ornelas, 2000). This prejudice toward mestizo Catholics would play a major role in the formation and expansion of the United States and contribute to the emerging origins of the formation of the indigenous as "the other" on the American frontier at a time of violent westward expansions into Indian lands in North America.

There is no question that these new American attitudes toward Indians, Spaniards and mestizos were an important and often overlooked factor in the Texas Revolt of 1836 and the U.S. Mexican War 1846-1848 and has continued to be an instrument of oppression well into the present. The racism that would justify dejure segregation in the twentieth century would endure throughout the early years of Mexican and American conflict. Major William H. Emory stated in a Report on the United States and Mexican Boundary Survey in 1859: The "white race" was "exterminating or crushing out the inferior race." (Larralde & Jacobo, 2000, p. 25)

Others echoed his remarks. A United States soldier in the same year noted, "The Mexican, like the poor Indian, is doomed to retire before the more enterprising Anglo-Americans." Frederick Olmsted noted that Mexicans were seen "not as heretics or heathens to be converted ... but rather as vermin, to be exterminated." (Larralde & Jacobo, 2000, p. 25)

Mexicans were bitterly despised for their amalgamation or assimilation through racial miscegenation. Edward B. Foote wrote in his renowned bulky medical reference book on the subject of marriage that the Mexican, "population is divided between Mestizos, Mulattoes, and Zambos, many of whom are but little above the savage, go naked, have no established forms of marriage ... Those who do not associate with and imitate the customs of the whites, are omnigamic, and governed by their impulses." (Larralde & Jacobo, 2000, p. 25)

Distinguished scholars such as Joseph Simms, who compiled a massive celebrated college textbook that went through ten editions, often supported these racist statements. Those of Indian background, Simms wrote, had a face that "clearly betrays a degenerate nature." He stressed that "Dark races, like the Indian and Negro, are naturally revengeful, like the elephant; and black eyes evince more or less a revengeful disposition." He concluded that dark people especially those of Indian blood had "a wide mouth, and a narrow face, [that] may safely be defined as indicative of animal imitation." (Larralde & Jacobo, 2000, p. 25)

Since Mexicans were viewed as inferior, they were summarily excluded from the human race. Their physical appearance and conduct made it possible to regard them as repulsive. In 1874, Edward King and J. Wells Champney noted how the Mexican in San Antonio could not be made to see that "his slow, primitive ways, his filth and lack of comfort, are not better than the frugal decency and careful home management of the Germans and Americans who surround him." (Larralde & Jacobo, 2000, p. 26)

This racist rhetoric dominated social and political circles well into the twentieth century, justifying segregation and violence against the Mexican community in all sectors of American society. Rodolfo Acuña (2007) quotes a congressional report in 1930, which read.

> Their [the Mexicans'] minds run to nothing higher than animal functions- eat, sleep, and sexual debauchery. In every huddle of Mexican shacks one meets the same idleness, hordes of hungry dogs, and filthy children with faces plastered with flies, disease, lice, human filth, stench, promiscuous fornication, bastardy, lounging, apathetic peons and lazy squaws, beans and dried chili, liquor, general squalor, and envy and hatred of the gringo. These people sleep by day and prowl by night like coyotes, stealing anything they can get their hands on, no matter how useless to them it may be. Nothing left outside is safe unless padlocked or chained down. Yet there are Americans clamoring for more of this human swine to be brought over from Mexico. (Acuña, 2007, p. 209)

[handwritten annotation: "Mexican Problem" Idea that this will be brought over to the U.S]

Even when foreign threats loomed, discrimination, including in education, persisted against Mexicans. In 1943 at the height of the Second World War despite Mexican American contribution to the war effort, Acuña (2007) finds an official report by the Los Angeles police department, which read:

Although the report admitted that discrimination against Chicanos in employment, education, schooling, recreation, and labor unions was common, it concluded that Chicanos were inherently criminal and violent. Ayres stated that Chicanos were Indians, that Indians were Orientals, and that Orientals had an utter disregard for life. Therefore, because Chicanos had these inborn characteristics, they were too violent. The report further alleged that Chicanos were cruel, for they descended from the Aztecs who supposedly sacrificed 30,000 victims a day! Ayres wrote that Indians considered leniency a sign of weakness, pointing to the Mexican government's treatment of the Indians, which he maintained was quick and severe. He urged that all gang members be imprisoned and that all Chicano youths over the age of 18 be given the option of working or enlisting in the armed forces. Chicanos, according to Ayres, could not change their spots; they had an innate desire to use a knife and let blood, and this inborn cruelty was aggravated by the liquor and jealousy. The Ayres report, which represented official law enforcement views, goes a long way in explaining the events around Sleepy Lagoon." (Acuña, 2007, p. 253)

It is apparent that the perception of people of Mexican origin as animal-like and sub-human was reflected in all sectors of American society including the educational institutions. It is not surprising therefore, that Mexican students who were victims of such prejudice were transformed into agents of change in demanding educational justice and the construction of social-political spaces. Mexican origin children and their parents were at the forefront in the struggle against segregation in American schools (Darder, Torres, and Gutierrez, 1997).

Institutional Racism and the Mexican-American Education

Americanization, Roberto Alvarez vs Lemon Grove School Board, Mendez vs. Westminster, LULAC, Brown vs. Board of Education, Racialization, Xenophobia, Civil Rights

A long struggle for equality and equity in education marks the history of American schools in the Mexican origin community. A series of court cases document this struggle for a just education. In 1931, the case of Roberto Alvarez vs. the Lemon Grove School Board in San Diego County, California, is perhaps the earliest example of this struggle.

On January 5, 1931, Jerome T. Green, principal of the Lemon Grove Grammar School, acting on a school board decision barred 75 children of Mexican descent from entering school. According to the school board and the Parent Teacher Association these children caused health and sanitation problems and they came from homes where ignorance and poverty prevailed. Full of cultural prejudice the Lemon Grove School District in California secretly established a separate school for students of Mexican ancestry in the hope of "Americanizing" them (Griswold del Castillo, 2008).

Outraged that their children were being segregated from the Anglo children in a school they referred to as "una caberiza," the Mexican American community of this San Diego suburb sued the Lemon Grove School Board and won. The victory was based on the principle that Mexicans were officially Caucasians. State law, only allowed segregation of Black, Asian, and Indian children, Caucasian students could not legally be segregated from other Caucasians (Griswold del Castillo, 2008).

Another important case was Mendez vs. Westminster and the California Board of Education. In March of 1945, Mexican parents in Orange County, California confronted the segregation of their children into "Mexican schools" with the help of the League of United Latin American Citizens (LULAC). Aware of the Lemon Grove outcome mentioned earlier, the school's rationale for segregating the Mexican-origin children was language necessity, a pedagogical necessity. The Mexican parents and LULAC sued four local school districts for segregating their children (Acuña, 2007). They were also victorious. This landmark case challenged segregation in California school districts and gave support to the Brown vs Board of Education Supreme Court Decision of 1954.

The Mendez case was a victory for equality in education in California (Velez-Ibanes, 1996). The national victory would come with Brown vs. Board of Education. In 1954, the U.S. Supreme Court ruled that compulsory segregation of races in public schools was unconstitutional. The court held that separate facilities for Black and White students were "inherently unequal," and in 1955, ordered states with segregated schools to open them to all races with deliberate speed (Acuña, 2007).

The racialization and marginalization of the Mexican American in such areas as education and the return of Mexican ancestry soldiers from World War II and the Korean War provided background and impetus for change and the Chicano movement. This historical experience gave birth to the roots of the Chicana/o quest for civil rights in the United States as well as the creation of Chicana/o socio-politico space. Mexican origin people demanded equality and justice in all sectors of society especially in education, (Acuña, 2007; Chavez, 1991; Gutierrez, 1988).

The awakening of social consciousness during the 1960s and 1970s produced social movements which led to reforms in education including the introduction of bilingual education and the creation of Chicano Studies departments in the Southwest. The legacy of discrimination however, continues to permeate the American landscape. It reshapes itself, taking new social political dimensions. Presently, like in the past, this includes debates over Mexican legal and illegal immigration and access to education (Acuna 2007; Chavez 1991; Gutierrez, 1988). In Texas, for example, school districts were required to charge tuition to parents of suspected undocumented children until this practice was overturned in Doe v. Plyler (1982) where it was ruled that states cannot constitutionally deny students a free public education on account of their immigration status, nor enact practices which impose immigration-derived penalties.

The current social divide over immigration policy in the United States suggests that social fragmentation and xenophobia continue to permeate American society. It is also clear that engaging in any discourse over these divisions cannot be separated from discussions on race and class in American society. In fact, race and class are at the core of the recent attacks on immigrants, their families and their supporters (Mariscal, 2006).

Protest in the Mexican origin community must be seen as much more than a form of unrest against a failed immigration policy that targets the undocumented population in the United States. It is also an explosion of emotions against a system and ideology that continuously marginalizes and criminalizes the Mexican origin community (Mariscal, 2006).

As we have entered the 21st century the global economic profit driven markets have brought the issue of immigration policy into debate once again. On the one hand the need for inexpensive labor, and on the other, the issue of controlling the borders of the nation (Gaona, 2006).

Dependency on Mexican Labor and a Failed Immigration Policy

Push and pull factors, Economic Vortex, Una Vida Mejor, Chinese, Exclusion Act, Gentleman's Act, Enganche, 1917 Immigration Law, Bracero Program, Amnesty, Proposition 187

Regrettably, immigration and in particular illegal immigration especially from Mexico, is rarely seen as a human and humane issue in the United States. More often it is only associated with economic cost of benefits to "illegal aliens." It is also safe to say that for most Americans the immigration debate is held in a contemporary capsule. It is seen as a current problem. Legal and illegal immigration from Mexico to the United States, however, has persisted for over one hundred years and it has often been triggered by American demand for easily exploitable labor (Acuña, 2007).

In addition, most Americans see immigration as one-dimensional in terms of its causes, and take no responsibility for its existence. This again, is particularly true of undocumented immigration. Few people are aware of historical immigration patterns established by the demand of American labor markets. Fewer take responsibility as consumers for its existence (Balderrama & Rodriguez, 1995).

Migration is often contextualized as patterns governed by push and pull factors which activate population relocation. Simply stated, the push factors are those that are driving people out of the country of origin. They can be subdivided into social, political and economic factors with unemployment, war, and repression often at the head of the list (Acuña, 2007).

The pull factors on the other hand, are the forces that pull people into a place. This is often associated with employment opportunities, freedoms, or what Mexican and Central American immigrants simply call "una vida mejor," a better life. The idea and ideal of "una vida mejor" is found continuously in the narratives in the general immigrant voice (Jacobo, 2006).

The historically consistent dominating pull factor has been an American economic vortex. The formal and informal American economy, and in particular its labor-intensive sectors, have historically fed on the inexpensive labor pool south of the border. The pull factor can be developing economic spaces, un-enforced immigration policy, and the general American standard of living. From the chicken farms of the Midwest to the maquiladoras (assembly plants of selected products located near the U.S. Mexican border) to maintenance of neighborhood lawns are examples of the pull factor in effect (Acuña, 2007).

It is nevertheless, simplistic to address these push and pull factors as migration patterns. A host of conditions and challenges as well as a range of emotions marks the exodus of millions of people around the world. Behind are left loved ones, homes, and the battered dreams and aspirations of entire populations. Perhaps it is the reason that despite the years in economic exile, Mexicans in the United States still see Mexico as home (Jacobo, 2006).

A brief examination of immigration policy in the twentieth century can attest to America's appetite for Mexican labor and its dire consequences. Simply put, historical demand for inexpensive goods and services as well as corporate desire for increased profits has created an economic vortex which functions as a lure for immigrants, both legal and illegal, from across the border (Balderrama & Rodriguez, 1995).

The United States, however, has historically failed in implementing practical and viable immigration laws that regulate the legal status of immigrant populations and their families. As a result this phenomenon created serious problem with families who have members especially children illegally in the country (Darder et. al., 1997).

The interdependency between Mexican labor and American industry began late in the 1800s as the American Southwest was transformed from a local plaza economy, to a national and international one. It should be pointed out that industrialization highlighted by the railroad system facilitated such a transition. This is also true of land reclamation acts that transformed deserts into agriculturally productive areas. Three industries experienced unparalleled growth: mining, agribusiness and transportation (Acuña, 2007). All three labor-intensive industries would depend heavily on Mexican labor, from the formative years to its modernization and the adaptation of technology to agriculture..

Accompanying the development of these industries were changes to traditional labor in the form of anti-Asian immigration policy such as the Chinese Exclusion Act of 1882 and the Gentleman Act of 1907. The Gentleman's Act curtailed Japanese immigration. The curtailing of Asian immigration was to have a direct impact on Mexican immigration, as Mexico would become a labor pool for many American industries. Those industries became more and more dependent on Mexican labor throughout the 20th century (Acuña, 2007).

Mexican labor was very appealing. What made it so attractive was its low cost and presence of skilled and unskilled labor. Availability was also an important attraction as Mexican labor was easily accessible and easily discarded. This dependency on Mexican labor cemented in the late 1800s is demonstrated by a number of programs, laws, and social environments which emerged early in the 20th century such as the Enganche System, the 1917 Immigration Law, and the Bracero Program (Gutierrez, 1998).

The mining companies of Arizona are a clear example of this early dependence on Mexican labor as they engaged in what was known as the Enganche system. The Enganche system was a form of direct recruitment by American mining companies. Mining companies in southern Arizona were aware of skilled Mexican miners and sent Enganchadores to hook the Mexican workers by offering jobs in the Arizona mines. The hiring of Mexicans to work in the United States through this system was in violation of American law but it rarely led to criminal charges. The profits to be made were too great (Balderama & Rodriguez, 1995).

Mexican families were lured by the possibility of employment and attracted by the dollar. What they encountered, however, was exploitation, segregation and hostility. Mexican workers were frequently paid half of the wages of white workers and given the most dangerous and undesirable jobs in the industry. This occupational segregation was accompanied by social segregation that divided the towns and services by race. It was also clear that while the Mexican origin population was vital to the economic interests of the region; their presence was also seen as a social threat. Schools were not safe from racism and segregated schools for Mexican origin children were common in the southwest during this period (Darder, et al., 1997, Acuña, 2007).

The lack of enforcement or the tailoring of immigration laws by the American government throughout the 20th century also indicates the historic addiction to Mexican labor. A clear example of this is the 1917 immigration law. The 1917 immigration law placed taxation and a literacy exam on "appropriate" immigrant populations (Gutierrez, 1988).

Due to pressure from corporations, the law was temporarily suspended for Mexicans. Some scholars believe that the law was postponed for the duration of World War I because enforcing the law on Mexicans would have had a negative effect on America's operations during the war (Acuña, 2007). As with the Enganche

Program, the Mexican origin population faced blatant discrimination and schools were often the vehicles by which discrimination was disseminated.

However, no law or program reflects the reliance on Mexican labor and its social consequences more than the Bracero Program, which lasted from 1942-1964. The Bracero Program began as demands for cheap labor increased in the United States once the country had been propelled into the Second World War and many Americans abandoned cheap labor industries in favor of urban wage and industrial occupations. As a result, the demand was especially high in the agricultural and railroad industry.

Arguing that they faced with a labor shortage, farmers quickly turned toward Mexico, demonstrating a continuing pattern of dependency on Mexican labor by agribusiness and other sectors in the United States that had existed prior to the war. The Bracero Program was conceived of as an emergency wartime measure but was renewed after the war and continued until 1964, providing a huge stimulus for Mexican immigration to the United States. During the Bracero Program almost five million Mexican workers came to the United States (Jacobo, 2000).

The program had various consequences on the struggle for civil rights. One effect was that it increased the numbers of Mexicans who came to live in the United States since many Braceros did not go back to Mexico and many more crossed into the U.S. without documents because of the unmet demand for farm laborers.

The Bracero Program, however, also perpetuated discrimination and exploitation. Bracero camps were segregated from whites and even from the Mexican American sections of town. Braceros lived in extreme poverty and worked in dangerous conditions. When they ventured outside the camps on weekends they frequently were the victims of racially inspired beatings and robberies (Gutierrez, 1998; Jacobo, 2000).

Some scholars suggest that the Bracero Program established the contours of modern Mexican immigration flows and gave rise to the social, political and cultural issues that dominate discourse over immigration in the present (Jacobo, 2000). As stated, many

Braceros stayed in the United States illegally at the end of the program. They eventually brought their families hoping that one day the immigration laws would change.

More recently the Amnesty Act of 1986 known as the Immigration Reform and Control Act of 1986 (IRCA) not only proved the need to secure foreign labor but also created much of the turmoil we are currently experiencing in the last decade of the 20th century. The law offered permanent residence and opportunities for citizenship for immigrants who entered the U.S. before January 1st 1982 and resided here. While the law placed some two million people on a path to citizenship it did little to legally unite families thus creating a wave of children into the United States. These children eventually lived among us and were the target of Proposition 187 in California (Acuña, 2007).

California's Proposition 187 was a controversial but popular proposition that passed in 1994 by 58.8 % of the vote. Its goal was to bar illegal immigrants from receiving social services, health care and public education, under the SAVE OUR STATE initiative. Persons wishing to receive public benefits had to prove their legal immigration status. It allowed law enforcement to investigate the legal status of anyone suspected of being illegally in the country while seeking state aid in the areas mentioned above. The law was soon overturned by federal courts because immigration jurisdiction does not reside with the states. But Proposition 187 had already amplified the legacy of anti-immigrant sentiment in the United States (Acuña, 2007).

In theory, the Immigration Reform and Control Act also made it illegal to hire or recruit undocumented immigrants and created a climate that promoted discrimination, especially toward Latinos. Legal Latinos were forced to settle for lower wages and worse working conditions. The act was highly criticized for not solving the immigration problem. Many critics use it as proof that amnesty agendas do not solve the problem since the illegal immigrant population has increased since its passage in 1986 (Acuña, 2007).

All of these programs and laws are a consequence of labor demands in the United States but no serious and concrete effort has been made to regulate the status of undocumented workers and to provide for reunification with their families. Thus, one result is the influx of undocumented children to the United States to be with their families with the hope that one day the laws will change. This brings us to the challenges of today affecting dreamers.

When undocumented children enter school, they face a world of uncertainty and fear. At a very young age they must confront the reality that they are illegally in the United States and could very well be detained and deported. The separation of families is real and common occurrence in the United States. For many of these children, however, years can go by without ever being detained. Nevertheless, they consistently struggle having to negotiate their lived spaces. They live shadowed lives.

Undocumented

Dreamers, Dream Act, AB540, California Dream Act, NCLR, Macroaggressions, ICE

The Mexican-origin population in the United States has long been engaged in a struggle for justice and the creation of social, political, and cultural space. Being undocumented in the United States, however, adds a distinct and new dimension to this struggle particularly in the formative years of one's life. Regrettably, despite its enormous need there is scant literature on this subject and a tremendous need to contribute to this important but neglected area of study (Acuña, 2007; Chavez, 1991; Soja, 1996;).

While there are limited studies on this population, data suggest that undocumented youth and those who have undocumented parents are particularly under severe psychological strain. They suffer from extreme isolation, are vulnerable, and easily exploited (Strong & Meiners, 2007). Undocumented youth tend to live in fear and shame, feelings that are often fueled by political discourse and biased media in the United States. Current activity by immigration law enforcement in raids of low-income communities looking for undocumented persons have raised concerns by human rights groups and immigration reform activists.

Border Patrol raids have incited debates over accountability of child welfare as raids have resulted in the separation of hundreds of children from their parents. According to reports, many of these children are American citizens but have undocumented parents and make up the youngest and most vulnerable segment of our population: infants, toddlers and preschoolers. The reports suggest that millions of children could face the peril of being separated from their parents. It is estimated that some five million children born in the United States have at least one undocumented parent.

It is not hard to imagine the short and long-term impact on the immigrant children population, as a result of the separation from their parents. Immediate concerns include lack of supervision as well as lack of basic necessities such as food, baby formula, diapers, and clothing. The separation of the family is without a doubt a central concern. Such has become the fear of these raids that cases have been documented of families hiding in the basement or closets of their homes for days and sometimes weeks.

The article, "The Impact of Immigration Raids on America's Children," postulates that long-term impacts were experienced through "difficulty coping with the economic and psychological stress caused by the arrest and the uncertainty of not knowing when or if the arrested parent would be released" (Capps, et al., 2007 p. 3). In general, children experienced symptoms of emotional trauma such as fear, feelings of abandonment, isolation, depression, separation-anxiety and other forms of post-traumatic stress disorder (Capps, et al., 2007).

The daily life of an undocumented person is one of perpetual fear, stress, physical hardship and often traumatic physical abuse. Often in fact, these traumas can be reproduced internally in the family in the form of domestic violence. Most undocumented people live in fear of detection and subsequent deportation. As such, most endure violence, near subsistence wages, unsafe working environments, and unsanitary working and living conditions (Diaz et al., 2007).

Undocumented people avoid public safety institutions and

police, and hence are the victims of harassment, theft, assault, domestic abuse and frequently rape. There exists a pervasive sense that the undocumented population has no voice, no say, and no rights. These are feelings that resonate deep and influence the negotiation of lived spaces of the unauthorized population in the United States. The recent failures of immigration reform including DACA and the Dream Act further alienated this population as their legal and academic status continues to be unresolved due to recent presidential elections.

We can posit that tensions over the immigration debate are often higher in border cities as these are perceived by the anti-immigrant faction as the frontline against what they perceive is an invasion taking place through unauthorized entry into the United States. Groups like the Minutemen operate under a creed that advocates vigilante actions to effect dominion over American borders. Given these tensions, one can also deduce that the trauma experienced by the unauthorized population is higher as they are consistently harassed and threatened (Acuña, 2007). Simply put, proximity to the U.S.-Mexico border creates an environment where traumatic conditions can flourish (Capps, et al., 2007).

In short, historical prejudice, American appetite for inexpensive labor and an unfeasible immigration policy have produced an array of problems. Two of the major problems produced are the criminalization of the Mexican community and virtual incarceration of unauthorized youth. The heated debate, the failure of immigration reform, and in particular the stalling of the Dream Act have left these youth in a state of confusion, despair, and uncertainty.

6

From Revolution to Economic Depression

Richard Griswold del Castillo

Since 1848 it has been impossible to fully understand the history of the Mexican American or Chicano people of this region without taking into consideration the Mexicanos in northern Baja California. Many Mexican American families are bi-national and have grown up on both sides of the border. Thousands of Mexicanos from Baja California, Norte have come to live in San Diego and Imperial Counties, as permanent residents. Many more thousands have crossed the international frontier to work in the fields, on the rail roads, in factories, hotels and private houses in "el otro lado." Derogatory and racist attitudes directed towards Mexican immigrants also affect Mexican Americans who are U.S. citizens. Mexicano immigrants and Chicano U.S. citizens work side by side in construction, the service industry and in agriculture, competing for the same jobs and experiencing the same kind of discrimination. With this inter-relationship acknowledged, this chapter discusses the formative historical events in the creation of a bi-national Chicano/Mexicano community in San Diego, a society that is constantly evolving and changing. This chapter develops the theme of the influence of the U.S. Mexican border in the construction of a transnational community, a people who increasingly asserted their rights as Americans.

Others have researched how the events of the early twentieth century affected Chicano communities in the U.S. Mexican border region. Mario T. Garcia's pioneering study of El Paso's Mexican barrios during the Mexican revolution showed how immigrants contributed to the economic development of this city and managed to create a new kind of border society while organizing themselves socially and politically to protect their families. The same kind of dynamic took place in other border cities. In San Antonio the immigration of thousands of Mexican upper and middle class refugees from the revolution gave them intellectual and political leadership of the community, a leadership that native-born Tejanos contested. In Los Angeles thousands of immigrant laborers established a new community in East Los Angeles while they struggled against Americanization programs and economic inequalities. These and other community studies of Mexican barrios for this time period indicate that the immigration from Mexico which began even before the revolution of 1910 increased the activism of the community, through labor unions, mutual aid societies (mutalistas), and in reshaping ethnic identity to be more critical of the injustices that were the daily life of Mexicanos in the U.S. The theme of the importance of the border in the development of community life for Mexicans in the United States was prominent in the history of the Mexican and Chicanos in San Diego during this period as well.

The Mexican Side of the Line
Before the Revolution of 1910

The Kumeyaay people are bi-national, having indigenous communities on both sides of the international boundary. Before the construction of the fence and the military policing of the boundary, the Kumeyaay people freely moved from one side to the other, particularly those groups who lived near Tecate and Jacumba.

In 1848 very few Mexicans lived in Baja California along the present day border. It was a land composed mostly of brush and desert, suitable for stock raising but little else. In the Spanish and Mexican period the rolling hills which today are beneath the city of Tijuana, was the rancho land grant owned by Argüello family, descended from Santiago Argüello the comandante of the San Diego presidio. Before the U.S. Mexican war, portions of Rancho Tijuana passed to Pío Pico, who had grown up in San Diego with his brother Andrés. The Argüellos continued to own most of what today is Tijuana, as well as rancho lands comprising the present day communities of Lemon Grove, La Mesa, and East San Diego. Tijuana, the town and later city was officially founded on July 11, 1889, formed out of a portion of the Argüello lands. The official name for Tijuana was the Villa de Zaragoza (later changed to Tijuana in 1929). Initially this community was a small settlement of ranch houses. Later it would grow to include a customs house and a few trading stores. Not until the 1920s would it start to grow into the metropolis it is today.

Other portions of Mexican rancho land immediately adjacent to San Diego County was owned by the Bandini family, and, for the next 150 years, their descendants along with the Picos and Argüellos frequently crossed the border to visit with family members or to live in either country for periods of time. They were the first bi-national Mexican American families.

Adjacent to the Mexican ranchos and settlement, across the Tijuana River on the U.S. side, another rancho by the name of San Ysdiro was established in 1873. In 1874 the first customs house was built and by 1889, "Tijuana could display the baths of the Tia Juana Hots Springs Hotel at Agua Caliente, a cemetery, the customs house, a school, an adobe church, and the curio store . . . . and the ranches . . . .. The beginning village consisted of some twenty buildings, grouped along a sandy street on the bank of the river." The people who lived on Rancho San Ysidro depended on Tijuana's small settlement for supplies and for the next 100 years San Ysidro became more a part of Tijuana's economy and culture than that of San Diego.

El Valle Imperial

Mexicali, now the capital of Baja California Norte, is today a metropolis of close to a million people. Located in the midst of a vast desert, Mexicali's growth has been due to the development of irrigated farming in the early 1900s. The entire agricultural complex of the Imperial Valley, including the towns of Indio, El Centro, Brawley, and Calexico took place in the twentieth century, largely as the result of the investments of U.S. railroad and land corporations along with the labor of thousands of Mexicanos, Chinese and Hindus.

Today the people of the Imperial Valley region are vitally dependent on Mexican green card workers and Chicano laborers, who make up the bulk of the field workers. Many upwardly mobile Chicanos and Mexicanos, have moved to San Diego in search of better jobs and educational opportunities. Others have attended Imperial Valley College in El Centro or at the San Diego State University's extension in Calexico and then moved across the mountains to San Diego. There is thus a historical link between the Chicano communities of "El Valle" and the Chicano communities in San Diego.

Mexicali, Calexico and all the other towns in the Imperial Valley owed their origin to the construction of irrigation canals which brought Colorado River water to the desert. In 1892 Charles Robinson Rockwood, an American engineer working for the California Development Company, began studying the feasibility of constructing a canal east to the Imperial Valley. Because of the topography it was cheaper to build the canal mostly on the Mexican side of the border following the old riverbed of the Alamo River, and then enter the U.S. territory near Calexico. At the time, the Mexican government had given vast land grants to American corporate interests and they supported this project. In 1901 the first water entered the Imperial Valley and immediately a small farming community sprang up, named Mexicali. On the U.S. side hundreds of settlers rushed to file for sections of land and more than 100,000 acres were under plow within a few years. Soon the communities of El Centro, Calexico and Brawley were born.

In 1905 a disaster took place that would change the geography of California. Engineers had constructed a new intake gate on the Colorado River to avoid the problems of silting. Spring floods that year, however, washed away their temporary dams, and despite valiant efforts to stop it, the Colorado River changed course and began flowing, in its entirety, into the Imperial Valley following the Alamo canal. The river soon created a huge lake, called the Salton Sea. The river continued on its rampage for two more years, until it was finally re-channeled by the efforts of the Southern Pacific Rail Road, subsidized by the U.S. government. Thereafter the irrigation run off from the fields of the Mexicali and Imperial Valleys flowed into the Salton Sea making it extremely saline.

Of course water and land meant little unless there were workers available to clear the fields, plant and harvest the crops. From the beginning the majority of the workers in the valley were Mexicans, although the corporations who bought up most of the land, imported other nationalities such as American Indians, Chinese, Hindus, Filipinos and Japanese. In addition small numbers of African Americans and Anglo Americans worked in the fields. The crops they planted and harvested were of every conceivable kind: cotton, melons, alfalfa, barley, wheat, vegetables. Because of the weather and water usually three crops a year were possible. The population on both sides of the international border depended on the largess of the agribusiness corporations which controlled the economy. Paul Taylor, studied the Imperial Valley's labor conditions during the 1920s. He found that "Despite the richness of soil and high financial yield of crops in good years, the agriculture of the valley is characterized on its economic side by tenant farming, absentee ownership, and a general condition of instability and impermanence." That is to say the Mexicano and Mexican Americans in the Valley lived in colonial conditions of poverty at the mercy of the farm owners. With racist assumptions and stereotypes about Mexicans, the white growers constantly "preferred" them over other workers because of the low wages they were able to pay. Said one grower: "Mexicans are much to be preferred to whites. Once fixed, they are permanent and reliable. I do not think they are good for other types of work." During the 1920s occasional labor organizers tried to improve conditions for Mexicans in the Valley, but they were jailed, beaten and run out of town.

The Mexicans and Mexican Americans from El Valle looked west as a way out of conditions of semi-slavery. Until after World War II, few were able to make the move up out of the ranks of laborers and to escape the colonial conditions. Many of the most dynamic activists of the Chicano movement came from El Valle. They brought with them a heritage of struggle and hard work.

Filibusterers and Revolutionists

Violence periodically erupted along the border and it affected the lives of Mexican Americans living in San Diego and the Imperial Valley. In 1853 William Walker, an American from Tennessee led a group of 45 adventurers men to try to conquer Baja California and Sonora. This was the first of many efforts by soldiers of fortune to take over portions of Baja California, reflecting a continuation of ideas of Manifest Destiny and anti-Mexican sentiment. In November 1853, Walker sailed by ship From San Francisco to La Paz where they briefly took over that town. Then, forced to depart by Mexican military forces, he and his men sailed up the coast to Ensenada and captured that settlement along with several other small towns in the vicinity. Again forced out by the Mexican military, Walker and his men attempted to cross the desert to invade Sonora, but this expedition failed miserably in the dry and scorching desert. Finally Walker and remnants of his band walked back to Tijuana and crossed the border to surrender themselves to U.S. authorities in San Diego. Walker was subsequently tried and convicted of violating U.S. neutrality laws (in San Diego) It is said that the Walker unsuccessful invasion of Baja California angered then president Santa Anna who was in the process of selling the U.S. the Gadsden Purchase. As a result he refused to sell Baja California.

The next major invasion of northern Mexico from California took place in 1910 when partisans of the Partido Liberal Mexico, led by Ricardo Flores Magón, captured Mexicali and went on to take over Tecate and Tijuana in 1911. Magón's forces were comprised mostly of Anglo-American radicals, Wobblies, socialists and anarchists, who supported the ideas of the PLM enough to risk their lives in the opening battles of the Mexican Revolution. Although there were some Mexicanos who were in the invading army in Baja California, the whole group were branded as being "filabusteros" of the same stripe as William Walker, despite the fact that their leader, Magón, was well known in Mexico as a revolutionary who was opposed to the dictator Porfirio Díaz.

Although only about 100 people lived in Tijuana at the time, and a good portion of them were American merchants, the PLM invasion was traumatic for the border residents. In the battle for control of the small settlement the Mexican army lost 32 dead and 24 wounded. In the meantime the entire civilian population fled across the line to take up temporary residence in the Little Lander's Colony (today San Ysidro). Joe Montijo was a boy living in Old Town San Diego when the battle took place. He remembered his father taking him to Tijuana after the battle where he was told to select a warm jacket from among the dead. He wore his jacket with bullet holes to school the next day. Meanwhile the children and adults living in tents in San Ysidro wondered when they would be able to go home. The insurrectos control of the town was short lived, just long enough for them to allow San Diegans to loot the stores and for the rebels to collect border crossing fees from curious tourists. During this occupation Dick Ferris, a local promoter hired by the city of San Diego, sought to publicize the upcoming California-Panama Exposition (to be held in Balboa Park) by sending the president of Mexico a letter declaring Ferris the ruler of an independent Baja California. Meanwhile Mexicans complained that Ricardo Flores Magón had allowed himself to be allied with Americans who "call us greasers, "cholos," dirty Mexicans, etc. . . ." Finally in late June 1911 the Mexican troops recaptured the town. The ultimate casualties were Magón's revolutionary credentials and American good will along the border.

The Magonista rebellion affected the lives of some of the native peoples living in along the border. Both the Magonistas and the Mexican Federal army recruited Indians from both sides of the border to fight for them. These included the Guaycure, Cocopa and Yuma Indians as well as Indians who lived around Mexicali. Indian scouts were used by General Celso Vega to spy on the Magonistas, and Indians soldiers were credited with wounding the Magonista commander near El Alamo, Baja California. On the other side Emilio Guerrero was a captain commanding a group of Indians within the Magonista army in Tijuana. Some believe as many as 30 Indians served in the army. After the Magonista defeat the Mexican army pursued the Indian rebels and were reported to have executed nine to twelve men near Jamau. According to one historian, the Indian involvement in this rebellion had more to do with traditional hatreds between different Indian bands than to an appeal to ideology. The alliance of various partriliniages show that they chose the side they did hoping to exact revenge on rival groups.

San Diego During the Mexican Revolution

As already noted, the Magonista take over of Tijuana and Mexicali in 1911 was a dramatic event affecting Mexican-US. Relations and attitudes towards Mexican American border dwellers. During the subsequent years of the Mexican revolution, which lasted until the 1930s, Mexican Americans in San Diego were influenced by the increased numbers of immigrants crossing the border and by the fears of the Anglo Americans about Mexican radical revolutionaries.

Throughout Southern California there was a growing need for Mexican laborers who were hired at low wages to work in construction, light industry, and agriculture. San Diego, experienced a boom in population and the construction of new homes. Mexican immigrants were hired at the National City rail road freight terminal and in the lumber yards and new home construction sites thought out the city. They were needed in the waterfront district to work in the California Iron Works, the San Diego Marine Construction Company, and the new tuna packing sheds that were being built. Needing to be close to their work many Mexican families moved into Logan Heights, previously a middle class suburb. This was the origin of the present day Barrio Logan.

During this period, Paul Taylor, a noted agricultural economist studied the Mexican laborers of San Diego. In a sample of 100 workers he found that Mexicans worked in low skilled jobs such as day laborers, cement workers, maintenance laborers, etc. Semi-skilled laborers worked as gardeners, truck drivers, firemen, and janitors. Mexicans were also in skilled occupations such as carpenters, blacksmiths, and business owners. Children also worked as paperboys, junk collectors, odd jobs, and later worked along side women in the canneries. Almost a third of the employed men were members of labor unions or employee associations. This was despite a long prejudice within the AFL-CIO against Mexican and black

members.   The white members felt endangered by the Mexican
workers willingness to work for long hours at low pay and they
considered the Mexican as a threat to the "American Way of Life."
Nevertheless the Mexican population continued to grow in San
Diego.   Between 1900 and 1920 the Mexican origin population
of the city rose from 638 to 4,028.   Compared to day's population
this seems like a minuscule group, but for the time, it represented a
huge relative increase in the Chicano population. There was a large
floating or temporary population as well.   Many came to San Diego
by boat, since travelers by rail were in constant danger of being
attacked by Mexican revolutionists. Southern Pacific Rail Road
sent labor contractors (enganchistas) to Mexico and brought 500
Mexican workers at a time to San Diego by boat. These laborers were
then sent to the Imperial Valley to work in Mexico constructing
the Mexicali-Sonora line. The down town area between 8th and
Thirteenth had hotels, pool halls, and bars where these transitory
workers spent their leisure time.

Those Mexcianos who settled down with families and jobs in
San Diego developed a community life. One of the main institutions,
formed by Mexicano immigrants throughout the Southwest during
this time, was the mutualista. This was a mutual aid society, where
members gave weekly contributions and in return had the right
receive benefits in case of death.   The mutualista was also a social,
patriotic, and cultural institution including the families of the
workers. In San Diego the Unión Patriótica Benéficia Mexicana
Independiente was one such mutualista.   The families who were
members sponsored periodic fiestas to celebrate Mexican cultural
events, such as Cinco de Mayo and Día de la Revolution (November
20th).   Other groups such as La Junta Patriotica Mexicana became
bi-national in celebrating both American and Mexican holidays.

Mexicanos and Mexican Americans suffered the same kinds
of discrimination. The San Diego Union, for example did not
distinguish between the two groups in their articles. All were
"Mexicans." Added to the hostility that traditional labor unions felt
towards Mexican workers was the stereotype of the violent border
revolutionist/bandit. The San Diego Union helped fuel the paranoia

in reporting about the violent incidents that regularly took place along the border. In an article on March 14, 1914, for example, the headline screamed, "San Diegan Murdered by Border Bandit," while reporting that three suspects "were thought to be Mexican." Another headline on November 12, 1910 was "Death for Gringos is Cry of Rioters" reported the news of beginnings of the Mexican revolution.

Fears of Mexican revolutionists in San Diego led to calling out the National Guard to protect lives and property along the border. More than 18,000 troops were stationed in San Diego and Imperial counties along the border. On April 24, 1914, some dynamite was found near the Sweet Water Reservoir and, suspecting sabotage, ten Mexican employees were fired. Periodically rumors were reported that Mexican revolutionist were planning to poison the water supply. Accordingly 160 soldiers were dispatched to guard Otay Dam. The city of El Cajon created its own militia, the San Diego Home Guard, to protect that community from Mexican terrorists. The San Diego newspaper regularly reported about the movement of Mexicans who crossed the border going back to Mexico to fight in the revolution. Fears reached such a height in 1914, that the San Diego Police Department issued orders that Mexicans in San Diego were to be kept under strict watch and that they were not to be allowed to have weapons or ammunition. The police conducted a series of raids of the down town pool halls looking for seditious individuals. All during this period, the Justice Department employed agents to survey Mexican nationals in the U.S. who were suspected of violating U.S. neutrality laws. Hundreds of reports of the comings and goings of Mexican businessmen, politicians and workers ended up being part of massive "Mexican File," This resource gives even more detail to the fears surrounding the Mexican population in San Diego.

Tijuana: The Growth of a Metropolis

During the period of the Mexican Revolution and up to the 1930s, Tijuana experienced a period of economic and demographic growth largely due to tourist enterprises owned and operated by Americans. One of the first was one centering on the natural hot springs, the Tijuana Hot-Spa Hotel, built in 1885 and owned by P.L.Carle. This was followed by the construction of dog and horse racing tracks, casinos and other hotels. Mexicano entrepenuers opened the first bull ring by 1910. When tourists visited San Diego during the Panama Exposition in 1915, they also traveled to Tijuana which had recreation activities that were illegal in California. The Tijuana attractions, the Jockey Club, Trivoli Bar, the Foreign Club, the Sunset Inn and Agua Caliente Casino were all owned by Anglo-Americans and employed mostly American workers. This was a source of constant resentment with the Mexican labor unions and government.

A tremendous impetus for the growth of tourism was the enactment of Prohibition in the U.S. Over night Tijuana became a Mecca for those who wanted to drink liquor and have a good time. By the end of the 1920s there were more than 260 businesses located in the downtown area, many of them along Revolucíon. These included many service businesses besides bars. Besides liquor Tijuana also had the attraction of almost unregulated prostitution and related vice establishments. This period in the city's growth engendered many negative stereotypes about Mexicans and border towns in the minds of visiting American tourists. These attitudes were generalized to Mexican Americans who lived in San Diego.

It was not until the presidency of Lázaro Cárdenas that Mexico moved to end gambling and American control of the tourist industry in Tijuana. In 1934, by presidential decree Cardenas outlawed gambling and in 1937 the government expropriated American owned property in Tijuana. Some of the casinos were converted to schools and those Mexicanos who lost their jobs were given government employment.

San Ysidro: The Other San Diego

Bordering directly on the international line adjacent to Tijuana, San Ysidro has always been linked to México. San Ysidro's early urban development came from a visionary group of people who came to settle in the valley in 1909 and founded an agricultural utopian colony called "Little Landers." They were a group of people who believed that with "a little land," people could growing their own food and provide their surpluses to others within the community. They, appropriately, christened their community with the name of the patron saint of farmers, Isidro, "a virtuous farmer who had fallen asleep and had his fields plowed for him by angels."

Today San Ysidro still looms large in the dreams of many people. Immigrants "without papers" fleeing the U.S. border patrol ask breathlessly when they come across if they have arrived--if they have crossed "la linea" and entered the land of milk and honey. For long-time San Ysidro residents, who love their community and live, feel and appreciate the social relations that make up their community, their vision of San Ysidro goes beyond the limitations that some outsiders have.

Little Landers founder, William Smythe described the high ideals of brotherly love and the fullest development of human potential he held for the cooperative farming venture he founded. He foresaw the ideal colonist as: "a man who... is a scientist... an artist. ... a man with initiative. ... He is an independent, self-employing man. To his trees, his plants, and his vines he gives the ineffable touch of love. He is the spiritual man of the soil." Smythe's idealism was reflected in the colony's symbol: a flag bearing a white star on a field of blue, the "star of hope." The Little Landers Colony prospered largely by trading with the settlements in Tijuana, but in 1916 the Tijuana River flooded and destroyed most of the houses. Most of the Little Landers departed for other locales, but a few hardy pioneers remained. Until the 1930s most of the residents were Anglo Americans, farmers, ranchers and individual who worked in the booming tourist industry in Tijuana.

Ermanie Celicio was born in San Ysidro in 1912 and was one of the few Mexicans who lived in the Little Landers Colony after the flood. He recalled that "Everyone was friendly. We all knew each other and everybody talked." Ermanie's father worked in various jobs, for the San Diego and Arizona Rail Road, which connected San Diego with the Imperial Valley, loading and unloading trains, and as a dealer at the Monte Carlo Club in Tijuana. She recalled that San Ysidro was where the jockey's lived and the race horses and dogs were boarded. "Back then, San Ysidro was a jockey town. They kept horse and dogs here. The jockeys used to send their kids to school here." San Ysidro in the 1920s was home for 50 soldiers and some Chinese farmers. No one paid much attention to the border but freely crossed back and forth.

In another interview Edward M. Cuen described what it was like growing up in San Ysidro. "San Ysidro was a beautiful community. I think I knew everybody in town then. ... It was just farmland, and a lot of people had cows, goats, horses, chickens."

Between 1929 and 1969, many things changed in San Ysidro; but the strong sense of community remained. Lydia Armenia Beltran, who arrived in 1969, describes her reception:

> "It was a very beautiful community. We found people ... who were very much involved with the community. They ...told us what was going on and they said that if we worked hard and involved ourselves . . . the community would be that much better off. ... A little girl, . . . who's now my goddaughter... came out and welcomed me and took me over to her house.... My neighbors became all my compadres.... Everybody's compadre here."

Joyce Hettich, long-time San Ysidro resident and considered its unofficial historian, remarks about inter-ethnic relations in San Ysidro: "My experience of 49 years in San Ysidro is that we have all gotten along just fine." In describing relations between the Community Church and the Catholic Church, she explained how the churches would help each other out:

> "The Community Church minister would say to his congregation -- 'go over today to the Catholic Church-- they're having a fundraising drive.' When the Community Church was having a drive, the Catholic Church pastor would say, "Go over to the Community Church today, they're having a drive."

Today San Ysidro is a predominantly Latino community. Mexican music is heard, and Spanish is the principal language spoken. Yet San Ysidro contains an ethnic and cultural representation that many people are not aware of. It is a community that has undergone major demographic change, particularly since the 1950s and 1960s. Andrea Skorepa, director of the Centro Familiar in San Ysidro, observed that the community became "a lot more predominantly Latino, but we've also had an emerging African-American community . . . we've gotten an influx of African-Americans, Pacific Islanders, especially Filipino."

Steven Andrew Gomez describes his own family's background and social-cultural activities:

> "Me myself, being Mexican Indian, Tohno-O'odam, Yaqui and Papago, that's who I relate to more.... Our entertainment is Pow-wows. The Gathering of the people. These are my ways. Singing [in ceremonial drums] is another way. I attend, not a church, but a circle of friends, a Native American sweat lodge, which is our church."

San Ysidro is also home to an ancient equestrian tradition going back to the Moorish days in Spain and to the Spanish-Mexican frontier days: the Charreada, a form of rodeo, with elaborate dress, highly skilled horsemanship and beautiful lasso techniques performed by both male "charros" and female "escaramuzas". The Lopez brothers of San Ysidro were involved in forming an association of charros. Their charreadas drew people from as far away as Los Angeles and as far south as Rosarito.

This proximity to the border, which drew people from above and below the border, has been an important element in the life of San Ysidro, just as its proximity to the ocean and the salt beds once attracted Indian peoples from as far away as present-day Sonora and Arizona.

A New San Diego

As a result of the pressures of the Mexican revolution and the growth of the economy in Southern California new Mexican colonias and communites were established, in Logan Heights, San Ysidro, Calexico, and Brawley. These places became the nucleus for the flourishing of Mexicano and later Chicano culture in San Diego. The revolutionary period fueled fearful stereotypes and the close association of Tijuana with the Mexicans in San Diego added to Anglo American racist prejudice. In the next decade these attitudes would be used to justify a repatriation campaign to ship Mexicans back to Mexico.

By 1930 the Mexican population of San Diego and Imperial Valley had grown due to the changes in the economy and the demand for workers. The construction of the San Diego and Arizona Railway in (expand) opened up trade and travel between San Diego and the Imperial Valley, as well as with northern Baja California. Mexicano workers helped build this bi-national railroad and the continued to work its maintenance up to the 1950s. The rail road was a symbol of the interconnectedness of the people of the border, a fact that would become more and more important in the lives of average Mexican Americans.

The 1920s and Mexican San Diego

During the decade following the most violent years of the Mexican revolution, San Diego's Mexican origin population increased due to immigration and the economic development of the region which created a demand for more workers. As in other cities and towns in California, the native Californio families all but disappeared through inter-marriage and by being outnumbered by thousands of new immigrants from Mexico. In the period 1920-1930 the Mexican immigrant population began to settle outside of the Old Town barrio in Logan Heights, an area of San Diego known as the "East End,' a former upper and middle class residential neighborhood. From there Mexicanos traveled to work in the service and laboring jobs around the city, and women found jobs working for the fish canneries which were constructed along the harbor. Other settlements of immigrants grew where the jobs were located, near the yards of the San Diego and Arizona Rail Road, and in small agricultural colonias in Lemon Grove, Escondido and San Ysidro. The Mexican immigrant population in the Imperial Valley exploded in this period as they replaced Indian and Japanese workers. Seasonally these workers traveled to San Diego to work in the citrus and vegetable fields.

Along with the growth and dispersion of the Mexican population was the beginning of their efforts to challenge discrimination and economic exploitation. Two major movements were the Imperial Valley strikes 1928-1933 and the Lemon Grove incident in 1930-1931. In these confrontations San Diego's Mexicanos demonstrated that they to make sacrifices, and they also wanted to be shape their own destiny. Accordingly they organized unions, parent associations, neighborhood groups, and mutual aid societies attempting to fight for justice. This was the first significant community effort by the Mexicano and Chicano people to challenge their subordinated status within San Diego and Imperial Counties. It was a precursor for many subsequent "luchas" in the fields of labor, community organizing, and education.

Imperial Valley Strikes

The Mexicano communities in the Imperial Valley have been historically linked to San Diego's Chicano communities through immigration and economic development. The children of many immigrant farm workers from the Valley aspired to go to San Diego to get a college education and obtain better jobs. Simultaneously hard working, tenacious, and socially consciousness of the Mexicanos from "El Valle" became an important stimulating force within the Chicano and Mexicano communities of San Diego during the Chicano movement of the 1960s and 1970s.

The first Chicano/Mexicano labor activism in the San Diego-Imperial Valley region stemmed from the grueling experience of the farm workers. As the Imperial Valley's agriculture expanded so too did the demand for workers. Initially, in the construction of the irrigation canals and the clearing of the land, a succession of groups were recruited: American Indians, Japanese, Hindu, Filipino, and Chinese laborers were the majority of farm workers in the valley until the 1920s when large industrial size farms began to dominate. There after Mexicano immigrants became the major labor force. In 1927, Paul Taylor, a noted economist visited the Imperial Valley and report on the conditions. He found about 20,000 Mexican immigrants working in the fields and that about half of them had been born in the United States. Working 9 to 10 hours a day in the spring and fall, and suffering in temperatures over 110 degrees in the summer, the seasonal workers suffered from low wages and an abusive system of labor contractors. As Taylor remarked, "the agriculture of the valley is characterized on its economic side by tenant farming, absentee ownership, and a general condition of instability and impermanence." The changing seasonal crops meant fluctuating demands for workers. In the spring many farm workers would leave the valley looking for work in the Coachella Valley and San Diego. The average family earned about $600 a year and was constantly on the move following the crops. Taylor found that the most common complaint was against tenant farmers and labor contractors for failing to pay the wages due to the farm workers. In April 1928 the Mexicano workers formed a union to try to challenge the wage abuses they had been experiences. As was to be the case in hundreds of other Chicano unions, the original organizational efforts to unionize came form a "mutualista," a mutual aid society, the Sociedad de Benito Juarez led by Felemon B. Gonzales. The new union was called "the Imperial Valley Workers Union." Gonzales stated that the idea for the union came originally from the Mexican consul in Calexico who had been besieged with complaints of Mexican nationals against corrupt labor contractors and tenant farmers.

In May 1928 the union sent out letters to all the growers respectfully asking for 15 cents a crate for picking cantaloupes or 75 cents an hour for the labor. They also requested an improvement in working conditions: ice for drinking water, picking sacks, lumber to build out-houses and legal compensation to injured workers. Within a few days the sheriff arrested 36 workers for refusing to leave the fields where they refused to work unless their demands were met. The arrests provoked community meetings in the Mexican colonias. In one instance, Sheriff Gillette entered a pool hall where laborers were meeting to discuss the strike and Francisca Rodriguez, a farm worker, tried to force him to leave, aided by several others. They were promptly arrested. While most Mexicanos returned to work, at the old rate, the Anglo Americans began to fear a communist plot and rumors circulated about a possible Mexican uprising. The Sheriff then began making indiscriminate arrests of Mexicans on the streets and in pool halls and this led to criticism in the Mexican newspapers in Mexicali, an appeal to President Calles for intervention, the dispatch of a state official to investigate the situation, and ultimately to the farm workers getting most of their demands. More than sixty union activists were jailed for a short periods of time and the union continue to survive for four more harvests.

The final report of the state investigation into what was termed the Cantaloupe Strike was issued as part of Governor C.C. Young's special committee report on Mexican immigration in 1930. That report concluded that, contrary to allegations by the sheriff, that "reds" had been responsible for the strike, there was "no tangible evidence to support this view" and that the worker's demands needed to be seriously considered. Among these were the need for better housing, regulation of labor contractors, and better compliance with Workmen's Compensation Insurance. The investigation concluded that "future amicable relations between the growers and their laborers will be assured only by directing attention to the fundamental causes of the strike, rather than by resorting to the easier expedient of hurling time-worn and ineffective accusations of radicalism and red propagandism."

Unfortunately this advice was not followed in subsequent years. Early in 1930 organizers from the Trade Union Unity League (TUUL), a Communist led group dedicated to overthrowing the factory agricultural system, entered the Imperial Valley and organized the Agricultural Workers Industrial League. This organization then sought to piggy back on the efforts of Mexicano and Filipino workers who had a spontaneous strike during the lettuce harvest to gain wage and working condition concessions. The Mexicano workers, however were opposed to such Communist influence, and forbid the TUUL representatives from speaking at their meetings. Other individuals and organizations opposed the TUUL intervention into strikes in the Valley: the Mexican consul supported repatriating Mexicanos who sided with the TUUL and the Mexican union, the Confederacion Regional de Obreros Mexicanos worked to undercut the Communist organizers influence. Thereafter strikes that local Mexicano workers sought to organize during the cantaloupe harvest were squashed before they began by the joint efforts of Mexican and American authorities who feared Communist influence.

The final burst of labor organizing in the fields occurred in 1933-1934 during the worst days of the depression. A new militant union, partially influenced by communist organizers, emerged, the Cannery and Agricultural Workers Industrial Union (CAWIU). Their organizers found a receptive farm labor force, exploited even more than previously by falling wages. They were in turn opposed by the Mexican consulate who, fearing communist influence, organized a rival worker's union, La Asociación Mexicana del Valle Imperial. Ultimately the growers decided to support the worker's association in order to destroy the CAWIU.

In October of 1933 and June 1934 there were many strikes that resulted in violent reactions by the police and growers. More than once thousands of workers walked off their jobs only to be convinced to return by the Mexican consul. In 1934 the CAWIU called for a general strike of lettuce and vegetable workers and the authorities reacted by mass arrests and prohibitions against meetings. Scores of individual were arrested only on suspicion of supporting the strike. Isolated instances of violence and wholesale violations of civil liberties continued until the federal government sent a special conciliator to the Imperial Valley to try to mediate a peace. General Pelham D. Glassford sought out Joaquin Terrazas, the Mexican consul in Calexico who had organized La Asociación Mexicana and had personally intervened to prevent strikes in the past. Under Terrazas guidance the growers agreed to a new wage agreement and a number of other provisions, among them only to employ members of La

Asociación. For their part the workers agreed to keep communists out of their union and not to strike.

For the next year the CAWIU and La Asociación competed for support. For many observers the Mexican association was nothing more than a company union designed to promote the interests of the grower. The growers refused to conduct elections to allow the workers to choose which union they wanted and they were supported in this by California authorities. Ultimately the CAWIU lost the battle, overwhelmed by the combined alliance of growers, and the Mexican and state governments. The Mexicano agricultural workers of the Imperial Valley would have to wait more than 30 years for another unionization effort, one led by Cesar Chavez himself a farm worker.

The Lemon Grove Case

During the labor struggles in the Imperial Valley the children of Mexican immigrants throughout Southern California were increasingly segregated into separate schools. The boards of education in scores of towns and cities followed a policy of establishing "American Schools," which were separate facilities or class rooms where Mexican students were be given special instruction in English and American culture. Behind the supposed pedagogical benefits of this policy was a racial agenda, of separating Anglo and Mexican children in order to insure the purity of American children. The Los Angeles School District, for example, justified segregation by saying that Mexican children "are more interested in action and emotion but grow listless under purely mental effort." Other educators, such as Merton Hill, principal of Chafee Union High School, argued that Americanization school's curriculum would be where "girls should be trained to be neat and efficient servants. . . boys should be taught to make use of discarded tin cans in the development of useful kitchen tinsels." As it developed the Americanization program was wide-spread throughout the Southwest and it promoted inferior education. It lasted until the Supreme Court declared this kind of segregation illegal in the Mendez v. Westminster case in 1947

It is not known how wide spread segregated schools were in

San Diego. Due to the demographic concentration of Mexicanos in certain towns in the Imperial Valley, it is certain that many elementary schools there were de facto segregated. Taylor compiled a 1927 school census in the valley and found that Mexican school children comprised more than 50 percent in the towns of Brawley, Calexico, Glamis, Niland, and Heber. In semi rural regions of San Diego it is probable that segregation prevailed.

One notable challenge to the Americanization school came from the Mexican immigrant parents living in Lemon Grove, a rural hamlet near San Diego where the main employers were citrus growers. This has come to be known as the Lemon Grove Incident, thanks to the research of Robert Alvarez, Jr. and the documentary film produced by Paul Espinosa. This was the first successful legal challenge to the segregation of Mexicanos in the public schools in the United States.

The growers of Lemon Grove had attracted hundreds of Mexicano families, mostly from Baja California to come and work in the citrus fields. Many of the Mexicano residents were related by blood having come from the same region of Mexico. Their children, born in the U.S. began to enter the local school system in the late 1920s. On July 23, 1930 the Lemon Grove school board began to discuss what to do with the more than 75 Mexican students who were attending the local grammar school. It was decided to build a separate school for them but no notice was given to the parent of the Mexicano students.

On January 5, 1931 the principal of the Lemon Grove Grammar School, Jerome T. Greene stood at the door of the school and directed the incoming Mexican students to go to the new school building, a wooden structure that came to be called "La Caballeriza," (the barn). Instead the students returned home and thereafter their parents refused to send their children to the separate school. This became known in the press as the "Mexican student strike," but in reality it was their parents who, with the support of the Mexican consul in San Diego, decided to oppose segregation of their children. They formed a group called La Comite de Vecinos de Lemon Grove and asked the Mexican consul, Enrique Ferreira, for advice. Ferreira put the parents in touch with Fred C. Noon and A. C. Brinkely, two lawyers who had worked for the consul in the past and from there they filed a writ of mandate to prevent the school board from forcing their children to attend the segregated school. They chose a student, Roberto Alvarez, to be the plaintiff in the class action suit.

The Comite de Vecinos sought support for their actions from other Mexicano communities by contacting the Spanish language press in Tijuana and Los Angeles. La Opinion, the largest Mexican newspaper in California, published an editorial stating, "We are not in agreement, which is very natural, nor do we consider just, the separation of our children, without any reason, to send them to another establishment that distinguishes Mexican children from children of other nationalities . . .." Soon donations began arriving from Mexicanos throughout California to help with the costs of the litigation.

The battle lines were being drawn. The president of the Lemon Grove school board responded to La Opinon by claiming that the strike was being orchestrated by "an intense Mexican national organization." The San Diego District Attorney decided to defend the school board in the impending case. Simultaneously Assemblyman George R. Bliss introduced a bill to legalize the segregation of Mexican children and others announced that if the Lemon Grove school board lost their case, they would see to it that other bills would go to the legislature." Eventually the Bliss bill was defeated as were other segregationist measures.

The court case proceeded to trial. The Writ of Mandate that went through the Superior Court called on reinstatement of the Mexican children and argued that the board had ". . . no legal right or power to exclude (the Mexican children) from receiving instruction on an equal basis . . ." The court in turn indicted each member of the school board for illegal segregation.

The San Diego district attorney argued that the new school was appropriate because it was in the Mexican neighborhood and large enough for all the students; that most of the students were below grade level in their knowledge of English; and that they would receive better instruction in this Americanization school.

Incidentally they suggested that American students would benefit by not having contact with Mexican students.

On February 24, 1931 Judge Claude Chambers began hearing the case. Fred Noon, the Mexican parent's lawyer called ten witnesses to the stand to challenge the school board's contention that the Mexican children were educationally backward. Most of the students had been born in the United States and spoke English. At least one student spoke no Spanish at all. In the interrogatory Judge Chambers dramatically revealed the injustice of the differential treatment of Mexican students:

Judge Chambers: When there are American children who are behind, what do you do with them?

Answer: They are kept in a lower grade.

Judge: You don't segregate them? Why not do the same with the other children? Wouldn't the association of American and Mexican children be favorable to the learning of English for these children?

Answer: (silence)

In the final arguments, the judge was convinced that there was no reason to segregate the Mexican children and that the separation would probably hurt them academically in terms of learning the English language and customs. He ruled against the Lemon Grove school district and ordered them to reinstate the children in the regular school. While it was a victory for Mexicano students, the Judge had held that their segregation violated state law which allowed for the segregation of African and Indian children. Thus the logic underlying the verdict did not challenge racial segregation, and it would remain for later court cases to outlaw that kind of injustice.

The Lemon Grove case was the first legal victory of Mexicanos to challenge their separation in the school system. Unfortunately the case did not set a precedent in other districts and segregation continued outside of Lemon Grove. Nevertheless, the dramatization of the incident in the documentary film "The Lemon Grove

Incident" served to educate new generations about the struggles of their ancestors to achieve justice.

The Neighborhood House

During the period following the Mexican revolution and the first World War Anglo American liberals and social reformers sought to "uplift" Mexican and European immigrants who were streaming into the city. One of the efforts to reach the impoverished immigrants was the settlement house movement. The settlement houses provided basic services to the working poor and was the initiator of the concept of kindergarten schools in the United States. The settlement houses, located in the poorest sections of the cities, became centers for immigrant education and social activities as well as a place where immigrants could celebrate their native language and culture. While many settlements had as their goal the Americanization of the immigrant, through the teaching of English and "American" customs, sometimes they became centers of cultural pluralism and opposition to assimilation.

In San Diego the settlement movement began as a charitable outreach program of the College Woman's Club in 1914 and later was incorporated as The Neighborhood House of San Diego in 1923 with its main building located at 1809 National Avenue. The Neighborhood House had been preceded by the San Diego Industrial School, an after school and weekend school staffed by volunteer who taught Mexican immigrants industrial and domestic arts. It has little social or cultural outreach to the growing Mexican barrio. The Neighborhood House directors and staff shared in a nation-wide philanthropic movement which sought to ameliorate the evil effects of industrialization and modernization on the lives of the immigrant and working classes. During the 1910s the settlement house staff had been concerned with practical issues of abolishing child labor and other labor abuses. But by the time the Neighborhood House of San Diego was organized in the 1920s, the settlement house movement had moved away from concern with reform issues and now concentrated almost exclusively on public health, education and cultural and social activities.

The Neighborhood House official literature from 1920 stated the goals of the settlement house which the Woman's Club had constructed in Logan Heights:

"To understand its Mexican Neighbors.
To interpret the needs of the community.
To perform the intimate and friendly service of a good neighbor.
To direct needed educational and recreational work."

To many Anglo Americans, especially those who contributed money, the most important role of Neighborhood House was to be the Americanization of the Mexican immigrant. One reporter in the San Diego Union called Neighborhood House an "Americanization Factory." And it was true to that the directors sought to rationalize the budget of the Neighborhood House in terms of Americanization. But not all of the clients served were Mexican, perhaps 20 percent were African Americans and European immigrants. The funding for the Neighborhood house initially came from the Community Chest and later moved to the city. The range of activities sponsored by this barrio settlement house included classes in drama, English, and math, along with summer school for children and lectures, dances and community sings for the entire family. The Neighborhood House received some city funding during the 1920s to sponsor a nurse, a pre-natal and well-baby clinic and Red Cross classes. The clinic was immensely popular because many of the Mexican immigrants were reluctant to use the County hospital for illnesses. During the 1920s the Neighborhood House sponsored a milk station for mothers, who received free formulas and milk for their families. There was also a small library of donated books which the barrio residents could check out. Annually the Neighborhood House sponsored a traditional production of Los Pastores, a Mexican folk play about the shepherds and the Christ child.

One of the major obstacles to the Neighborhood Houses' outreach was the reluctance of Mexican men to allow their women to attend social and educational activities by themselves. In the 1920s and into the 1930s the barrio women succeeded in establishing a Mother's Club where they could gather to discuss issues of common concern and to participate in social and cultural activities. By the 1930s Neighborhood House had become a center for immigrant education with classes in English, Math, and health as well as a kindergarten.

Except for some community-wide events most of the programs of the Neighborhood House were segregated by race and gender with separate workshops and classes being given for African Americans, Mexicans, and Anglos as well as for girls and boys.

In the 1930s the Neighborhood House's programs expanded to include the construction of a community oven for the use of those who could not afford utilities and a class in how to be a hotel maid for young girls. In 1933 they built a new adobe building to house the baby and mother's clinic. Later in the 1940s the Neighborhood House expanded its facilities and programs even more to include a dental clinic and nursery.

The Neighborhood house was administered by Anglo Americans whose charitable desire to help the poor was laudable. Spanish speaking nurses and program aids were hired in an attempt to reach the Mexican population and it must be said that many of the programs that they offered were sorely needed. One of the early well-known directors of the Neighborhood House in the 1930s was Anita Jones who had worked at Hull House in Chicago, a noted progressive institution. She had been Director of the Mexican Immigrants Protective League there and had a degree form the University of Chicago. As director of the San Diego resettlement house she continued to administer to the Mexican immigrant community, by now more than 90 percent of the cliental were Mexican born with the balance being Greek, Portuguese, Japanese, and Italian. Old timers, including Laura Rodriguez, who was later an administrator for the Chicano Free Clinic, remembered that the Neighborhood House staff were kindly well-intentioned individuals who sought to learn the language and culture of their Mexican clients.

Although the Neighborhood house served most of the estimated 5,000 Mexican immigrants in San Diego during the 1930s, the city and county agencies almost completely ignored the economic and public health problems of Mexican immigrants. In fact in this period the government was trying to deport and repatriate Mexican immigrants and so was openly hostile towards their economic and social plight. The Neighborhood house consequently became a well known and respected community resource regarded by many Mexican Americans as a barrio institution. This was despite the sometime heavy handed efforts at Americanization and the administrator's failure to promote and encourage Mexican culture.

This all changed during the 1960s when the Neighborhood House administration came under attack by Chicano activists who wanted a different kind of locally controlled service agency. The origins of the take over of the Neighborhood House facility on National Avenue and the new Chicano oriented program will be the subject of a later chapter. For now it is important to note that during the Depression years the Neighborhood House was the only public agency devoted to improving the lives of Mexican and Chicano residents in Logan Heights.

The Mexicano Community during the Depression.

Estimates as to the numbers of Mexicans and Mexican Americans who lived in urban San Diego during the 1920s vary. Local officials estimated that there were approximately 20,000 Mexicans in San Diego by 1928 but the U.S. Census in 1930 only counted 9,266 Mexican born. The discrepancy may be due to the notorious undercounting of Mexicans by the Federal Census Bureau, as well as to migratory patterns of employment and residence. Also the 1930 Census did not include the Mexican American children of Mexican parents, a group that probably tripled the actual figures. During the 1930s the Mexican born population of San Diego declined because of the repatriation drive and the difficulties of finding employment.

What was it like living as a Mexicano in San Diego in this period? Constantine Panunzio, a sociologist who was an Italian immigrant and Director of the Neighborhood House in 1930 studied the community. He wrote one of the few social-scientific surveys of the Mexicano community of this era, published by the University of

California as How Mexicans Earn and Live: A Study of the Incomes and Expenditures of One Hundred Mexican Families in San Diego, California. This depression era study was done to determine the degree of "national adjustment" undergone by Mexican immigrants and their offspring who were living in San Diego. Panunzio studied the consumption patterns of one hundred "Mexicans" and found "habits of living of a group not yet wholly adjusted to the American standard." He described the Logan Heights barrio in 1930:

> "Mexicans live in San Diego under conditions that are, possibly, more than usually favorable. Most of them are in the southwestern portion of the city along the waterfront close to the factories and canneries. The streets are wide; sanitation is moderately good. Mexican stores, churches, pool halls, and the Neighborhood House are part of the district. Living conditions are reasonably good. There is little or no serious congestion. The cottage type of house prevails. There are no slum tenements."

This optimistic description is at odds with that of the Community Welfare Council which reported in 1928 that there were ". . . a multitude of undesirable conditions" in the barrio that housing was substandard and that the residents suffered from malnutrition unemployment, lack of education, communicable diseases, and a high infant mortality rate. The Welfare Council lamented that the Mexicans were responsible for creating ". . .un-American conditions. . ." that led to disease and poverty. This early indictment of Mexicans as being responsible for their own misery would emerge again and again in the popular mind.

What was the truth of the conditions in the barrio? No doubt conditions were better than what many had left in Mexico but at the same time probably shocking to middle class officials. Panunzio preferred to accentuate the positive in his report; others such as the Americanizers in City and County government saw the Mexican section of town as alien and un-American. As to who was to blame for the substandard conditions? It would be forty years until the Chicano movement would indict the real culprits: racist officials, apathetic bureaucrats, exploitative employers, and slum lords.

Another impression of barrio life in the 20s and 30s comes from those who actually lived there. In the 1930s Luis Alvarez lived in Logan Heights as a little boy. His father was a painter and his mother worked in a local fish cannery. He was sent to a parochial school were he remembered being in class with Anglo kids. When he attended the public school he recalled that it "was more or less segregated on a voluntary basis, the people seemed to stay in tune with their race of their own will. In those days they used to kind of look down on the Italians, they were known as "Diegos" and the Mexican people were known as "greasers" and the colored were known as "niggers." Alvarez remembered Logan Heights as a neighborhood where he felt safe. "People were very united, very friendly; you could leave your home without having to bolt it down or lock it down and feel pretty safe that no one would bother you. There was more respect between people especially the younger people towards their seniors."

Logan Heights during the 1920s and 1930s was in transition becoming a community of Mexican immigrants and African Americans. One of the indications that change was the beginnings of mural art. The first Mexican inspired murals in San Diego were done in 1934 by Jose Moya del Pino, a Spanish artist who had been commissioned by Aztec Brewery in Logan Heights to illustrate the interior of the building with scenes from Mexico. Pino was a Spanish immigrant who lived in San Francisco and who had been commissioned to paint murals there. During the 30s he was an instructor at the California School of Fine Arts. In San Diego the Aztec Brewery was owned by Edward Baker and Herbert Jaffee who had moved the brewery equipment from their original plant in Mexicali into the building that was formerly the Savage Tire Company. The images Pino painted inside the brewery in Logan Heights included a large Aztec Calendar, scenes from the daily lives of the Mayans and Aztecs, and the flora and fauna of Mexico. In addition to the murals the brewery had a good deal of wood work with hand painted pre-Columbian motifs and framed art pieces depicting aspects of Aztec culture. This building with its art remained hidden in the barrio until 1989 when the city gave permission for it to be destroyed to make way for construction. Prior to its demolition some samples of the mural and art work were stored in Chuey's Restaurant nearby were people could view them. Today no one knows where the murals are. The Pino murals were the precursors of later murals that would adorn the concrete pillars of the Coronado bridge, the expressions of Chicano art that would be part of Chicano Park.

Repatriation

During the depression conditions for Mexicans in San Diego became worse as unemployment increased and it became harder to find and keep a job. Adding to the oppressive situation was a political campaign to force Mexicans to go back to Mexico. This was a nation-wide repatriation movement that broke up families, disrupted the lives of hundreds of thousands of individuals, and violated the civil rights of many U.S.-born Mexican Americans. In the early 1930s more than a million Mexicanos were forced to leave the United States.

The pressures to "get rid of the Mexicans" mounted because of the economic hard times during the depression. Encouraged by the Immigration and Naturalization Service as well as American Federation of Labor, local municipalities were encouraged to deport undocumented Mexican residents and to mount campaigns of terror to frighten others into returning to their homeland. In early 1930s numerous round ups or raids were conducted within Mexican colonias throughout the United States. Families were separated, children traumatized and the civil rights of Mexican Americans who were citizens were violated. The Mexican consul generals in most of the major cities where the raids took place, complained about the beatings and terror but were not able to stop the campaign.

In the popular imagination, then as now, it was assumed that the Mexican population was taking welfare services and jobs from U.S. citizens. In reality, Mexican nationals were among the least likely to rely on county welfare, and the vast majority of them were already unemployed. (Local governments passed laws making it illegal to hire non-citizens.) Groups such as the San Diego based National Club of America for Americans, Inc. drafted anti-alien ordinances for local governments. In reality few Mexican immigrants took advantage of welfare or charity services and avoided contacts with officials.

Meanwhile thousands of the older children of the immigrants who were citizens of the United States were forced to make a decision whether to go to live in a country they had never seen, or to stay behind without their family. Women without their husbands and children in orphanages were forced to be repatriated as well as people who were mentally ill. Often employed healthy citizens were coerced into leaving by threats of physical violence and unemployment.

Once they arrived in Mexico the Mexican government tried its best to resettle them on agricultural lands, but the planning and resources for such an effort was inadequate. Most of the repatriados had a hard time adjusting to their new country. They encountered some discrimination against them by native Mexicans and found the government's promises of economic assistance unfulfilled. Most of the new colonies were economic failures.

In San Diego charitable organizations worked with the Mexican consulate to arrange the transportation of immigrants back to Mexico. Many began asking the consulate for financial help to make the move. Consul Enrique Ferreira reported in 1931 that most of those asking for help had been unemployed for months and were desperate for jobs. Ferreira managed to help waive the entry fees for those who wanted to return and help get funds for others. In August 1931 the County Welfare Commission working with other local agencies told Ferreira that a train would be available for indigent Mexicans and soon 35 families departed. In 1932 the Mexican government decided to use the Mexican warship ironically named "Progreso" to transport repatriados from San Diego and Los Angeles to Mexico. The plan was to land in the port of Topolobambo, Sinaloa and from there to distribute the repatriados to various land grants in the surrounding states. Far fewer than the envisioned 800 people took advantage of this "cruise." The consul estimated that only about 250 departed. One passenger, Jimeno Hernandez, a fourteen year old, wrote about his experienced on the ship. He recounted how the Mexican officials at Manzanillo extorted money from the passengers claiming that their baggage exceeded the limit.

Camille Guerin Gonzales, who has done the only study of repatriation from San Diego, found that the typical repatriado was a family of more than three people headed by a man of about 40 years old. Half of the repatriates were children. Very few extended family members traveled back to Mexico. About half of the San Diego repatriados ended up settling in the border states. Colonia Libertad, for example, in Tijuana was settled by repatriates from San Diego. For the next sixty years this colonia adjacent to the international boundary fence would be the jumping off point for generations of immigrants heading north.

Conclusions

During the period 1920-1930 Mexicano immigrants in San Diego and Imperial Counties contributed the sweat of their brow, their blood, and life spirit to building the economic infrastructure of a modern society. The construction of the San Diego and Arizona Railroad, the agricultural ranches and irrigation canals in the Imperial Valley, the trolley car system, new housing developments in eastern San Diego, and the growth of the fish canning industry all were done with Mexicano and Chicano laborers. The challenge of the new immigrants was to first survive economically, given the low wages and hard living conditions. Segregated in Mexican colonias and barrios they relied on their families, compadres, and neighbors to make it from day to day. They experienced racism, discrimination, and hostility from teachers, employers, officials. Sometimes they benefited from the sympathetic efforts of groups like those working with the Neighborhood House. But ultimately they were expected to give up their language and customs to become Americans in order to receive the basic rights entitled to all residents regardless of citizenship status, skin color, or language. Mexicanos not only endured but they also organized to improve their children's lives, during the labor strikes in the Imperial Valley and in the Lemon Grove struggle. These actions were the beginnings of Chicano activism in San Diego and Imperial Valley. Later generations would draw from these traditions in community and labor organizing. The depression of the 1930s increased the hardships they had to endure and resulted in a campaign to repatriate Mexican immigrants and their children back to Mexico. The Mexicano community declined in these years but those that remained or returned during World War II continued to struggle for a justice and equality. Unfortunately it would take the cataclysm of the World War to truly begin to change these conditions.

7

San Diego's Ku Klux Klan, 1920 - 1980

Carlos M. Larralde
& Richard Griswold del Castillo

During the 1920's, San Diego, along with many other
Southwestern cities and towns, witnessed a new emergence of
the Ku Klux Klan, a rebirth of the older secret organization that,
in the nineteenth century, had targeted newly freed slaves in the
South. The new Klan of the 1920s was a racist as well as an anti-
immigrant organization targeting new immigrants and Jews as well
as African Americans. In San Diego, the Ku Klux Klan particularly
targeted Mexican immigrants. Thousands of Mexican newcomers
were crossing into California every year lured by the demand for
laborers in the fields and in the newly developed suburbs. There
the Mexicans encountered other immigrants, white Midwestern
Protestants, who were eager to find fortune in the west. For many of
these white immigrants the Klan, as well as fundamentalist religious
organizations, offered a solution for the anxieties they felt as they
encountered a new environment and new peoples.[1]

While there have been several monographs on the Klan in the
1920s, Klan activities in Southern California have been ignored by
most scholars. The Klan continues to exist under a new name, the
White Aryan Resistance, and some of its main forerunners are from
San Diego. There is an unbroken narrative of this hateful association
in San Diego and its legacy has never been told.[2]

This is one of the first attempts to trace the activities of the
Klan in San Diego using newly available records. Most of the San
Diego Ku Klux Klan materials were donated to the San Diego
History Center by local businessman Wayne Kenaston, Sr. in the
1980s. Also, the San Diego History Center's oral history project

interviewed Wayne Kenaston, Jr. gathering further documentation on the Klan and his father's role in it.[3]

Needless to say, it is difficult to get reliable primary documentation about the Ku Klux Klan since they have attempted to keep their membership and many of their organizational activities secret. Their public actions have surfaced periodically in the press. But during the 1920s, Klan crimes were rarely recorded. Newspapers refused to investigate cases of Klan hatred because editors feared that negative publicity might create a bad image for San Diego and hurt its commercial growth.[4]

The resurgence of Klan activity in San Diego in the 1920s was led by descendants of old American stock.[5] They presented themselves as defenders of Christian morality and law enforcement, and they were also chosen to be members of grand juries where they were able to influence district attorneys.[6] About 1922, the active branch of the K.K.K. in San Diego was the Exalted Cyclops of San Diego No. 64. It flourished throughout the county.[7] The Klan center was a large hall west of 30th Street near Idaho Street and University Boulevard in North Park. The San Diego chapter flourished even while the national Klan headquarters was overwhelmed with problems of graft, mismanagement, and personal clashes.[8] The Los Angeles chapter also seemed to prosper as colorful pamphlets poured from their office and, used-automobile-parts dealer John Porter thrived as Klan leader and became mayor of Los Angeles in 1928.[9]

The San Diego Klan members paid $10 to join and usually met on the second Wednesday of every month. Faithful participants included Fred Crandall, a prosperous paint store owner, E. D. Goodwin, a mechanic who worked in Gilmore's Bicycle and Toy Store, W. J. Simpson and his wife Myrtle, Earl S. Barr, and John S. Burbank. Actually, these cardholders were hard working, thrifty, middle class church-going individuals. Nevertheless, the Klan used the Bible and the old concept of manifest destiny to see themselves as superior and Mexicans as inferior and in need of control. "Keep in mind that some harmless members envisioned a gregarious Klan, ignoring its grim horrors to those it detested," stated the attorney Carey McWilliams.[10]

San Diego Klan participants formed their own traditions. V. Wayne Kenaston, Jr., whose parents were members of the Klan, reminisced, "If my memory serves me correctly, my mother made me a miniature Klan outfit with a little hood...."[11] A number of women joined the Klan and were strongly encouraged to participate so as "to propagate in or through such meetings, either directly or indirectly..." the Klan's message.[12] The San Diego Klan affiliates saw themselves as humanitarians, similar to other Klans who established schools and hospitals.[13] The testimony of Kenaston, Jr., revealed white Catholic voters, mostly from the Blessed Sacrament Church on 56th and El Cajon, supported the Klan's political committee. As Kenaston, Jr., stated, "I'm wondering if, in San Diego, there were actually Catholic Klan members of the Klan, or whether they were referring to the fact that Klan members might have voted for the people that the Catholics might have liked."[14] The Klan did influence some religious groups. In parts of Southern California, "Many [Catholics and Protestants] who were suspected of being Klansmen at first denied their affiliation, but when confronted with their official Klan and number and date of entry, they could do nothing but admit membership."[15] Some of them were members of Catholic War Veterans and the Knights of Columbus.

"Most Irish-American clergy had no sympathy for Mexicans who were seen as an endangerment to traditional American values," noted economist Ernesto Galarza. "They often ignored the Klan's abuses toward Hispanics."[16] McWilliams noted, "For the most part, the Church later ignored Klan atrocities and focused on Communism. One was Father Thomas J. McCarthy, editor and scholar, who later provided funds to the Klan to continue its anti-Communist crusade." Also, the Klan received comfort from anti-Semitic, right-wing broadcasters: Gerald L. K. Smith, Father Charles Edward Coughlin, and William Pelley, a self-professed fascist.[17]

Anti-Mexican Activities in the 1920s and 1930s

Kenaston, Jr., somewhat disingenuously, avowed that the Klan never intimidated any ethnic groups even as he admitted that their main zeal was in "chasing the wetbacks across the border." [18] Most

Klan activities were clandestine, aimed at keeping recently arrived Mexicans from participating in community politics. As McWilliams noted, "They opposed white-collar jobs for Mexicans, who at one time were merchants or professionals in war-torn Mexico, and demanded a policy to force them into manual labor." [19] Luisa Moreno, a labor union leader, stated, "The California Fruit Growers Exchange, the tuna cannery industry that had its base in San Diego, and other local businesses enthusiastically supported this concept."[20]

There are some testimonies as to Klan activities by their intended victims. Kenaston, Jr. remembered that years ago east of 55th Street and El Cajon Boulevard, past College Avenue, there were lemon orchards.[21] Among these citrus orchards in suburban San Diego and in the rural areas, Mexicans were occasionally discovered dead, sometimes disfigured by torture. An expatriated soldier of the Mexican Revolution, Mercedes Acasan Garcia, reminisced that in San Diego, "any Mexican worker who challenged authority or appeared suspicious of one thing or another would forfeit his life."[22] Garcia, who was a young maid for Mrs. Alice Victoria Hamilton, recounted, "At first the Mexican field hands were curious at the sight of these strange men on horses shrouded with snowy gowns and huge, spotless cardboard hoods over their faces. Others had white cone shaped hoods to add height and also disguise their faces. They had painted red crosses on them." The workmen believed that they were pious Catholics who were penitents and wanted alms.[23]

In response to the danger posed by the Klan, Mexican workers sought the support of their local mutual benefit societies. Garcia was active in one of them. In tears, she described how she saw Mexican laborers being dragged and lynched; others whipped or burned. "Since they were ragged Wetbacks, nobody cared who they were and nothing was done about it."[24] When traveling to visit her relatives, Garcia took back roads to cross the U.S./Mexico border to avoid contact with the Klan who were trying to intimidate immigrants. Farm owners who required immigrant workers often opposed Klan harassment tactics. She recounted how, "These laborers in rural areas had their homes or barns burned. Several growers patrolled their fields to calm their sad and worried field hands; their crops were worthless without Mexicans."[25]

Carey McWilliams, a Los Angeles Times writer, explained that Mexicans who were transported from the farm regions "probably saw conditions better than those in their homeland until they were exposed to the erratic temper and violence of the Klan."[26] Several groups like the California Cavaliers, the American Legion, and the Associated Farmers of California favored stopping the influx of Mexican foreigners into the United States. McWilliams characterized the Associated Farmers as "Farm Fascists."[27] The Klan's publication, The Imperial Night-Hawk, noted that "foreigners are taking the places of our native sons.... These foreigners want a place in the sunlight, and our money, but when we trade with them, we build them up at our own expense...."[28] The Klan Imperial Wizard H. W. Evans proclaimed, "To the South of us thousands of Mexicans, many of them Communist, are waiting a chance to cross the Rio Grande and glut the labor marts of the Southwest." This Klan ideology influenced government officials and indeed some members of the local county and city bureaucracy were members of the Klan.[29]

During the depression of the 1930s, numerous Mexicans were deported from Southern California. Known as the repatriados, or repatriated ones, they were sent to Mexico. Some families were shipped from Northern California in trucks or cattle trains to San Diego and then dumped at the Mexican border. In several cases, mothers or fathers were separated from children. Some families never found their relatives.[30]

Under the leadership of Wayne Kenaston, Sr., from 1930 to 1931, the San Diego K. K. K. expanded. As a reward for his effective leadership and service, he received the title of "Klan Giant" from T. S. Moodie, the Grand Dragon of all Klans.[31] An "Organizing Committee" met regularly in the 1930s to inquire about how to further expand the Klan. As their questionnaire and application stated, "The purpose of this investigation, being conducted among the membership, is to increase our attendance, strengthen our organization, and to further the spirit of the Klancraft...."[32]

Political and religious pamphlets and books such as Coin Harvey's Tale of the Nations, published in 1894, which glorified the White Race as the custodian of civilization, were distributed as part of the educational program of the California Knights of the Ku Klux Klan. Another book was Madison Grant's The Passing of the White Race, warning that unrestricted immigration would create a degenerate nation of different races like Mexico.[33]

During this era, Frank G. Ellis of the U.S. Immigration Service in Calexico, recalled how he obtained information about immigrant smugglers. "We used to pay the informants out of our own pockets — I spent a lot of money for the government along that line."[34] He also related how some of the Mexican smugglers got Chinese immigrants across the border. Ellis was a Catholic family man who belonged to the Elks Lodge in Calexico. He soon dropped out of it because, "it became too much control by the Ku Klux Klan."[35]

Even while K.K.K. activities threatened the safety of immigrants, Mexican families fought against discrimination. In 1931 in Lemon Grove, parents of 75 Mexican American students refused to send their children to an all-Mexican school built for them by the school board. The parents sued the school board and won in a landmark case. The Lemon Grove case was the first legal victory by Mexicans in challenging their separation in the school system.[36]

The San Diego Klan, meanwhile, announced it had a new leader, Richard A. Floyd. As one account reported, "He is fearless, honest, devoted to the cause of Protestantism, and I consider him an outstanding man among men of high repute and capable." He and other new officers were installed in 1933.[37] Floyd suffocated the Klan with his fierce iron will and pitted Klan individuals against each other in order to control the organization. Active in the local Republican Party, Floyd also dominated the American-Mexican Republican League, organized on July 2, 1934. Ironically, the league was designed to promote business relations with Mexico. Distinguished Mexican merchants joined it and their dues and other funds secretly went to the Klan.[38]

In 1937 Mexican President Plutarco Calles was exiled to the United States. According to historian Enrique Krauze, Calles stayed in San Diego for five years. Despite his cold and firm personality, Calles made friends with the influential Mexican businessmen of the American-Mexican Republican League. They all shared the same traits: anti-Communism, anti-Semitism, and anti-liberalism, sentiments the Klan also held. Carlos Montalvo, a local community activist, stated, "While reading Hitler's Mein Kampf with interest and respect, Calles disregarded the Klan's crimes against Mexicans as a frivolous matter. His biggest concern was getting back to Mexico."[39]

Ironically, numerous Mexican Cristeros were also exiled in Southern California. They were named after their battle cry of "Christ is King," and had bitterly fought Calles's government. In 1934 the Cristeros carried huge crucifixes and other religious relics during several parades in Los Angeles and San Diego against the atheistic Russian and Mexican governments. At first most of them supported the Klan. They believed that the Klan's painted crosses on their white gowns and their burning crosses symbolized Christ, Mary, and the saints. As Montalvo explained, "A few of the Cristeros attempted to join the Klan, only to be rejected. To their sorrow, they later discovered what the Klan was all about."[40]

Bitter conflicts meanwhile erupted between Floyd and the Klan. In August 1939, Kenaston received an urgent letter from organizer S. E. Mendenhall, stating that "There will be a special Klan meeting at Hawthorne Hall...on August 25.... We wish to talk about reorganizing here, and wish your attendance."[41] To Mendenhall's regret, Floyd prevailed as the Klan leader. He saw himself as the father of a family of minors that needed to be disciplined. With Floyd's parsimonious budget and strict rules of discipline, the Klan survived by gaining respectability.

During the 1930s, the Klan began to merge with like-minded organizations such as the Silver Shirts League, the MinuteMen, and the White Guards. Historian Stephen Schwartz affirmed, "Many adherents of the Silver Shirts were former members of the Ku Klux Klan." The San Diego Silver Shirts League, "a deadly fascist inspired group," was planned with the purpose of attacking blacks, Hispanics, and Jews. Inspired by the Nazi SS mystique, the Silver Shirts saw themselves as an American counterpart, enforcing Aryan racial superiority through intimidation and violence.[42]

The Silver Shirts had other branches scattered throughout the United States. The San Diego chapter was well-known but ignored by most city officials who did not consider their anti-Semitic and anti-Mexican propaganda a problem. The San Diego Silver Shirts soon split into two groups, one under the leadership of Donald J. Niswender and the other led by C. T. Lee.[43] Niswender's groups held clandestine meetings where they performed mysterious rituals before a flag with the swastika. One confirmed tactic of the Silver Shirts was to seize governmental weaponry and learn military tactics that would enable them to "cleanse society of undesirable characters."[44] For the Silver Shirts the Mexicans were considered particularly undesirable, for in addition to being non-Aryan, they were from a country that, in their opinion, had a socialist president, Lazaro Cardenas.[45]

By the late 1930s the U.S. government was concerned about the activities of the Silver Shirts and Corporal E. T. Gray of Marine Corps intelligence was assigned to infiltrate and report back on the activities of the San Diego Silver Shirts. Soon Niswender discovered that Gray was an undercover agent and five Silver Shirts attacked Gray in downtown San Diego between C and Broadway Streets. They slit his face, fractured his skull, and sent him to Balboa Naval Hospital for two weeks. Later, two Silver Shirts shot at him.[46] Cherishing the spirit of the Klan, the Silver Shirts rehearsed war games and practiced shooting their rifles, reportedly using Mexican wetbacks as targets. During their rallies, they dressed in blue corduroy knickers and a silver gray shirt with a crimson "L" (for liberator). They also wore blue ties and jackboots.[47]

Despite Hispanics' attempts to avoid the Klan and the Silver Shirts, labor organizer Luisa Moreno vividly recollected how the groups helped the tuna industry, a major employer of Latinos, combat unionization by breaking up unions, and physical intimidation and violence. The Klan fight against unionism enabled the tuna packing companies to pay low wages. Companies like California Packing Corporation, Marine Products Company, Van Camp

Seafood Company, and several others, financed the Klan to battle against union leaders like Moreno. Also, the Associated Farmers of California, the American Legion, and other extremists supported the Klan. In the end, Moreno was convinced that some of the tuna executives and the growers had employees that were members of the Klan and the Silver Shirts. Although she openly fought them, Moreno privately feared the Klan and other right wing radical groups. As she later recalled, "With the Klan, you never knew what they planned to do next or who they actually were. With the Silver Shirts, their ugly mouths were their worst enemies."[48]

Bert Corona, another labor organizer in Southern California, stated, "The Klan and other radical groups were ruthless and intimidated many of our people with fear. They broke up our union strikes and clubbed several of our members."[49] Mercedes Garcia admitted, "Most Mexicans were staggered by the obstacles to stay in Southern California. The greatest adversary to stay alive was not the Klan but one's determination to go on."[50]

A Zealous Renewal

The 1940s saw a growth of Klans in California, with Los Angeles serving as its western headquarters. In 1940, it offered to aid the House Un-American Activities Committee and passed out anti-Communist brochures in downtown Los Angeles.[51] The Klan burned a cross protesting Harry Bridges speaking in Huntington Park and attempted to sabotage a speaking engagement he had later in San Diego.[52]

During World War II, San Diego grew into a major port for the U.S. Navy and a center for the aircraft industry. Old prejudices endured, however. Several religious leaders throughout Southern California, like Methodist Bob Shuler, propounded a fundamentalist message from the pulpit defending the Klan against its Jewish opponents. He castigated the Mexicans who he thought were guilty of lewdness. To prove his point he labored over the rumor that Reverend Sister Aimee Semple McPherson had been kidnapped at Agua Prieta, Mexico. Later it was revealed that she had eloped with a lover.[53]

Klan associates like V. W. Kenaston, Sr., stayed active against Hispanic labor and civil rights activities. While a member of the Klan, he was on the Building Trades and Labor Council and also an affiliate of the Federal Mediation Service.[54] Kenaston was well acquainted with the city's mayor and councilmen, and with local bankers and merchants. With the friendship of Senator Jack Tenney, head of the California Un-American Activities Committee, it put Kenaston in an ideal position to incapacitate Mexican American civil and labor rights.

Meanwhile in war-time Los Angeles, former K.K.K. leaders ran for Congress and State Attorney General Robert W. Kenny was concerned how to prevent a resurgence of Klan activity.[55] Fiery crosses were discovered in the front yards of some African Americans in Los Angeles and Kenny persuaded Superior Court Judge Alfred A. Paonessa to move to limit the Klan's ability to organize since it "taught social hatred through violence." Finally, on May 21, 1946, the Klan's charter was revoked and it was denied the right to obtain a permit to operate in California. As Kenny affirmed, "The real victim, [of the Klan] the final victim is American democracy."[56]

Following World War II, the Mexican American community was politically divided. A super-nationalist group arose, composed of members of the Alianza Hispanico-Americana, and was led by John B. Calderon. Another conservative group was the "Loyal Democrats," which included figurehead Hispanics such as Oceanside resident, Hollywood actor Leo Carrillo. Together they ignored Klan activities and sided with Senator Jack Tenney, who conducted a witch hunt for Communists and militant labor organizers like Luisa Moreno.[57] The Hispanic nationalist group, "Loyal Democrats," simplified their views in a leaflet: "Leave us Mexicans out of your Communistic sneaky underhanded [activities].... Any Mexican with a religious background would grind you...into meat."[58] Petrified by the threat of deportation, most Mexicans refused to testify against the Klan or discredit Tenney's California Un-American Activities investigations. Moreno was soon brought before the committee and subsequently deported to Mexico. Tenney meanwhile concluded that most Mexicans in the civil rights organization, Mobilization for Democracy, "deliberately manufactured Ku Klux Klan acts of terrorism for political purposes. The Communist plan to utilize this front for agitational purposes in California..." was aided by the labor movement.[59]

To avoid deportation, discrimination, or the Klan, several Mexican aliens attempted to "whiten their skin" with the chemical hydroquinone. The San Diego lawyer, Alfredo Montoya, hated by the Klan and Loyal Democrats for helping Mexicans, tried to stop these dangerous skin treatments. According to Bert Corona, "He was a very self-sacrificing individual, with an almost priest-like dedication to his work." Loyal Democrats and the Klan opposed Montoya as he assembled evidence of abuses against Mexicans by the Klan and the Immigration and Naturalization Service. Another effort to combat hate crimes was the work of two trade union leaders in San Diego, Phil and Albert Usquiano. Together in the 1950s, they founded the Hermandad Mexicana Nacional (Mexican National Brotherhood), an association dedicated to helping immigrants preserve their civil rights. They chartered chapters throughout San Diego County, and were also affiliated with the Carpenters' Union and the Laborers' Union.[60]

They warned their members about the Klan. Moreno noted that "The Klan operated where there were few witnesses. One of their areas was remote farms. As before, they preyed on innocent, defenseless Mexican field workers. Local law enforcement refused to do much about these foreign Mexicans when they were murdered."[61] Even during the 1950s and 1960s, the F. B. I. refused to devote funds to curtail the Klan violence. Instead, they infiltrated those labor unions which they saw as supporting "extreme left-wing activities associated with violence."[62]

Not much was heard about the Klan until the 1970s. People believed that the Klan in San Diego County was dead. Nevertheless, San Diego's Police Chief Bill Kolender was aware that strong Klan groups had resurrected in San Diego and in Oceanside. A state of California report declared in 1980 that the Klan was stockpiling weapons, "allegedly preparing for the race war its members believed to be inevitable." The United Klans of America put up posters that declared, "Don't be half a man: Join the Klan."[63] Several Klan demonstrations took place in San Diego in this period.

By the late 1970s, a San Diego television repairman, Tom Metzger, emerged as California's Klan leader. In the early eighties Metzger and forty Klansmen provoked a riot in Oceanside when they marched into John Lander's Park to rid it of Mexicans and other aliens. In the ensuing melee, several people were injured as the Klan encountered a rock-throwing mob.[64]

Metzger warned in his publications, "Our nation will sink into the swamp of racial pollution known as the third world." He preached that Mexico was the real threat since its population doubled every twenty years. By the year 2000, when Mexico's population would expand to 125 million it would, in his words, "create a racial attack on the United States."[65]

Chicano leaders like Chole Alatorre, Roberto Martinez, Bert Corona and others were active in the Hermandad Mexicana Nacional during the 1980s to protect minorities from Klan abuses. They were confronted by several ghastly revelations. On December 10, 1983, the Klan boasted of beheading undocumented aliens. Alatorre declared, "Several Mexican men in remote regions disappeared. Their wives saw them for the last time when they were driven out to work in the fields. Nobody saw them again. I believe that the sadistic Klan had fun with them and dumped their bodies in a crevice."[66] A former police officer, Douglas K. Seymour, testified at a six-hour hearing of the state Fair Employment Housing Commission in Oceanside on December 9, 1989, that the San Diego County Klan remained "one of the strongest chapters in the country." As a reserve officer he attended Klan rallies, demonstrations, and cross burnings throughout Southern California. He rose in the organization to become one of the Klan's leaders, Tom Metzger's right-hand-man, a member of the inner circle of the white-supremacist organization. Seymour admitted that members frequently boasted of beheading and burying undocumented Mexicans. Roberto Martinez, a leader of the San Diego Chicano Foundation's Law and Justice Committee, said most of the complaints he received from Mexican immigrants were police harassment and Klan beatings. "What we have here in

North County is selective law enforcement," Martinez announced.[67]
The police infiltrator, Seymour, kept undercover in the Klan in the late 1980s. As he declared, the Klan attempted to "adopt a more low-key underground type of activity" chiefly to undermine Mexican aliens and Chicanos. Eventually Seymour alleged that the San Diego Police refused to acknowledge his activities, declaring that his supervisor "ordered him to lie to the F.B.I., the county grand jury, Escondido police officers, and Palomar Hospital, who treated him for a gunshot wound."[68] Finally, Seymour was awarded $531,000 in a lawsuit against the police, claiming that the top command of the San Diego Police Department "had disavowed its undercover officer inside the Klan and destroyed his intelligence reports to deny allegations that police were illegally spying on a [mysterious] right-wing congressional candidate."[69]

The full story of the Ku Klux Klan in San Diego and Southern California has yet to be told. What emerges from the scanty evidence drawn from the archives is a tenacious legacy of hate toward Mexican immigrants, Jews, and others who were branded as un-American. San Diego's proximity to the U.S.-Mexican border along with its growing population drawn from all over the United States has made for a favorable environment where the Klan could recruit and sustain an organization that has died out in other areas of the country. The persistence of the K.K.K. and its offshoots thriving in "AMERICA'S FINEST CITY" is one of the disturbing realities of twenty-first century California.

Notes

1. The classic work on the rebirth of the KKK is Charles Alexander, The Ku Klux Klan in the Southwest (Lexington: University of Kentucky Press, 1965).

2. See Richard Melching, "The Activities of the Ku Klux Klan in Anaheim, California, 1923-1925," Southern California Quarterly, LVI, 2, Summer, 1974.

3. V. Wayne Kenaston, Jr., Interviewed by Nancy B.Cuthbert, 8 February 1978, San Diego History Center Oral History Program. Hereafter, Kenaston, Jr.

4. House Executive Document, Hearings before a Subcommittee of the Special Committee on UnAmerican Activities at Los Angeles, California. 73rd Congress, 2nd Session, 1934, 4-6, hereafter, Congressional Hearings. See also, Cater Tarrance, "San Diego Silver Shirts," 12, seminar paper, 1976, San Diego State University, item S.S., SDHC.

5. Arnold S. Rice, The Ku Klux Klan in American Politics (Washington, D.C.: Public Affairs, 1962), 13. See also "Well Organized New California Klans," The Imperial Night-Hawk, June 13, 1923, 5. This illustrated magazine was one of the official KKK publications printed in Atlanta, Georgia.

6. The Klan and other radical groups flourished in Southern California. See the Los Angeles Times, April 23, 30, 1922; Santa Ana Register, May 1, 1922; Anaheim Bulletin, December 31, 1924, June 4 and November 16, 1925; La Habra Star, July 2, 1924; Balboa Times, January 27, 1927.

7. The K.K.K. in San Diego was formed about 1922. See Constitution and Rituals, 1927-1928, Mss 203, V. Wayne Kenaston Papers, San Diego Historical Society, Research Archives, Box 1, File 1, Item 3, hereafter KKK, SDHC. For California Klan activities see, Ed Cray, Chief Justice: A Biography of Earl Warren (New York: Simon and Schuster, 1997), 52-54, 56-57.

8. "Imperial Kloncilium Brands Charges Against Klan Officers 'Absurd False and Malicious,'" Imperial Night-Hawk, June 27, 1923, 2-3. See also Kenaston, Jr. 3.

9. Kevin Starr, Material Dreams: Southern California through the 1920's (New York: Oxford University Press, 1990), 138-139. Starr has written several books on California history. He said, "I have a deep respect for Carey McWilliams and Robert Kenny for their struggle against the Klan in Southern California. As attorneys they curtailed Klan abuses against Mexicans." Interview with Kevin Starr, October 12, 1994. See, Carey McWilliams, It Can Happen Here: Active Anti-Semitism in Los Angeles (Los Angeles: Privately Published, 1934), 11. Interview with Carey McWilliams, June 12, 1979.

10. "Letters, Miscellaneous, 1931-1939," KKK, SDHC. See also item 19, a portion of a Klan member list, ibid. On several of these members' occupations, see the San Diego City and County Directory from 1929 to 1935. Interview with Carey McWilliams, September 12, 1978.

11. Kenaston, Jr., 3.

12. "Knights of the Ku Klux Klan Recognize Combine of Women's Orders as Auxiliary," The Imperial Night-Hawk, June 13, 1923, 5.

13. For example see "Will Break Ground for $125,000 Hospital to be Erected by Klansmen at El Dorado, Ark.," The Imperial Night-Hawk, June 27, 1923, 8.

14. Kenaston, Jr., 4.

15. Rev. Donald Montrose, ed., The Story of a Parish" Its Priests and Its People, 1860-1960: The Centennial of St. Boniface Church, Anaheim, California, Anaheim, CA: St. Boniface Parish, 1961), 153.

16. Interview with Ernesto Galarza, January 12, 1978. With few Latinos as priests or nuns, Latino Catholics remain largely segregated from other Catholics in the nation's parishes. In this country, there is just one Latino priest per 10,000 Latino parishioners. See Margaret Ramirez, "Study Finds Segregation of Latinos in Catholic Church," Los Angeles Times, March 1, 2000. See also David Rieff, Los Angeles: Capital of the Third World (New York: A Touchstone Book, 1991) 164-165.

17. McWilliams Interview, September 12, 1978. Interview with San Diego civil rights leader Luisa Moreno, April 17, 1971, and Carlos Montalvo, January 7, 1992. For more on Thomas J. McCarthy see Carolina Walker, "Speakers Assail Reds," Los Angeles Evening Herald & Express, March 10, 1949. On anti-Semitism, see Arthur Herman, Joseph McCarthy: Reexamining the Life and Legend of America's Hated Senator (New York: the Free Press, 2000), 81, 82.

18. Kenaston, Jr., 5.

19. McWilliams Interview, June 12, 1979. The Klan used the same policy on Mexicans in El Paso. See Mario T. Garcia, Desert Immigrants: The Mexicans of El Paso, 1880-1920 (New Haven: Yale University Press, 1981), 250. See also Shawn Loy, War, Revolution, and the Ku Klux Klan: A Study of Intolerance in a Border City. (El Paso: University of Texas, 1985). Loy wrote about how the Klan dominated El Paso during the 1920s.

20. Interview with Luisa Moreno, April 17, 1971. Some of the same conditions could be applied to regions like El Paso. See, Desert Immigrants, 84.

21. Kenaston, Jr., 8.

22. Interview with Mercedes Acasan Garcia, June 12, 1979. For her military activities see Josefina Rendon, Justo Homenaje al Valor Herocio: Album 1911 (Tijuana: Artes Graficas, 1976), 28. She was fifteen years old when she aided the army with water and bullets.

23. Garcia Interview, June 14, 1979. In F 1, Garcia Papers, there is a thank you note from Mrs. Hamilton "for Coming." Apparently, Garcia did some extra chores for her.

24. Ibid.

25. Ibid. Another Klan victim was Heliodoro Barragan. See his testimony in Marilyn P. Davis, Mexican Voices American Dreams: An Oral History of Mexican Immigration to the United States (New York: Henry Holt and Company, 1990), 11-15. For a comparison see the interview with Wally Sanchez, July 15, 1994, interviewed and edited by Robert Gonzalez, transcribed by Kathleen Case, conducted for the Redlands Oral History Project, AK Smiley Public Library Heritage Room, Redlands, CA.

26. McWilliams Interview, June 12, 1979.

27. For more on this era see Kevin Starr, Endangered Dreams: the Great Depression in California (New York: Oxford University Press, 1996), 161-162.

28. "Every Influence Needed on Side of Restrictive Immigration Bill," The Imperial Night-Hawk, March 5, 1924, 5.

29. H. W. Evans, Attitude of the Knights of the Ku Klux Klan toward Immigration (Atlanta: Imperial Palace, c1926), Imperial Instructions, p. 7. See also Evans's The Practice of Klanishness (Atlanta: Imperial Palace, 1924), Imperial Instruction, Document No. 1 Series AD, 5.

30. George Kiser and David Silverman, "The Mexican Repatriation During the Great Depression," Journal of Mexican American History, 3, 1973, 153; Abraham Hoffman, "Stimulus to Repatriation: The 1931 Federal Deportation Drive and the Los Angeles Mexican Community," in Norris Hundley, ed., The Chicano (Santa Barbara, CA: Clio, 1975), 110.

31. Letter form T. S. Moodie, Grand Dragon, to V. W. Kenaston, April 14, 1932, Los Angeles. K K K SDHC, file 3, item 4.

32. Questionnaire from the KKK Committee, June 7, 1933, KKK, SDHC, Item 12A. See also eight copies of a card advertising KKK, no date, ibid., item 13AH.

33. Paul Johnson, A History of the American People (New York: Harper Collins Publishers, 1997), 667. See also, "Body of Minutes," February 2, 1933, Exalted Cyclops, San Diego, No. 64, KKK, SDHC Item 10.

34. Edgar F. Hastings interview with Frank Garfield Ellis, March 28, 1961, 17, San Diego History Center Oral History program. Hereafter, Ellis.

35. Ellis, 17.

36. Annie Reynolds, The Education of Spanish Children in Five Southwestern States (U.S. Department of Interior Bulletin No. 11 (Washington, D. C., 1933) in Carlos E. Cortes, ed., Education and the Mexican-American (New York: Anno Press, 1974), 13.

37. Exalted Cyclops to the Knights of the Ku Klux Klan, San Diego, January 3, 1933, KKK SDHC, Item 7. See notice of Election of Officers, no date, Item 18A-C, ibid.

38. "Spanish G. O. P. Group Formed," San Diego Sun, July 2, 1934; McWilliams Interview, August 12, 1979.

39. Interview with Carlos Montalvo, January 7, 1992. See Enrique Krauze,

Mexican Biography of Power: A History of Modern Mexico, 1810-1996 (New York: Harper Collins Publishers, 1997), 412, 436. See also Jean Perier to A. Poincare, April 29, 1924, Box 25, File 1, Correspondencia Diplomatica Francesa, Paris.

40. Montalvo Interview. See also, Jack Williams, "Carlos Montalvo, 82; active in early days of Chicano Movement," San Diego Union-Tribune, February 15, 2000. See also Rieff, Los Angeles, 163-164.

41. Letter from S. E. Mendenhall to Klansman Kenaston, August [no date], 1939, Item 8A, KKK, SDHC.

42. Los Angeles Examiner, August 6, 1934. See Henry Schwartz, "The Silver Shirts: Anti-Semitism in San Diego, 1930-1940," Western States Jewish History, XXIV, 1, October 1992, 52-60. See Stephen Schwartz From West to East: California and the Making of the American Mind (New York: The Free Press, 1998), 296. For more on these radical groups, see A. B. Magil and Henry Stevens, The Perils of Fascism (New York: USA International Publishers Co., 1938), 106-111.

43. San Diego Sun, August 6, 1934.

44. San Diego Union, August 8, 1934. A unique source of San Diego's Silver Shirts was C. Leon de Aryan, the eccentric editor of San Diego's The Broom. See the report of how the Silver Shirts were fighting for "Christian control," The Broom, February 12, 1934. See also another issue with the headline, "Silver Shirts-Second Edition-Why?" The Broom, August 27, 1934.

45. Life, September 20, 1937, 37; Time, August 29, 1938, 19; McWilliams Interview, August 12, 1979.

46. Interview with Luisa Moreno, April 17, 1971; Montalvo Interview, January 7, 1992. See Congressional Hearings. Richard M. Sola, "The Case of Silver Shirts: Criminal Proceedings Against two San Diego Fascist Leaders, 1934-35," legal history category, miscellaneous manuscript, SDHC.

47. San Diego Evening Tribune, October 25, 1934.

48. Moreno Interview, April 17, 1971. See also the Waterfront Worker (San Francisco), January 2, 3, 1933; March 5, 1934. See also Mss. 009 Box 16 of 27, Harry Bridges Legal Collection, Southern California Library for Social Studies and Research, Los Angeles (SCL). In this collection, see Box 19, File 1, letter, June 22, 1939, Los Angeles lawyer Lee Coa to San Francisco attorney Aubrey Grossman concerning the Klan and the Silver Shirts.

49. Ibid. Interview with Bert Corona, April 25, 1980. The Klan remained active in San Pedro. See the Waterfront Worker, March 5, 1934, and Waterfront Worker, January 2, 1933. On page 3, it stated, "Ben Gusick and his gang were fired for this accident, and a Ku Klux Klan organizer, scab-herder, and a tool who helped to break the 1923 strike was put in his place...." For copies of this Southern California periodical see Mss. 009, Box 16 of 27, the Harry Bridges Legal Collection.

50. Garcia Interview, June 14, 1979. Even McWilliams wrote, "In short, the history of labor in California is really not a history of the struggle of unions to achieve recognition but of a struggle for power between organized labor and organized capital...[which] accounts for the periodic convulsions in the state's social history." See Carey McWilliams, The Great Exception (New York, A. A. Wyn, Publisher, 1949), 130.

51. Los Angeles Times, March 31, 1940.

52. Los Angeles Times, May 5, 1940. McWilliams Interview, January 12, 1979.

53. McWilliams Interview, January 12, 1979. Daniel Mark Epstein, Semple Aimee: The Life pf Aimee Semple McPherson (New York, Harcourt Brace Jovanovich, Publishers, 1993), 264, 296, 314. For more on Shuler see Starr, Material Dreams, 136-137. Klan supporters used proverbs from the Bible, such as Deuteronomy, 7:3, 23:2 and Joshua 23: 12, 13. One Klan defender, the Rev. Bertrund L. Comparet, abused Biblical Proverbs in his pamphlet, "God Commands Racial Segregation" (Los Angeles: privately published, 1980).

54. Kenaston, Jr., 2.

55. See the commentary columns in Los Angeles Times, April 9, 10, 12, 1946.

56. New York Times, May 23, 1946, p. 23. See "Attorney General Robert W. Kenny's Address Olympic Auditorium, June 14, 1946," Box 22, Miscellaneous Files, I-M, file Ku Klux Klan, B 22, F 6, in Civil Rights Congress, Los Angeles Collection (SCL). Un-American Activities in California, 1947 (Sacramento, CA: Government Printing Office, 1947) 57-58.

57. Robert E. Burke, Olson's New Deal for California (Berkeley: University of California Press, 1953), 22. Interview with Emil Freed, March 12, 1980. Carrillo remained a friend to Tenney and helped him with conservative causes. For more on Tenney's blacklists, see, "Give Filmsters Chance to Erase Their Names Off Tenney Reports," Variety (Los Angles), July 23, 1954. In the end, he destroyed the careers of many people in the film industry, both Anglos and Mexicans. As McWilliams said in a UCLA conference in October 1976, "If Tenney did not like you, your career was in danger."

58. See "FREE CLEAN AMERICAN MEXICANS 100%" to Civil Rights Congress, August 8, 1950, Miscellaneous Files, I-M, Ku Klux Klan Clippings, B 22, F 7, Civil Rights Congress, Los Angeles Collection, (SCL) Most Free Clean American Mexicans were composed of G. I. Form members, LULAC associates, and several religious groups like the Knights of Columbus. As McWilliams stated in an interview January 12, 1979, "Jack Tenney played on their sympathies to promote his career and destroyed those who questioned him"

59. For more on Moreno see Steve Murdock. " A Question of Deportment," in Our Times (Los Angeles and London), 1949, p. 3; Evening

Tribune (San Diego), 27 June 1950, Sec. B, 1. See also, Carlos Larralde and Richard Griswold del Castillo, "Luisa Moreno: A Hispanic Civil Rights Leader in San Diego," Journal of San Diego History, vol. 41, no. 4, Fall 1995, 285-311, and "Luisa Moreno and the Beginnings of the Civil Rights Movement in San Diego," Ibid. Vol. 43, no. 3, Summer 1997, 159-175. See California Senate, Un-American Activities in California, 1947, (Sacramento, CA: Government Printing Office), 369.

60. See "From Black to White: Chemicals Lighten Dark Negro Skins," Los Angeles Times, August 16, 1949, P-11. See also Ann M. Simmons, "Quest for Light Skin is Darkening Lives in Africa," Los Angeles Times, August 15, 2000. Different methods are still being used in an effort to bleach dark skin. Mario T. Garcia, Memories of Chicano History: The Life and Narrative of Bert Corona (Berkeley: University of California Press, 1994), pp. 290-291. Interview with Bert Corona, April 25, 1980. See "Meeting Proceedings," April 30, 1950, Box 8, F 15, Conference and Convention, Park Manor, 1950, Civil Tights Congress, Los Angeles Collection (SCL). It reveals how effective Luisa Moreno, Frank Lopez, Henry Schmidt, Carlos Montalvo, and others were fighting deportations, loyalty oaths, intimidation, police brutality, and other issues. Their attempts were later sabotaged by the McCarthy era.

61. Moreno Interview, April 17, 1971. See the California Eagle (Los Angeles), November 7, 1946; see the Los Angeles Sentinel, September 19, 1946, and October 31, 1946.

62. The F. B. I. continued to do the same thing during the 1970s. See Bryce Nelson, "Violence by Informants Indicated in FBI Memo," Los Angeles Times, April 8, 1971.

63. Joe Gandelman, "Racism: Infiltrator requests federal investigation of Klan," San Diego Union, December 10, 1983; Bill Callahan, "Kolender doesn't recall approving KKK Spying," San Diego Tribune, April 27, 1988. For more details see "Klan Storing Weapons in State for Race War, Deukmejian Says," The Ventura County Starr-Free Press, (Venture, CA), September 30, 1980.

64. Bill Olsen, "Racial Discrimination hearing due in Oceanside," Blade-Tribune (Oceanside), November 3, 1983; Eric Bailey, "O'side Police Prepare for Racial Hearing, " Blade-Tribune, December 11, 1983.

65. Tom Metzger, "Viewpoint from the State Organizer," in Ruben Botello, "Chicanos in Ventura County: A Demographic Analysis of Oppression," (Ventura County Community Action Organization, 1983), 12.

66. Interview with Chole Alatorre, April 12, 1992.

67. Elizabeth Wong, "Klansmen here boasted of beheading aliens, infiltrator says," San Diego Tribune, December 10, 1983. See also Tom Gorman, "Klan Infiltrator Settles With City, Takes His Story to Television, " Los Angeles Times, March 1, 1989. Seymour had dreams for a best-selling book of his infiltration of the KKK for use as a movie or television miniseries.

68. Bill Callahan, "KKK Spy Seymour Claims Police Boss Ordered Lies," San Diego Tribune, April 13, 1988; Richard Serrano, "Police Kept Infiltrator in Klan Despite Political Race," Los Angeles Times, April 27, 1988.

69. Andrea Estepa, "Klan Infiltrator Is Awarded $531,000 in Suit Against Police," Los Angeles Times, May 10, 1988.

8

Luisa Moreno and the Beginnings of the Mexican American Civil Rights Movement in San Diego

Carlos M. Larralde & Richard Griswold del Castillo

Famous as a political and labor activist in the United States, Luisa Moreno loved San Diego and lived there the last three years that she was in the United States from 1947 and 1950. While she and her husband lived in a small house in Encanto, she had a slogan inscribed over her door. "We are created to serve others. The sad thing is that we die only for ourselves." This was to be a fitting epitaph for Luisa herself, since it was in San Diego that she was underwent one of the most trying periods in her life and would later live in exile as a result. During this period, the San Diegans who met her found her to be cheerful and outgoing, a model for a perfect lady. But behind that pleasing personality was a strong inner core. She would not allow herself to be intimidated, not even by the United States government.[1]

Luisa Moreno was born on August 30, 1907 in Guatemala City. Her upper class father, Ernesto Rodriguez, a serious and bookish man, and her fragile mother, Alicia Lopez Rodriguez, gave the new baby the christened name of Blanca Rosa Lopez Rodriguez. In 1916 young Alicia came to the United States with her parents to attend the College of the Holy Name in Oakland, California. After completing her studies she returned to her homeland. Developing an interest in social issues, she worked at different newspapers and published a volume of poetic verse. Later she came to the United States for a second time in 1928 where she lived until her voluntary deportation in 1950.[2] During the early years of her career as a labor organizer, because of her family's disagreement with her political position and to avoid embarrassing the family name, she changed her name to Luisa Moreno, in honor of a famous Mexican labor organizer of that era, Luis Moreno.

Luisa Moreno was a small woman, about five feet tall and she had a talent for persuasion. As a forceful speaker, she convinced others by the weight of her logic and her ease in using the right words. Yet in public, when not speaking, this passionate lady was reserved. Her mysterious nature and her silence was such that people yearned to know more about her. Throughout her adult years, Luisa Moreno took care of her appearance and visited a hairdresser whenever she had the opportunity. A long time labor activist and friend, Bert Corona recalled, "Even if you knocked on her door at 8 in the morning, you'd find her well put together ... She was always proper and rarely complained."[3]

Moreno's career as a labor organizer began when she and her first husband, the Guatemalan artist Miguel Angel de Leon, migrated to New York City on August 28, 1928. When she arrived, she was appalled to see how minorities were treated by segregation within the city. During the Great Depression, she supported her infant daughter and unemployed husband by working in a garment factory near Spanish Harlem. According to historian George Sanchez, "Here she had contact with socialist Puerto Rican workers, an experience that radicalized her and pushed her toward professional labor activism."[4] Toiling for hours over her sewing machine, she experienced first-hand the deplorable working conditions of the Latin sweat shops of that era.

Her first experience with labor activism, however, was during a cafeteria strike in 1930. She found a job in Zelgreen's Cafeteria in New York City and soon was involved with her co-workers in a strike. Together they faced a contingent of police who intended to prevent them from picketing. Luisa, in a fur collar coat, strolled through the cordon of policemen as if she was going to enter the cafeteria. When she was directly in front of the door she pulled a picket sign from under her coat and thrust it in plain view. Two burly policemen grabbed her by the elbows. They lifted her off the sidewalk and hustled her into the entrance way of a nearby building.

She came out with her face bleeding and considered herself fortunate that she was not disfigured.[5]

On June 25, 1937, Moreno and her husband were divorced and she now had to raise an infant daughter named Mytyl alone. A few years before Moreno had become a labor union activist. In 1935 the American Delegation of Labor hired her as a professional organizer. Moreno was shaped by the liberal intellectuals and activists of that era and she had a faith in the idealism that molded the new Soviet state. In the 1930s, many liberals loathed Nazism and were disillusioned with capitalism's failures, so evident during the Great Depression. Along with many other labor organizers she believed in Marxist ideology and was attracted to the American Communist party due to the attention it devoted to Latinos and labor issues in factories and in agriculture.[6]

In 1930, Moreno had joined the Communist Party in New York. The Party was active not only in organizing workers but also in community issues: working for school desegregation, opposing segregation in public facilities such as swimming pools and housing, protesting police abuse, obtaining relief aid, and preventing the deportations of Mexicans during the 1930s.[7] Even actors joined the Communist Party. As Marlon Brando wrote, "During the thirties, several members of the Group Theater . . . joined the Communist party-largely, I suppose, because of an idealistic belief that it offered a progressive approach to ending the Depression and the increasing economic inequity in the country, confronted racial injustice and stood up to fascism."[8] An additional attraction of the Communist Party to Luisa Moreno was that it took an active part in championing the cause of women workers.[9]

During the early 1930s Luisa Moreno worked in a variety of areas. She unionized Blacks and Latina cigar rollers and other tobacco workers in Florida. While in Tampa, Luisa helped a dwindling cigar workers union that the Ku Klux Klan had been terrorizing. Then she organized cane workers in Louisiana. Through the years she gained valuable experience that she would later use in the fields and packing houses of California and finally among the Latino tuna packing workers in San Diego. By 1934 Moreno joined the Congress of Industrial Organizations, a newly formed alliance of unions devoted to organizing unskilled workers. She soon was elected as the first woman and the first Latina member of the California CIO Council. A few years later, in 1938, Luisa Moreno became an international representative of UCAPAWA [United Cannery Agricultural Packing, and Allied Workers of America]. That year Donald Henderson, a Communist, had organized the UCAPAWA-CIO. Throughout her career Moreno insisted that "UCAPAWA was a left union, not a Communist union." In the 1930s UCAPAWA was a major organizing force among Latino field, shed and cannery workers.[10]

In 1937, Luisa moved to San Diego to help the fish and cannery workers organize unions in the tuna industry. At that time tuna packing was a major employer of Latinos who mostly lived in Logan Heights. The canneries, which dominated the south bay water front included the California Packing Corporation, the Marine Products Company, the Old Mission Packing Corporation, the Van Camp Sea Food Company, and Westgate Sea Products. They operated around the clock in sweatshop conditions.

The workers found Luisa to be trustworthy and likeable. Few realized that she was an astute politician. She was never beholden to any political party or business interest. The challenge of the San Diego canneries made her tough-minded and pragmatic about how unions could benefit the common, poorly educated worker, who found her optimistic and "very down-to-earth."[11]

Like most parts of California, organizing was difficult in San Diego County's fields and factories. Poverty-stricken Anglo Americans had come from other states during the Depression by the thousands and settled there. As labor historian Sam Kushner noted, "The Anglos, many of whom had been brought up to believe in rugged individualism were not as amenable to union organization. Even so, their bitter experiences educated many of them quite rapidly and they, too, were among those who joined in some of the struggles of those days."[12]

In San Diego, Moreno enjoyed the extensive gardens in Balboa Park. It made life pleasant for her. She recalled, "The beauty of the city made me forget the stupidity, ignorance, prejudices and paranoia of the world." Even her nature garden walks had a larger purpose, "to reinforce humility so that I don't have to nurse later a bruised ego."[13]

During the first part of 1938, while still in San Diego, Moreno helped to organize a Hispanic civil rights assembly called El Congreso de Pueblos que Hablan Español (the National Spanish-Speaking Congress). This would be the first ever conference that would bring together Mexican American unions, mutual aid associations, political clubs and other organizations. The purpose of the meeting would be to exchange information, establish a network of Mexican American organizations, and to discuss a civil right agenda. After months of planning and some frustration, Moreno working with Josefina Fierro de Bright saw their dreams realized when El Congreso met in Los Angeles on April 29, 1939.[14] With her union contracts throughout the nation, Moreno was a key organizer but she strongly believed in sharing responsibility. In her words: "One person can't do anything; it's only with others that things are accomplished."[15] As a result of El Congreso's conference, the House Un-American Committee in Washington, under Congressman Martin Dies, decided to investigate its organizers, including Luisa Moreno. Dies accused the Congreso of being affiliated with communists and suspected their anti-agribusiness stance. He accused the Congreso organizers as attempting "to separate the Mexicans of the Southwest from the rest of the United States and either form a new republic or return the Southwest to Mexico." He also charged the Congreso with fermenting "violent riots and revolutionary activities."[16]

Pending the full investigation, Moreno decided to go to Texas to organize women working in the pecan shelling factories. She arrived with her child, Mytyl, in 1938 and rented a small house in San Antonio. When she visited the barrios she saw the vicious cycle of poverty and hopelessness ravaging the Hispanic community. "I could detect the harshness and cruelty of the system everywhere." There she helped the militant Emma Tenayuca organize the women. Soon Moreno was arrested for her labor activities but was "released without charges."[17]

Following this, Moreno spent three months in the Lower Rio

Grande Valley where she saw the harsh life of the farm workers. Naturally, she worked as a union organizer, and made contacts with vegetable, fruit canning, and packing industry workers. Also she helped to organize the field workers who harvested beets, sweet corn, cabbage, spinach, and other vegetables for only fifty cents a day.[18]

In September 1939, Moreno moved on to organize sugar beet workers in Colorado and then returned to California. For the next few years she lived in Los Angeles and was involved in historical events that shaped Mexican American history. At first she joined the Anti-Nazi League. It sponsored a labor rally, organized with her help, at the Los Angeles Coliseum and a Quarantine Hitler rally at the Shrine Auditorium.[19]

After 1940, Luisa Moreno was the chief organizer of UCAPAWA in Los Angeles and San Diego. She traveled constantly trying to break the discriminatory hiring habits of canneries and factories. In San Diego she was successful in getting non-discrimination pledges from the Royal Packing plant that processed Ortega brand chiles. She also traveled to Los Angeles where they got a pledge from the California Walnut Growers Association. As the general manager of the California Walnut Association, W. T. Webber wrote, "For a period of four years during the middle 1940s. ..[Moreno] held a position of authority in a labor union with which the California Walnut Association had a contract." He noted that he had "a high regard for her character, ability and honesty."[20]

In San Diego Moreno spent most of her time organizing cannery operatives. With the patience of a saint, Moreno tackled the most routine and boring tasks in order to reform California canneries. She put all her energy into every detail. Finally, after a much effort her dedication paid off and contracts were signed with most of the canneries. This affected thousands of cannery workers, seventy-five percent of whom were women.

Moreno was moved by the sufferings of these women and men when she saw life inside the San Diego canneries with its segregated policies and terrible working conditions. If a female operative cut her finger slightly while paring or canning fruit, she hesitated to bandage it. She was afraid to fall behind because she was being paid the piece rate (so much per box). As a result, the finger became infected and pus oozed out of the wound and contaminated the fruits.[21]

Repeatedly, Moreno declared, "These people are not aliens — they have contributed their endurance, sacrifices, youth and labor to the Southwest. Indirectly, they have paid more taxes than all the stockholders of California's industrialized agriculture, the sugar beet companies and the largest cotton interests that operate or have operated with the labor of Mexican workers."[22] During this period, she coined the motto of UCAPAWA, "An Injury to One is An Injury to All." Years later Dorothy Healey said, "A strong sense of national identity held these workers together, but did not prevent them from making common cause with others, like their Jewish and Russian fellow-workers."[23]

While in San Diego, Moreno worked with the activist attorney Carey McWilliams. There were very few labor lawyers in San Diego and Los Angeles. Both were violently anti-labor towns. McWilliams worked to expose abuses done to farm field and factory workers by the agricultural industry. As David F. Selvin noted, "If there had been no Carey McWilliams back in the latter days of the 1930's, we would have had to invent one."[24]

Moreno, McWilliams and other labor union leaders organized minority and other farm workers in California's lush agricultural valleys. "Their efforts were met with violence from the growers and local police." As a lawyer, McWilliams defended striking citrus workers and wrote articles about their plight and other issues in several publications, especially in the San Diego Union.[25]

To Moreno's amazement, during World War II, San Diego transformed itself into a dynamic military and factory city. "The fear of Japan made San Diego in a few short years the greatest naval port in America."[26] Like a nest of ants, thousands of soldiers and sailors moved in and out of the region. Manpower needs were critical. Moreno spoke out against the relocation of the Japanese Americans to camps and saw that a disproportionate number of Chicanos were drafted because they lacked jobs which carried draft-deferral status. Once again thousands of Mexicans poured across the border and took the least skilled, low-paying jobs, for which they competed with other unskilled workers.

In San Diego, housing was in short supply. Rations became a nuisance. Transportation became a problem. The war triggered anxiety and people searched for scapegoats. Known as "Pachucos," eccentric Chicanos youngsters in baggy and extra long pants were prime targets. Moreno testified before the Los Angeles Grand Jury which was investigating the famous Sleepy Lagoon Case — a sensational trial in the summer of 1942 where nine teenage Mexican Americans were put on trial for murder. In her testimony she predicted that the tensions created by the media's sensationalism would result in violence unless corrective measures were taken.[27]

Her prophecy turned into a reality. In June of 1943, the Los Angeles Zoot-Suit riots began, sparked by violence between soldiers and sailors on leave and young Chicanos. They took place in the largely Spanish-speaking neighborhood close to the downtown sections of Los Angeles. For a series of evenings, sailors and soldiers organized fleets of taxicabs and roamed the streets looking for teenage Chicanos wearing zoot-suits "with reat pleat and stuff cuff."

Encouraged by police indifference, sensational news stories flourished. Mobs grew larger. During one evening, Zoot-suitors were dragged out of downtown motion picture theaters, their fancy suits torn from their bodies. They were beaten and chased through the streets.[28]

On the second night of the rioting there was an emergency meeting of several hundred citizens. One of the concerns was to stem the wild rumors that were sweeping through the communities of southern California. Fears of a "Pachuco war" were spread by hysterical and provocative reports that appeared in the press. Moreno pointed to the war stress, racism and paranoia that had caused this media over-reaction. The Los Angeles Times, for example, printed headlines, such as, "Ten Seized in Drive on Zoot-Suit Gangsters," and "One Slain and Another Knifed in Zoot Fracas."[29]

Luisa Moreno along with members of El Congreso and other Mexican-American community leaders sprang into action. They mobilized a defense committee on behalf of the youngsters who had been arrested by the police even though they had been attacked by the servicemen.[30] The San Diego Union also reported on the riots but Moreno was relieved that the newspaper refrained from blatant "yellow journalism." But they too were caught up in the stereotype. The San Diego Union reported that groups of servicemen, ranging in size from a dozen to several hundred, roamed San Diego's downtown streets, searching for "zoot-suited hoodlums reported to be infiltrating into San Diego from Los Angeles." About 100 sailors and marines stormed downtown San Diego on G Street below First Avenue to chase several youths wearing "the outlandish zoot-suit garb. The youths made their getaway in the darkness." About 300 other servicemen gathered at Third Avenue and East Street but they were quickly dispersed by city and military police before any zoot-suiters were discovered. Moreno learned that all of San Diego's police were ordered to search suspicious individuals who "appeared to be members of a Pachuco gang." Anyone found with possible weapons was to be booked on deadly weapons charges.[31]

After years of strikes, pickets, organizing, negotiating and fighting for labor unions throughout the Southwest and moving from town to town, Luisa Moreno finally moved to San Diego permanently to live with her new husband Gray Bemis. A U.S. Navy sailor from Nebraska, Bemis met Luisa during one of her organizing trips to San Diego. After a brief courtship they were married on February 1, 1947 in Yuma, Arizona.[32] Soon after they moved into an apartment by the beach in San Diego.

Luisa was attracted to Gray Bemis because of his intelligence and sensibility. It seemed now that she was ready to settle down in one place for the first time in her life. While Bemis worked as a manager for the Consolidated Pipe & Supply Company, she sat with her heavy, black typewriter and wrote a guidebook on how to organize labor unions. She wanted others to avoid her mistakes. Slowly her project turned into an autobiographical narrative of her labor union activities.[33]

Determined to be a traditional wife, Moreno withdraw from most of her major labor activities, resigning from the staff of the CIO. She remained, however, an active dues-paying member of the union and gave moral support and was involved in several local projects. Periodically she made Monday trips to Los Angeles to teach a class at the California Labor School with Ramon Welch entitled, "Mexican-Americans and the Fight for Civil Rights." Sometimes she would stay overnight with a friend to help Murray Korngold with a Tuesday class, "How the People Made Our History."[34]

In 1949, the soft-spoken Bemis built her a small frame house, painted red with white trim at 6426 Medio Drive. It stood on the side of a remote hill overlooking San Diego's harbor and downtown. The location with the view of the sea and the hills evoked a soothing sense of timelessness. In the back yard Luisa cared for an extensive azalea garden. The garden became her sanctuary from years of turmoil and a retreat for her meditations and intellectual pursuits.

As Moreno remembered, "That house symbolized some of the happiest moments of my life. He was a great husband and my best friend." Later, her daughter Mytyl Glomboske noted, "It was a marriage made in heaven. Not once did they raise their voice at each other or argue. They had a high regard for each other."[35] In their small house with huge windows, her husband furnished an office with an old oak file cabinet in one corner. Moreno looked out her office window at a scenic view of San Diego's harbor as she typed her reflections. Bemis even wall-papered the room for her with her favorite design. For her birthday, he bought her a fine Navaho rug and some Pueblo pottery. Ceramics sat on top of her huge cabinet — her memory bank — full of letters, reports and other narratives about her activities in labor unions.[36]

Luisa's husband loved photography and photographed his wife and Moreno's grandchildren. One bedroom was used for a well-equipped photo lab. Both of them loved company and they frequently had a variety of dinner guests. Luisa enjoyed cooking and gardening and hired a Mexican gardener to keep the landscape beautiful.[37]

Since she loved azaleas, Moreno joined the San Diego Organic Gardening Club. As a perfectionist, she extracted certain azaleas from her garden whose tint of color was not quite right. To rearrange her garden, she clipped sprigs of new azaleas in bloom and set them in Coke bottles. The bottles were then relocated about in the landscape until Moreno was content with the color and harmony. She was slowly forming a Japanese garden.[38] Moreno loved things well done. As she used to say, "If you do something, do it once and do it right."[39] Even this precise lady's house reflected her personality. She had numerous books and had a few Pre-Columbian objects and different types of wall masks and colorful Mexican rugs.

After three years of marital bliss in San Diego, her domestic world was shattered by Cold War fears and McCarthyist hysteria. Nation-wide an atmosphere of paranoia about Communist infiltrators prevailed. Because of her Marxist ideas and Guatemala origins, the California Un-American Activities classified Moreno as a dangerous alien.[40] Moreno was stunned at first and went to see attorney Robert W. Kenny, who had a law office in downtown San Diego. Kenny was a remarkable lawyer who sometimes antagonized other lawyers because of his legal successes. He was eventually appointed to the Superior Court of Los Angeles County. Moreno considered him a courageous man of ethics.[41]

In September, 1948, as she awaited confirmation of her citizenship application, Moreno was subpoenaed by the State Senate Committee on Un-American Activities. She attended the hearings of the Committee at the San Diego Civic Center from September 8 through 10, 1948. On September 10, a trim Moreno in a black dress and white gloves took the witness stand and faced Senator Jack B. Tenney's Committee, a statewide precursor to the national McCarthy-led witch hunt of radicals.[42]

The San Francisco Chronicle evaluated Tenney and the committee hearings:

> One of the Committee's troubles under Tenney's leadership was that it roamed and rambled into fields of assassination and guilt by association which had subversiveness. Anyone who was in favor of overthrowing the Government, was likely to be hauled up and smeared by inquisition and innuendo. His methods have done more

damage to the cause of intelligently combating Communism than almost any other influence in California . . . [43]

Luisa Moreno remembered her impressions: "While the members were cautious and passive, Tenney was a bully with a scathing tongue. He reduced his victims to tears. By the time he finished with them, they felt depleted."[44] When Moreno walked into the hearing room, she retained her dignity. She remained calm while suppressing her anger against the bigoted ignorance so apparent in the questioning. As she sat calmly, she felt that Tenney's sessions had become an unscripted soap opera. Moreno was asked directly if she had been a member of the Communist Party. She replied that question was an attempt to "smear" a labor union and she invoked her Constitutional rights.[45] Then she was found to be a hostile witness. The council persisted with the same question. Moreno's eyes glared. She made it explicitly clear to Richard E. Coombs, Chief Council for the delegation and Jack Tenney that they had no right to ask that question and that she had no intention of answering it.[46] Like most individuals who were subpoenaed by the committee, she protected herself by invoking the Constitution's Fifth Amendment.

Coombs asked her pointedly whether she might not be risking the right to become a full-fledged citizen by refusing to answer his question. "Citizenship," Moreno responded, "means a lot to me, but the Constitution of the United States means more."[47] Listeners applauded in defiance of the customary Tenney edict against displays of audience sentiment. One youth was even hustled from the room by officers. "I told Coombs," recalled Moreno "that I had taken an oath to uphold the U.S. Constitution when applying for naturalization and that was what I intended to do in the hearing."[48] More questions followed in a long, exhausting and emotionally draining session. Later she wrote, "During the testimony Sen. Jack Tenney threatened me with sending the transcript to the [U.S.] Immigration and Naturalization Service."[49] The irritated Coombs and other Tenney committee members agreed that Moreno was insubordinate and had failed to answer their questions. A transcript of her session was forwarded to U.S. immigration authorities.

After a few weeks after the San Diego hearing on September 30, 1948, the U.S. Department of Justice issued a warrant for Moreno's arrest as an alien "affiliated with an organization . . . and teaches the overthrow, by force and violence, of the government . . ."[50] While she appealed the order the INS asked Moreno to post $4,000 bail or report to the local office weekly.[51] Her citizenship application was not a dead issue. Historian George Sanchez wrote, "Ironically, Moreno would include herself and the other Latino labor leaders of the period as individuals who really loved America even while the U.S. government was trying to define her and others like her as aliens, outsiders to the American tradition."[52]

When considering her appeal the INS requested that witnesses appear on Moreno's behalf to testify about her character. Luisa was desperate to find witnesses, but many people were afraid of being smeared as communist sympathizers.[53] Finally a few friends came forward on her behalf. In a huge office in downtown Los Angeles, on February 14, 1949, Ignacio L. Lopez, editor of the Spanish language newspaper La Opinion, testified about her dedication to labor union and civil rights. But that was not enough.[54]

On March 14, 1949, Moreno traveled to the San Diego office of the INS to be interviewed to determine her immigration status. After the interview, the INS finalized her deportation. During all this, Moreno was offered citizenship by the FBI in exchange for her testifying at the Harry Bridges investigation. Bridges was an Australian-born International Longshoremen Labor Union leader who had been charged with being a communist. Moreno turned down the offer, refusing, in her words, to be "a free woman with a mortgaged soul."[55] Despite the deportation order, Moreno continued her labor activism while free on bail. She accepted an invitation from Paul Pinsky, director of the 12th Annual Convention of the California CIO Council in 1949. Speaking before this audience, Moreno criticized the "Witch Hunt" conducted by the Tenney Committee.[56]

Strange things are happening in this land. Things that are truly alien to traditions and threaten the very existence of cherished traditions . . . Yes, tragically, the unmistakable signs are before us — , who really love America. And it is we who must sound the alarm, for the workers and the people to hear and take notice. For it seems that today, as the right to organize and strike was fought for and won, as the new labor agreements were fought for and won, as the fight against discrimination is being fought but far from won, so the fight for the very fundamentals of American democracy must again be fought for and re-established.[57]

Later, Moreno was dismayed when she read that university professors were dismissed for refusing to submit to the Un-American Activities Committee Investigation. Even "distinguished scientists" were being "harassed and persecuted for no more than their opinions and associations." Moreno was upset that the Board of Regents of the University of California in Los Angeles voted to discharge 157 members of the university's staff for failing to make a formal declaration that they were never members of the Communist Party.[58]

Sometime after the hearings Moreno met Zero Mostel in San Diego. He was one of Broadway's great entertainers. Like her, his life was shattered. According to his biographer, "Mostel had been before the Un-American Activities Committee, and jobs for him had evaporated like a morning mist on a hot summer day."[59] Moreno and Mostel soon became friends and gave each other moral support to survive the oppression. Mostel had some savings and was exploring a career in art but Moreno was not that fortunate. Her life was shattered after the Tenney hearings.[60] She stayed mostly at home working on her autobiographical book. She pondered over the documentation with several files spread all over her table for quick references. While sitting at a black typewriter, she rewrote her pages, read and sorted papers. One morning, as she prepared in her kitchen a sandwich and coffee for lunch, she looked up and saw her Mexican gardener, Manuel, staring at her through the open window. Later she caught him reading some of her manuscripts by the window. The embarrassed gardener excused himself by saying that he had been looking for her to ask about how she wanted several plants arranged. Luisa questioned him and she discovered that her faithful Manuel, who could speak and read English, had been bribed by the

FBI to find things that could incriminate her and to testify against her. The FBI had promised Manuel and his relatives citizenship in exchange. After this confession Luisa told him to say whatever it took to protect himself and his family. She asked him to stay as a gardener and report what he wanted.

Manuel had also told her that the FBI had interviewed her neighbors and close acquaintances.[61] The FBI agents in San Diego had asked them what kind of automobile she drove and if she was living beyond her means. They inquired if she had ever been drunk or had loud parties with strange-looking visitors. They asked the neighbors if they had ever received her mail by mistake and noticed any foreign magazines. Had they ever seen the Daily Worker, a communist newspaper? One agent asked, "Just between us — this is off the record, of course — do you have any reason to suspect that she might not be, you know, 100 percent American?"

Frightened by Manuel's information, Moreno decided that her writings had put her former associates in danger. When her husband, Gray, came home from work, they sorted out family photos and burned all their confidential records in the backyard. Photos that depicted union groups perished in the blaze. Boxes of private papers went up in smoke. Years later, Moreno regretted not saving these papers which were really a priceless collection on early labor unions in San Diego.

This was not the first time that Moreno had encounters with the FBI. During her labor activities in San Diego during the 1930s, Moreno was under constant FBI investigation. Her friend Harry Bridges, a radical leader of the San Francisco Longshoremen's Union whom she had met during her organizing days with the CIO, had taught her how to detect their surveillance. She learned from him to have "fun with the FBI." For example, when she checked into a hotel, she rented an adjoining room so that she could see under the connecting floor and listen. She saw two pairs of men's feet moving around the room. Hearing no talk, except whispers, she knew it was FBI agents. Then she turned on the radio full blast and tuned it to a climactic soap opera or a thriller. Bridges told her to check on likely wiretapping sites and if the phone was bugged, blow a horn into it. As Moreno recalled, "I could spot agents in a room or in a hotel lobby. They had a unique habit of holding newspapers in front of them. They held the paper just below their eyes and their eyes peeped over the top of the paper."[62]

Other counter-strategies were to tear up meaningless envelopes and stationery and drop them in a waste basket in her hotel room. If she had the time, she would make elaborate paper dolls out of old union leaflets and leave them there; she knew that agents patiently reassembled them. In typing letters she used old carbon paper from a stenographer at a retail store. She knew that it was rushed to the FBI Lab in Washington, where technicians with smudged fingers spent hours trying to decipher them.[63]

In 1950, after almost a year of waiting for the results of her appeal, Moreno's immigration status took a grotesque turn. Local San Diego canneries, such as the Old Mission Packing Corporation and the San Diego Packing Company, had asked that Moreno and her closest friends in San Diego be questioned by the House Un-American Activities Committee, a new witch hunting committee that had been set up by the Congress. The committee questioned her and her friends Donald Henderson, John Tisa and Elizabeth Sausly. Much of the time the committeemen issued publicity-catching pronouncements such as declaring Moreno and her friends as "card-carrying members of the Communist Party" and "agents of Soviet intrigue." When her friend Elizabeth Sausly asked Moreno what to do, Luisa replied, "Stand up for the truth regardless of the consequences."[64] As the journalist Steve Murdock wrote, "The government's action appears to be linked . . . . . . to a whole series of deportation actions against union leaders on the Pacific coast particularly union leaders in the agricultural and food processing industry."[65]

Back at her San Diego home, Moreno realized she probably would be deported. Her friend Bert Corona noted that she wanted to fight deportation but only "if she had sensed that it would have been a collective struggle rather than just an individual one." But Luisa Moreno and other Latino activists were abandoned by the American left during this difficult period. Corona remembered: "Unfortunately, the efforts by the left — specifically, the Communist Party — to defend labor leaders in similar situations extended only to those of European descent and not to Latinos."[66] Chicano leaders like Josefina Fierro de Bright, Refugio Martinez, and others discovered themselves isolated and defenseless. Some were deported.[67]

Without the support of liberals, her husband Gray, and Ignacio Lopez, an activist and editor from Riverside, and Carey McWilliams set up a defense committee called the Provisional Committee for Luisa Moreno Bemis. As chairman, Lopez set up the committee headquarters in a small office on South Hill Street in Los Angeles and wrote solicitations for donations to the defense fund.[68]

Some individuals helped. Prominent figures joined the committee like Beatrice Griffin, author of American Me, and Joseph W. Aidin, a well-known Los Angeles lawyer. Later the committee opened another office at Encanto in San Diego, to raise money for legal expenses and to promote a Spanish language leaflet.[69] McWilliams, for his part, lobbied on Moreno's behalf. He wrote, "Are we to do nothing and say nothing while this fine human being who would make such an admirable citizen, is ignominiously deported from her friends, from her husband, her daughter and her granddaughter? For myself I can only say that I count it a privilege to support Luisa's case in every way at my disposal."[70]

Moreno felt that her fate was wrapped up in her union activism: "They can never deport the people that I've worked with and with those things that were accomplished for the benefit of hundreds of thousands of workers — things that can never be destroyed."[71] She considered racism a factor as well when she wrote on March 16, 1950, "We are right back in the pages of that revealing book on the 'Asiatic and the Alien . . .' No Constitution for us, who are neither citizens nor persons, but a freakish creation called 'aliens.'"[72]

Luisa Moreno was one of several militant Hispanic leaders who had never become citizens. Instead they took an American identity through their participation in unions and political organization, primarily in San Diego and Los Angeles. Now, in historian Sanchez's words, they "faced deportation for the political activities they had engaged in under the rubric of a newfound ethnic Americanism."[73]

Almost every week the San Diego newspapers accused her of being a subversive. For the San Diego Evening Tribune she was a woman who was part of a "subversive organization [who] is living quietly as a housewife in San Diego." When Moreno and her husband began receiving violent threats they moved to 1818 6th Street, San Diego. When the threats continued they decided to make out a will. She was now even forbidden by the INS to keep a copy of her deportation proceedings transcript. Depressed over her predicament that financially drained her, on November 15, 1950, she received another bill from her attorney, Robert Kenny, for "professional services."[74]

Hope again faded. She was arrested and detained in the Terminal Island Federal Prison in the Los Angeles harbor. She remained there for a few days. While seeing the majestic harbor from a prison window, she remained calm and realized that her friends could not help her anymore. She retained her protective glaze of discipline and never complained. Her husband Gray became her tower of strength during these desperate critical moments. Mytyl went to visit her at Terminal Island, which would be the last time she would see her mother for a long time.

Finally Moreno was released and given only days to gather her possessions and leave the country. Luisa and Gray drove a Studebaker to El Paso. On November 30, 1950, they went into Mexico through Ciudad Juarez.[75] The terms of her exit were listed as "voluntary departure under warrant of deportation" on the grounds that she had once been a member of the Communist party.[76] She never again stepped foot on United States soil. In fact, if she were to return without permission, she would be guilty of a felony, fined and imprisoned.[77]

Proud of his accomplishment, Jack Tenney spoke to a public gathering in San Diego and characterized Luisa Moreno as a "Parasitic Menace."[78] When the local Hispanic community heard about Moreno's deportation, they were grief-stricken. They respected this determined lady who had devoted her life to helping them and other disadvantaged groups throughout the country. They knew her extensive tradition of farm and factory labor organizing. The San

Diego Tribune printed error-filled articles about her and even the local radio stations perpetuated myths about her. As Moreno recalled, "One of the radio stories talked of a 'powerful labor leader living as a quiet housewife in San Diego.' Well, that's quite a discovery! What they will do to garnish their chatter!" It irritated Moreno to no end since there was even confusion about the elementary facts of her life.[79]

Moreno and her husband stayed in Mexico for almost a year. They were enchanted with Oaxaca and its Pre-Columbian ruins, Monte Alban and Mitla. They later moved to Guatemala and friends from the Guatemala Confederation of Labor welcomed them. On February 8, 1951, Moreno and Bemis registered as residents of the country. She was classified as a domestic. They opened a hardware business and became involved in activities associated with the progressive Jacobo Arbenz government until it was overthrown by the Central Intelligence Agency in 1954.[80] Later Moreno returned to Mexico. Cheerful about starting a new life in Mexico City, she promised herself never to get involved with labor organizations and politics again. In August 1956, Moreno and Bemis rented a place in Ixtapalapa, near Mexico City. There they operated a poultry farm. Carey McWilliams warned them "that it was an illusion to think that one could make a living from it."[81]

Shortly after, Bemis became ill from emphysema, aggravated by smoking. Luisa took him to Mexico City for medical treatments but his health disintegrated. A friend noted that Moreno and her husband "eked out less than a bare existence attempting to operate a small, ill-equipped poultry farm . . .She takes care of her bedridden husband, attends the household and looks after the farm-alone. She has no funds to hire help. What little is realized is quickly eaten up in medical needs."[82]

By 1960, Bemis required an oxygen tank to breath. Moreno continued to give him his medications — painful injections to the stomach. She became his twenty-four hour nurse. He finally died in her arms on February 1, 1960.[83]

In April 1960, a weak and grief-stricken Luisa Moreno went to Cuba to live in Fidel Castro's socialist society. She wanted to go somewhere totally different to ease her sorrow for Bemis. As she recalled, "I worked for six months as an English translator for a time in the new revolutionary educational system." After a period of mourning she went back to Mexico and worked in the Mexican border town of Tijuana. As she exclaimed, "I wanted to move to San Diego. But I realized that the deportation case was over me like an ugly cloud."[84] While in Tijuana, she renewed her immigration card and worked in the fashionable Arte de Salinas Art Shop, located at 1305 Revolucion Avenue in Tijuana. The large store with its polished marble floors appeared like a museum of contemporary art, depicting Pablo Picasso and other cubistic artists.[85]

During one afternoon in the art store, a friend brought Moreno some photographs of her home on Medio Drive in San Diego. Later when she was alone, she carefully saw the pictures of the home she loved so much. She wanted to cry. Instead she sat silently. Vivid memories with her husband, Gray flashed back. Thinking she was back in time, she thought she heard Gray's voice, calling her to come home. After a long interval, a customer dropped in the shop and her mind steadied again.[86]

In 1977, Moreno moved to Guadalajara where she managed apartments. Her health failed. One day she had a stroke while waiting for a bus by the cathedral. She felt dizzy and collapsed, injuring her head. Later Moreno had another stroke and her brother Ernesto eventually took her back to Guatemala. Luisa Moreno died in her native Guatemala on November 4, 1992.[87] For over thirty-five years, until 1985, Luisa Moreno served as a staunch worker in an array of social justice causes in Guatemala, Cuba, and Mexico. Despite her time in jail, her labor union obstacles, and the persecution of her friends, Moreno was free of bitterness. As Bert Corona remarked, "Luisa bore all of these conflicts, not only because of the cause of freedom in the United States for Hispanics, but because she is that rare human being for whom the human household is her family."[88] In Chicano history, Moreno remains enshrined in a civil rights pantheon. As Mytyl, her daughter said, "My mother was a good role model for me who taught me to be aware of discrimination and injustices that are inflicted on the working class."[89]

Years later, on October 16, 1994, Mytyl remembered her mother as she marched with 70,000 in downtown Los Angeles to protest Proposition 187, the anti-illegal immigration initiative.[90] Mytyl silently followed other protestors down Cesar E. Chavez Avenue near downtown. As she marched, she saw her mother as a spirit of her people who refused to be defeated. "I think of my mother and she is in my heart when I participate for the struggle of justice."[91]

A Note on Oral Historical Sources

During the 1970s, I met Luisa Moreno through her confidant and friend Bert Corona. At that time she lived in Tijuana as a sales lady in the elegant abstract art shop, Arte de Salinas. The interviews took place over a day while Corona and I visited her. Bert insisted that I not use a tape recorder, so I took prolific notes of the conversations. Most of these interviews drifted into recollections between Moreno and Corona about previous events.

At first, Moreno loved to talk about her preferred topic, art history. She enjoyed twentieth century art, that is why she liked her job. Abstract Expression [Action Painting] fascinated her, especially the contrasts of color and texture of Marc Chagall. Another choice was the variants of Cubism by Pablo Picasso and Georges Braque. In her spare time this lady read reference art books in her shop.

Luisa Moreno was mysterious about her past. She never talked about herself, except in relation to her union activities. To those who asked about her personal background, she politely changed the topic or ignored it. Even Corona admitted that he knew little about her personal life.

Her daughter Mytyl Glomboske gave me numerous insights to her complex mother. I met Mytyl in Los Angeles on April 17, 1994, at a book signing event. It turned out that she lived only a few miles from me and we met several times during that year during which time she gave me copies of letters that she had sent to her mother. Although she was not familiar with most of her mother's political activities, her revelations about Moreno's inner world were valuable. Through Mytyl, we understand more about Moreno's inner qualities, mainly her enduring discipline, that gave her the dynamic energy to demand civil rights opportunities that were unjustly denied to American minorities. Through Mytyl we realized that Moreno was an exceptionally strong woman who avoided irrational, misguided self-destructive battles of despair and defeat when the odds were against her. In the end, the eloquent Moreno managed to inspire others to continue her crusade for justice. We thank Mytyl for correcting and elaborating upon the facts in this article.

The notes of these interviews and others cited in the notes are available in the archives that are kept at my home in Long Beach, California. My personal archives are a collection of many materials given me by Moreno, Corona, and others who were active in the 1930s. These materials are available to researchers who are willing to use them in my home.

NOTES

1. New information about Luisa Moreno in San Diego was uncovered in the Robert W. Kenny Collection, Southern California Library for Social Studies and Research, Los Angeles in the file "Deportation and Related Activities: Individual Cases-Luisa Moreno Bemis," MSS 003, Box 7, Folders 53-59. As an attorney Kenny took cases of individuals who were indicted for questionable activities, such as Luisa Moreno Bemis. Regarding Luisa's name changes see "Data on Luisa Moreno Bemis" and the notes that Kenny took during an interview with her. This information was provided by Luisa herself to the attorney Kenny and his law partner Robert S. Morris on April 30, 1949, San Diego, Calif. Also in the same folder see A. R. Mackay, U.S. Department of Justice, Acting Assistant Commissioner, Washington D.C. to District Director of Immigration and Naturalization, Los Angeles, September 30, 1948, Warrant For Arrest of Alien. The documents states that Moreno was known as ROSA RODRIGUEZ-LOPEZ alias LUISA MORENO alias LUISA BEMIS alias ROSA DE LEON. When Jack Tenney realized that Moreno and other union labor activists had several names, he said, "You realize that you are dealing with people who are deceptive, who take assumed names, who disguise their activities and objectives....[It is part of] a Communist organization." See Edward L. Barrett, The Tenney Committee: Legislative Investigation of Subversive Activities in California (Ithaca, New York: Cornell University Press, 1951), 145. See Bert Corona, interview by Carlos Larralde, 12 May 1980.

2. Copy of birth certificate from "El Registrador Civil de la Capital [Guatemala City], certifica: que al folio 630 del libro 49-1 de nacimientos, se encuentra la partida 1611, donde consta que: Blanca Rosa, nacio en esta ciudad el treinta de Agosto de mil novecientos siete, hija de Ernesto Rodriguez y de Alicia Lopez, originarios de esta ciudad." The copy was made for the Servicio Consular Mexicano, No 92703 on November 26, 1976. Quoted from Carey McWilliams, "Luisa Moreno Bemis," August, 1949, Los Angeles, a biographical leaflet written for the "Provisional Committee for Luisa Moreno Bemis." Carlos Larralde Collection.

3. Mario T. Garcia, Memories of Chicano History: The Life and Narrative of Bert Corona (Berkeley: University of California Press, 1994), 116. Corona, interview, 25 April 1980.

4. Luisa Moreno, interview by Carlos Larralde, 28 May 1971 (Larralde Collection). George Sanchez, Becoming Mexican American: Ethnicity, Culture and Identity in Chicano Los Angeles, 1900-1945 (New York: Oxford University Press, 1993), 244.

5. Steve Murdock, "A Question of Deportment," Our Times (Los Angeles), 9 September 1949, p. 3. Our Times was a British newspaper. Murdock was a popular British journalist who gave Luisa Moreno early publicity. After

Murdock wrote this article, he gave lectures on Moreno and the Tenney Committee in Britain.

6. Rosa Rodriguez L. de Leon [Luisa Moreno] Plaintiff versus Miguel de Leon, Defendant, Final Judgment of Annulment, Index No. 11730, June 25, 1937, Supreme Court, New York City. Sanchez, Becoming Mexican American, 244. Luisa obtained the divorce on October 6, 1937. She then took her child Mytyl and boarded a bus for Florida. Mytyl never saw her father again. Years later she wanted to see him again but was afraid to antagonize her mother. For Moreno's early labor organizing career see "Data on Luisa Moreno Bemis," Folder 53, Robert Kenny Collection. Sam Kushner, Long Road to Delano (New York: International Publishers, 1975), 17.

7. "Data on Luisa Moreno Bemis," Folder 53, Robert Kenny Collection. Responding to an enquiry wrote that, "Held membership card in Communist Party from 1930 to 1935. Dropped membership for personal reasons." Bert Corona said, "It is not clear whether Luisa was in fact a member of the Communist Party, but even if she had been, membership in the CP was not in reality a subversive act." See Garcia, Memories of Chicano History, 119.

8. Marlon Brando, Brando: Songs My Mother Taught Me (New York: Random House, 1994), 193.

9. For literature on the CP advocacy of women's rights see Rosalind Rosenberg, Divided Lives: American Women in the Twentieth Century (New York: Hill and Wang, 1992), 120-121; Alan Brinkley, The End of Reform: New Deal Liberalism in Recession and War (New York: Alfred A. Knopf,1995), 201-205. Regarding Moreno's affiliation with the Communist party, to many Moreno stood out as an intellectual. Sam Kushner explained that "she was a teacher of Marxism to many when they sought answers beyond those provided by the trade-union movement or the organization of the Spanish-speaking workers." Kushner, Long Road, 92. In an interview with Carlos Larralde on May 12, 1971, Moreno said that she had an extensive library on Marxism that she kept in her home in San Diego. Some of the items were by Lenin, State and Revolution and Left Wing Communism and Infantile Disorder, Marx's Communist Manifesto, M.F. Olgin, Why Communist?, and The Struggle Against Imperialist War. These items and other books were listed as evidence for "Government Exhibits Introduced at the Luisa Bemis Deportation Hearing on November 10, 1949." The records said she "dropped her membership [in 1935] for personal reasons." Later Moreno told Larralde in an oral interview that she left because of ideological disputes, see "Data on Luisa Moreno Bemis," Folder 53, Robert Kenny Collection.

10. "For Clerk." Folder 53, Robert Kenny Collection. According to this record, Moreno resided in Tampa, Florida during the winters of 1935 and 1936. She was active in the East Coast off an on throughout the 1930s. She also lived for a time in Silver Springs Maryland between July 1939 and July 1940. See

Garcia, Memories of Chicano History, 117. For the California period see Vicki Lynn Ruiz, Cannery Women, Cannery Lives: Mexican Women, Unionization, and the California Food Processing Industry 1930-1950 (Albuquerque: University of New Mexico, 1987), 42.; Carey McWilliams, "Luisa Moreno Bemis," August, 1949, a biography written for the Provisional Committee for Luisa Moreno Bemis. Author's collection. Also quoted in Murdock, "A Question of Deportment," 3. For more on this period see Warren A. Beck and David A. Williams, California: A History of the Golden State (New York: Doubleday & Company, 1972), 395-396. On UCAPAWA and Moreno see Vicki Lynn Ruiz, "UCAPAWA, Chicanas, and the California Food Processing Industry, 1937-1950," (Ph.D. dissertation, Stanford University, 1982), p. 135; also Beck and Williams, California, 396.

11. Luisa Moreno, interview by Carlos Larralde, 17 April 1971; Murdock, "Question of Deportment," 3.; Corona, interview, 25 April 1980.

12. Kushner, Long Road, 90-91.

13. Moreno, interview, 12 May 1980.

14. Garcia, Memories of Chicano History, 109, 113, 117. For further information on Moreno and the Congreso see Mario Garcia, Mexican Americans: Leadership, Ideology & Identity, 1930-1960 (New Haven: Yale University Press, 1989), 146-153.

15. Quoted in Vicki Ruiz, Nuestra Cosa (Claremont, Calif), Spring 1993.

16. Garcia, Memories of Chicano History, 110. Even in the 1940s, Dies as investigator of the Un-American Activities continued his "grotesque attacks" on liberals to the point that Roosevelt's vice-president, Henry A. Wallace, compared Dies to Goebbels and declared that "the effect on our morale would be less damaging if Mr. Dies were on the Hitler payroll." Quoted in Brinkley, p. 150. See also Carey McWilliams, Witch Hunt: The Revival of Heresy (Boston: Little, Brown and Company, 1950), 304.

17. "For Clerk," Folder 53, Robert Kenny Collection.

18. Moreno, interview, 17 April 1971; Murdock, "A Question of Deportment," 3. Carey McWilliams' leaflet "Luisa Moreno Bemis Biography," August 1949, Los Angeles. It was written for the "Provisional Committee for Luisa Moreno Bemis." Larralde Collection.

19. Moreno, interview, 28 May 1971. Moreno retained an interest for Hispanics in South Texas. She kept a correspondence with Harry Koger, a journalist. See his article, "Sunshine, TB-Migratory Workers' Lot," FTA [Food, Tobacco, Agricultural and Allied Workers Union of America], (New York), January 1950.

20. W. T. Webber to those concerned, 5 August 1949, "Provisional Committee for Luisa Moreno Bemis," Larralde Collection; "Memo for Robert Morris on Character Witness," undated, Folder 54, Robert Kenny Collection.

21. Ruiz, Cannery Women, 36.

22. Luisa Moreno, "Caravans of Sorrow," address delivered at the panel on Department and the Rights of Asylum of the Fourth Annual Conference of the American Committee for the Protection of the Foreign Born, Washington, D.C., March 3, 1940, Folder 1, Carey McWilliams Collection, Special Collections, University of California, Los Angeles.

23. Quoted from Sanchez, Becoming Mexican American, 244.

24. See David F. Selvin's review in the section of "Carey McWilliams: Reformer as Historian," California Historical Quarterly 53 (Summer 1974): 173.

25. McWilliams, The Education of Carey McWilliams, 47. See also McWilliams' articles, "Getting Rid of the Mexican," American Mercury (March 1933): 322-324; "Once Again the Yellow Peril," The Nation (26 June 1935): 735-36, and "Race Business," New Republic (26 June 1944): 852-853.

26. Beck and Williams, California, 367.

27. Moreno, interview, 2 June 1971. See also Carey McWilliams, The New Republic, 18 January 1943.

28. McWilliams, The Education of Carey McWilliams, 113.

29. Carey McWilliams, "Zoot-Suit Riots," New Republic (June 21, 1943): 18-20. Moreno, interview, 20 April 1971; see also the Zoot-Suit Riots files in the Carey McWilliams Collection, Special Collections, University of California, Los Angeles. See also the Los Angeles Times, 25 May; 16, 18 June 1943.

30. Garcia, Memories of Chicano History, 143. For more information about the Zoot Suit riots, see Maurcio Mazon, The Zoot Suit Riots: The Psychology of Symbolic Annihilation (Austin: University of Texas Press, 1984).

31. Moreno, interview, 28 April 1971; "Zoot-Suiters Hunted in S.D.," San Diego Union, 10 June 1943, 1.

32. A copy of Luisa Moreno [Rosa Rodriguez] and Gray Dayton Bemis marriage Certificate is in Yuma County Courthouse, Arizona, Marriage Records, Book 129 on page 133. As for Bemis, he was born on April 15, 1906 in York, Nebraska. In 1930, he attended the University of Nebraska. Then he joined the U.S. Navy and became an Electrician's Mate Second Class. On November 25, 1945, he was honorably discharged in Los Angeles. Bemis had an interest in the civil rights of minorities and was part of the Citizens Committee for the Defense of Mexican-American Youth or those involved in the Sleepy Lagoon Case. See Report of the Joint Fact-Finding Committee to the Fifty-Fifth California Legislature, Un-American Activities in California, 1943 (Sacramento, California: Government Printing Office, 1943), 217.

33. As a rule, her business and personal correspondence, notes and even Christmas cards were always typed. She rarely used her clear penmanship.

34. Robert Kenny to Senator Sheridan Downey, 23 February 1950, Folder 54, Robert Kenny Collection. As Kenny explained in this letter, "As you will

recall, Mrs. Bemis had retired from labor activities some years ago, married an American citizen who is an overseas veteran, and was living quietly in San Diego when these proceedings against her were commenced." For additional information on her marriage see Section 8, "Data On Luisa Moreno," Folder 53, Robert Kenny Collection; See also the San Diego Evening Tribune, 27 June 1950, Sect. B, p. 1.; Moreno, interview, 12 May 1971. The goal of the California Labor School, 112 West 9th St, Los Angeles, was to help "to rout the union-smashers, the enemies of civil rights, the racial and religious bigots, the war-mongers." For more on this institution see the California Labor School Collection, Southern California Library, Los Angeles.

35. Moreno, interview, 17 April 1971; Mytyl Glomboske, interview by Carlos Larralde, 12 June 1994.

36. Ibid. As of 1995, Luisa Moreno's home is still standing and has changed little. An artist now lives there. It is hoped that as a result of this and other investigations, the City of San Diego may someday designate this home a historic site.

37. Moreno, interview, 20 April 1971. Her daughter Mytyl Glomboske used to visit them periodically. She said that Bemis and Moreno's marriage "was made in heaven. They truly loved and respected each other. As a stepfather, Gray was very good to me. To my mother he was an angel." Glomboske, interview, 5 January 1995.

38. "Data On Luisa Moreno Bemis," Folder 53, Robert Kenny Collection; Moreno, interview, 12 May 1971. One friend who admired her garden was Juliette A. Williams, a registered nurse and a Girl Scout leader. She wrote. "Since her marriage in 1947 Luisa has been living quietly with her husband. They built a little ranch house in San Diego and she has been happy and busy with her home and garden. Williams to Whom It May Concern, 4 August 1949, Folder 53, Robert Kenny Collection.

39. Moreno, interview, 17 April 1971.

40. Ibid., 20 April 1971.

41. In 1966, Kenny was appointed by Governor Edmund G. (Pat) Brown to this position. In 1970 there was an unsuccessful attempt to recall him and Jerry Pacht from the office of Superior Court Judge. Kenny retired from the bench in 1975. He died on July 20, 1976.

42. San Diego Evening Tribune, 27 June 1950, Sect. B, p. 1; Carl Morgan, "Destroying the California CIO Council," in edited by Ann Fagan Ginger and David Christiano, The Cold War Against Labor (Berkeley, Calif: Meiklejohn Civil Liberties Institute,1987), 433. Robert Kenny to Senator Sheridan Downey, 23 February 1950, Robert Kenny Collection. As Kenny explained in this letter, "These proceedings followed her refusal to be harassed by State Senator Jack B. Tenney and his Un-American Activities Committee. Since then, as you know, Tenney has been removed as chairman of that committee

but the damage he did continues to affect Mrs. Bemis and her family." See also Murdock, "A Question of Deportment," 3. Finally, see Arthur H. Samish and Bob Thomas, The Secret Boss of California: The Life and High Times of Art Samish (New York: Crown Publishers, 1971), 130.

43. Quoted in Samish and Thomas, The Secret Boss of California, 131.

44. Moreno, interview, 12 May 1971.

45. Ibid.; San Diego Evening Tribune, 27 June 1950, Section B.

46. Murdock, "A Question of Deportment," 3.

47. Ibid.

48. Ibid.

49. "Data On Luisa Moreno Bemis," Robert Kenny Collection.

50. A. R. Mackay, U.S. Department of Justice, Acting Assistant Commissioner, Washington D.C. to District Director of Immigration and Naturalization, Los Angeles, 30 September 1948, Warrant For Arrest of Alien, Folder 53, Robert Kenny Collection. See also letter of R. Kenny to Luisa Moreno Bemis, 25 November 1949, Folder 53, Robert Kenny Collection.

51. Carol King to Robert Kenny, 5 December 1949, Folder 53, Robert Kenny Collection. See also San Diego Evening Tribune, 27 June 1950, Sect. B, p. 1.

52. Sanchez, Becoming Mexican American, 251-252.

53. "Memo for Robert Morris on Character Witness," undated, Folder 54, Robert Kenny Collection.

54. H. R. Landom , District Director of U.S. Immigration and Naturalization Service and by George W. Scallorn, Chief Entry, Departure, and Expulsion Section to Luisa M. Bemis, File No. 246-121334, 15 December 1949, Los Angeles, Folder 54, Robert Kenny Collection.

55. Ibid; Glomboske, interview, 28 April 1994.

56. Luisa Moreno to Robert W. Kenny, San Diego, Calif, 3 October 1949, Folder 53, Robert Kenny Collection. Garcia, Memories of Chicano History, 116.

57. Address delivered by Luisa Moreno Bemis to the 12th Annual Convention, California, CIO Council, 15 October 1949, pp. 3-4, Folder 53, Robert Kenny Collection. Also quoted in Sanchez, Becoming Mexican American, 251.

58. Moreno, interview, 17 April 1971. See also the headlines "UC Regents Fire 157 Refusing to Sign Non-Communist Letter," Los Angeles Times, 24 June 1950.

59. Richard Fleischer, Just Tell Me When To Cry: A Memoir (New York: Carroll & Graf Publishers, Inc., 1993), 80.

60. Robert Kenny to Carol King, 4 October 1949, Folder 53, Robert Kenny Collection.

61. Moreno, interview, 12 May 1971. Mytyl Glomboske also recalled this incident about the gardener.

62. Moreno, interview, 17 April 1971. See how Harry Bridges handled the FBI in Curt Gentry, J. Edgar Hoover: The Man and the Secrets (New York: W. W. Norton & Company, 1991), 246.

63. For a comparison of Harry Bridges, see Gentry, J. Edgar Hoover, 263.

64. Moreno, interview, 12 May 1971; 28 May 1971.

65. Murdock, "A Question of Deportment," 3.

66. Garcia, Memories of Chicano History, 119.

67. Individuals like Fierro de Bright, who never became U.S. citizens left the United States voluntarily. She refused "to remain and possibly incriminate friends if subpoenaed. She also believed that she would soon be arrested." See Garcia, Mexican Americans, 173.

68. Ignacio Lopez to Friends, 6 August 1949, "Provisional Committee for Luisa Moreno Bemis" file, author's collection.

69. "Newsletter for Committee for Luisa Moreno Bemis," March 1950, Encanto Station. Copy in Larralde Collection.

70. Carey McWilliams, "Luisa Moreno Bemis," August 1949, a biography written for the Provisional Committee for Luisa Moreno Bemis. Larralde Collection.

71. Quoted in Murdock, "A Question of Deportment," 3.

72. Luisa Moreno Bemis to Robert Kenny, 16 March 1950, San Diego, Calif., Folder 54, Robert Kenny Collection.

73. Sanchez, Becoming Mexican American, 252.

74. San Diego Evening Tribune, 27 June 1950, Sect. B, p. 1. For a variety of newspaper coverage on Moreno see "Bemis Case Support Starts Rolling in North," Labor Herald, (San Francisco, Calif), 28 February 1950, p. 1. See also "Red Law Arrests," Los Angeles Evening, 25 October 1950, p. B 2 and "Judge Calls for Non-Red Proof," Los Angeles Evening Herald, 31 October 1950; Robert Kenny to Luisa Moreno Bemis, 10 April 1950, Folder 53, Robert Kenny Collection. As he wrote, "It will be necessary that you return to me the transcript in your deportation proceedings. I have been informed by the immigration people that they want it back. I have checked the authorities and find that they are correct in stating that I cannot let it out of my control even for the purpose of making copies." Kenny later tried to get a duplicate for her. He failed. Kenny and Morris Law Office to Mr. & Mrs. Gray Bemis, 15 November 1950, Folder 55, Robert Kenny Collection. In Folder 55, there are numerous legal papers on Moreno's deportation.

75. Luisa Moreno to Robert Morris, 1 December 1950, Folder 56, Robert Kenny Collection. Moreno and her husband first went to Chihuahua, Mexico and slowly drove their Studebaker to the interior of the country. Later they went

to Guatemala to see her family. Again in Folder 56, see the correspondence of Moreno to Kenny.

76. W. F. Kelly, Department of Justice, Immigration and Naturalization Service, Assistant Commissioner, to Robert Kenny, 1 November 1950; Luisa Moreno, "Application for Voluntary Departure," 1 November 1950, Folder 55, Robert Kenny Collection.

77. Ibid.; H. R. Landon, U.S. Department of Justice, Immigration and Naturalization Service, District Director, Los Angeles, Folder 54, Robert Kenny Collection.

78. Moreno, interview, 28 April 1971; Corona, interview, 12 May 1980.

79. Luisa Moreno to Robert Kenny, 30 June 1950, Folder 53, Robert Kenny Collection. Even recently, certain aspects of Moreno's life have been distorted. When the California Department of Education, Sacramento, did an exhibition during March, 1990, on "National Women's History Month," a brief biography with a picture of Moreno's was exhibit. It started, "Born in Guatemala, Luisa Moreno became a U.S. Citizen in 1937.....Although she was a U.S. citizen, she was deported in 1950 for refusing to testify before the House Un-American Activities Committee." The fact is she never became an American citizen.

80. Luisa Moreno to Robert Morris, 30 December 1950, Folder 56, Robert Kenny Collection. She sent him neatly typed letters. She rewrote her prose four or five times, before they were typed. She was careful about grammar and the appearance of her letters. Also she loved to send unusual thoughtful cards during Christmas, Valentine's Day or for special events. Again they were typed and neatly signed. Even the quality of paper was taken into consideration. To her a sloppy letter was an unpardonable sin. Wherever Moreno went, her old favorite, black Remington typewriter went with her. It was her most cherished possession; Luisa Moreno was issued as Blanca Rosa Rodriguez de Bemis Libreta de Ciudadania [Republica de Guatemala], Register No. 75060. Luisa Moreno Papers.; Garcia, Memories of Chicano History, 118.

81. Rosa Bemis to Robert Morris, 23 August 1956, Folder 56, Robert Kenny Collection; Gray and Luisa Bemis to Robert Morris, 11 January 1956, Folder 56, Robert Kenny Collection.

82. Quoted from a fund-raising leaflet. It also stated that Bemis suffered from "heart lesions, tuberculosis and arteriosclerosis." This statement was printed by James L. Daugherty, William S. Lawrence, and Philip M. Connelly in a huge, white leaflet, printed in October, 1957 to raise money to aid him and Moreno. Larralde Collection.

83. Death of Gary Dayton Bemis, Acta de Defuncion, Departamento del Distrito Federal, No 49901, Legalizicion No 01260, Registro Civil libro 1, a la foja 155-OF. 10. Filed February 15, 1960. Copy in Larralde's files.

84. Moreno, interview, 2 June 1971.

85. The attentive Moreno worked in this art store since the owner, named "Flor" was disabled. Flor had a disease in her lower legs and feet that Moreno thought could be infectious. Moreno told me and later also confided in her daughter Mytyl that she was afraid to get the ailment from Flor. Once a month Flor went to the store to check the records. When she left, the cautious Moreno mopped the marble floor with her favorite lemon fresh bleach and water.

86. Moreno, interview, 2 June 1971.

87. Glomboske, interview, 12 June 1994. Moreno stipulated in her will that she wanted to be cremated. Moreno's brother Ernesto opposed it. Instead she was buried in a family marble mausoleum. See Luisa Moreno Bemis' Will, 17 November 1950, Los Angeles, Folder 55, Robert Kenny Collection.

88. Corona, interview, 12 May 1980.

89. Glomboske, interview, 5 January 1995.

90. See Patrick J. McDonnell, "70,000 March Through L.A. Against Prop 187," Los Angeles Times, 17 October 1994, A1.

91. Glomboske, interview, 2 November 1994.

9

World War II and the Emerging Civil Rights Struggle

Rodolfo Jacobo

During the 1940s and 1950s the Mexicano and Mexican Americans of the San Diego and Imperial Valley border region underwent profound changes due to the cataclysmic events of World War II, a trauma that affected everyone's life. Thousands of young men joined the military and went off to fight in the war, many of them died heroes' deaths, others returned with a new commitment to rebuild their lives and those of their communities. Young Mexican women contributed to the war effort by getting jobs in the many war industries that were created in San Diego. They developed a new sense of independence and self-confidence that provided the basis for a later Chicana movement. Those who lived through these years later were part of the struggle to achieve the full civil rights that they were promised during the war. As a result of the changes in the war years, Chicanos and Mexicanos in San Diego gained valuable experience to continue the struggle against discrimination and segregation. The borders that they encountered in these years included segregation and socioeconomic exclusion yet they collectively never accepted these limitations but joined with others to eliminate these borders and establish a strong sense of community.

Although World War II was supposed to be a war against injustice and totalitarianism abroad, there were also struggles on the home-front as discrimination in employment, in public services, in schools, and by officials continued. Beginning in 1942 Mexican laborers were brought under contract to the U.S. as braceros and they influenced the development of the barrios and colonias. A new labor activism was born through the efforts of Luisa Moreno, an organizer who lived and worked in San Diego, fighting for labor rights and against the discrimination against Mexican youth, called pachucos. Racism continued to plague San Diego, and the Ku Klux Klan continued its anti-Mexican operations. In 1953 the federal government's sponsored Operation Wetback resulted in the repatriation of thousands of immigrants, creating a period of fear and intimidation. All of this ferment prepared the ground for a resurgence of community organizing and the civil rights activism of the 1960s.

Luisa Moreno: Labor and the Zoot Suit Riots[1]

One prominent example of a San Diego Latina who remained a leader in the struggle for civil rights during the war was Luisa Moreno. She was a Guatemalan-born labor leader who was active in organizing for the United Cannery, Agricultural, and Packing Workers Association (UCAPAWA) during the 1930s. In July 1940, Luisa Moreno moved to San Diego to work on a labor union newspaper and to continue her organizing activities among the women cannery workers. She and her friend Robert Galván helped organize the United Fish Cannery Workers Union, UCAPAWA, Local 64, and they soon organized hundreds of fish and cannery workers in the largest San Diego canneries: California Packing Corporation, Marine Products Company, the Old Mission Packing Corporation, Van Camp Sea Food Company, and Westgate Sea Products.[2]

While Luisa Moreno was working with the cannery workers, the United States entered into World War II on December 7, 1942. Within a short time, Southern California, and especially San Diego, was transformed into a military industrial center for the war effort. As a result San Diego became even more conservative, politically and culturally. Local Japanese Americans were sent to internment camps, officially called War Relocation Authority Camps, while at the same time, a disproportionate number of Chicanos were drafted because they lacked jobs that carried draft-deferral status. Lured by jobs in agriculture and in other businesses, thousands of Mexicans poured across the border. Forbidden to work in the petroleum industry, shipyards, and other vital industries, they took the least skilled, low-paying jobs.[3]

These immigrants were soon joined by bracero workers who were contracted beginning in 1943 to come to the U.S. to work in selected industries, mostly in agriculture and railroads.

As a union consultant for the cannery workers in San Diego, Moreno gave speeches saying that legal and illegal Mexican immigrants used fewer government resources than native-born citizens. She pointed out that they contributed more to the public coffers in taxes then what they took from the region. She was angered and annoyed when conservatives, including remnants of the KKK made public announcements against Mexican immigrants.[4]

Sleepy Lagoon and Zoot Suit: Effects on San Diego

Luisa Moreno was also active in protesting the mistreatment of Mexican American youth arising from the infamous Sleepy Lagoon case and Zoot Suit riots in Los Angeles. Both of these events outside San Diego had important implications for the civil rights of all Mexicanos and Mexican Americans in Southern California and beyond.

On August 2, 1942, José Díaz was found dead near a gravel-pit in East Los Angeles, a tragedy that would have far-reaching consequences. In Los Angeles, following the murder he police ordered a dragnet and arrested three hundred young Chicanos. Following days of sensational newspapers articles labeling all Mexican American youths as gangsters and Pachucos, there was an indictment of twenty-three youth for murder. Eventually twelve young Chicanos were convicted of murder and five for assault. The Sleepy Lagoon defendants were convicted on January 13, 1943, making it "the largest mass-murder trial even conducted in Los Angeles. The trial took place in an atmosphere of intense prejudice, before a biased judge, and with a stubborn and courageous but inadequate defense."[5] Newspaper, public and judicial bias as well as police prejudice and blatant mistreatment molded the jury verdicts.

As wartime stress mounted, tough police action against

Chicano youth gangs throughout Southern California was reported in newspapers.[6] During that year, UCAPAWA's Southern California official Luisa Moreno, Warehouseman's Union Bert Corona, California State Department Immigration and Housing's attorney Carey McWilliams, and others formed the Sleepy Lagoon Committee to rescue the convicted men. Moreno stressed that the grand-jury testimony, based on racially justified assumptions against the Chicano juveniles, created unavoidable conflicts. As she explained, "The Sleepy Lagoon Case is a reflection of the general reactionary drive against organized labor and minority problems. This case now shows all sorts of division among the various racial, national, and religious groups among the workers."[7]

Moreno sensed the war uneasiness in Southern California, primarily in San Diego. Housing was in short supply. Rations became a nuisance. Transportation was a problem. Racial conflicts in the U.S. Navy and in San Diego became intense. People searched for scapegoats.[8] The war triggered anxiety, ambiguity, and frustration. Several ships were shelled and torpedoed along the Southern California coast. Most people in 1943 felt the United States was losing the war. Her prophecy turned into a reality in Los Angeles. Known as pachucos, eccentric Chicanos, Blacks, Filipinos, and even white youngsters in peg bottom, long pants and long coats were prime targets. In Los Angeles, Chicanos were the majority who wore Zoot Suits. Their dark skin, accent and mannerisms were enough to set them apart from the average Angeleno. "Basically bilingual, they spoke both Spanish and English with an accent that could be mimicked by either or both groups," wrote McWilliams. Also an age-old heritage of ill-will resentment prevailed against Chicanos who had long been stereotyped. "The pachuco also had a uniform, the zoot-suit, which served to make him conspicuous."[9]

In early June 1943, about two hundred sailors took the law into their own hands. Coming from the Navy Armory in Chávez Ravine into the center of downtown Los Angeles, they formed a brigade of twenty taxicabs. Several young Chicano zoot-suitors were spotted. They were badly beaten and left bleeding on the pavements for the ambulance to pick up.[10] Later one of the sailors who led the expedition made a bland statement: "We're out to do what the police have failed to do…. [W] e're going to clean up this situation…." [11]

Sensational newspaper stories flourished for several days on the front pages. "The worse came from the Hearst Press, which in Los Angeles was represented by the L.A. Herald and the L.A. Examiner." As Luisa Moreno pointed out, "These papers assaulted Mexican pachucos and zoot suiters. They insinuated that Mexicans were the cause of all the crime and delinquency in California."[12] Mobs grew larger. "Squads of servicemen, arm linked, paraded through downtown Los Angeles four abreast, stopped anyone wearing zoot-suits or suffer the consequences." They were encouraged by police indifference. "Aside from a few half-hearted admonitions, the police made no effort whatever to interfere with these hoards of disorder."[13]

During one evening, zoot-suitors were dragged out of downtown motion picture theaters. Their fancy suits were torn from their bodies. They were beaten and chased through the streets. The Sleepy Lagoon case of the previous year and the excitement it had caused had, of course, created further anxiety.[14]

An emergency meeting of several hundred citizens was called. Moreno, Corona, and other Mexican-American community leaders sprang into action. "They mobilized a defense committee on behalf of the youngsters who were being arrested and detained even though they were the victims" of racist, paranoid servicemen.[15]

Intense emotions gripped Los Angeles. Military authorities declared downtown Los Angeles off limits. The city's police department was indifferent to the brutality. The Los Angeles Times meanwhile went berserk printing stirring headlines, such as on November 2, 1942: "Ten Seized in Drive on Zoot-Suit Gangsters." Then on February 23, 1943, another headline appeared: "One Slain and Another Knifed in Zoot Fracas."[16]

According to Alice McGraff, one of the women working on the Sleepy Lagoon Defense Committee, sailors from San Diego were among the instigators in the violence in Los Angeles. McGraff stated that bus loads of servicemen from San Diego convoyed up to Los Angeles to participate in the riot against the pachucos. Stories spread that Blacks, Chicanos and unpatriotic Whites abused military personal. In retaliation several taverns and other favorite spots were vandalized. As one report stated, "Damage done on the Fifth Street Landing in the way of malicious mischief possibly by enlisted men of USS Kilty."[17] Tensions prevailed. Places like La Reine Cafe on 2003 Logan St remained "a low class business frequented by civilians and service men of mixed races and by a large number of common unescorted women." The "general air of drunkenness" created fights over attractive prostitutes.[18]

Rumors spread about taverns like La Reine Cafe, owned by "a large hard Negress." Most of them were located on Mission Blvd, such as the Beach Club Cafe and the Casino Club. The San Diego County Council, consisting of veterans of foreign wars, concluded its investigation "that service men in the uniform of our navy, were being beaten, robbed, drugged, and subjected to other such acts, common to places of low repute."[19]

On June 10, 1943 San Diego Union reported that groups of servicemen, ranging in size from a dozen to several hundred, roamed San Diego's downtown streets south of Broadway. They searched for "zoot-suited hoodlums reported to be infiltrating into San Diego from Los Angeles."[20] About 100 sailors and marines stormed downtown San Diego on G Street below First Avenue to chase several youths wearing "the outlandish zoot-suit garb. The youths made their getaway in the darkness." About 300 other servicemen gathered at Third Avenue and East Street. They were quickly dispersed by city and military police before any zoot-suiters were discovered.

San Diego's police were ordered to search suspicious individuals who "appeared to be members of a pachuco gang. Those found to be carrying the usual pachuco weapons-knives, chains and clubs-will be booked in the city jail on charges of carrying deadly weapons, police reported."[21]

Charles C. Dail, a San Diego city councilman, was concerned about the violence and informed Rear Admiral David Bagley, commandant of the Eleventh Naval District in San Diego that the action taken by the sailors and marines against the so-called "zoot suit" was actually aimed at civilians in general. "There has been numerous instances in San Diego where members of the military forces have insulted and vilified civilians on public streets..." [22]

Admiral Bagley at first ignored Dail's complaint; he then tried to discredit him. Later he denied the indictments leveled by Dail, who was supported by W.J. Decker, Secretary of the San Diego Industrial Union Council. The navy kept a lid on the San Diego disturbances.

Inviting Bagley for a meeting with San Diego community labor and political figures, Moreno said, "Arrogance, pretense, and pride have no place in a commitment to serve the public. I wanted to have every avenue open to avoid blood and tears. In negotiations, you will never get everything you want. That is why you need to be flexible. You will need to get manipulative ways to get out of conflicts." [23]

Meanwhile ugly racial incidents continued to flourish. There were military reports from El Centro that sailors were "maliciously assaulted by Mexican police..." The Teddy Orias Cafe, 522 6th Avenue, refused to serve Blacks, and tensions escalated. [24] A frustrated Moreno wanted an investigation of racial issues that marred San Diego and the naval base. As she explained, "Without a stable political and social environment, nothing can be done. Political powers rests to those who can sustain growth and deliver prosperity. Then they can inspire loyalty and cooperation from the people." [25]

Finally on November 30, 1950, because of her involvement with Mexican American civil rights issues, the Sleepy Lagoon Case, and the protests of the Zoot Suit riots, Luisa Moreno was deported to Mexico. Representative Jack Tenney, who headed a committee hunting for communists, found Luisa Moreno a "dangerous alien." [26] Desperate for peace and rest, she and her husband went into Mexico through Ciudad Juárez. [27] The terms of her exit were listed as "voluntary departure under warrant of deportation" on the ground that she had once been a member of the Communist party. [28] She never again stepped onto United States soil. In fact if she were to come back without permission, she would be guilty of a felony, fined, and imprisoned. [29] For a time she lived in Tijuana, Baja California where she and her husband operated a furniture store. There she maintained contacts with friends and associates in San Diego. In her final years she lived in her native Guatemala where she died in 1992.

Mexican and Mexican American G.I.s

Despite the continued discrimination and racism at home hundreds of thousands of Mexican Americans and Mexicans joined the armed services to fight to defend the United States. Their experience served as a platform for later activism when they sought to redeem the promises that were made during the war for a more democratic society.

More than two and a half million persons of Mexican descent lived in the Southwestern part of the United States when the Japanese bombed Pearl Harbor on December 7, 1941. Of that number more than half were native-born U.S. citizens, and probably about one third, or just fewer than one million, were men of draft age. While there are no reliable statistics, impressionistic accounts indicate that large numbers of Mexican Americans either volunteered or were drafted into the armed services during World War II. It is estimated that about 500,000 Mexican American men joint the armed services during the war.[30]

They volunteered for a variety of reasons: some sought escape from poverty and discrimination at home; others wanted adventure, or did so out of pride and a sense of manhood. Some joined because their families expected them to contribute, some out of patriotic motives, and some because their friends or relatives had enlisted. Raúl Morín, a veteran whose book *Among the Valiant* is a personal account of Mexican Americans during World War II, put it this way:

> We felt that this was an opportunity to show the rest of the nation that we too were also ready, willing, and able to fight for our nation. It did not matter whether we were looked upon as Mexicans, Mexican-Americans, or belonging to a minority group; the war soon made us all genuine Americans, eligible and available immediately to fight and to defend our country, the United States of America.[31]

In addition to the U.S.- born Mexican Americans there were also hundreds of thousands of Mexican citizens who were residents in the U.S. and who were eligible for the draft. After June 1942, when Mexico declared war on the Axis powers, Mexican nationals living along the border crossed into the U.S. to join as well.

There are hundreds of stories that tell of the bravery and sacrifices of the Mexican American G.I.s during the war.[32] As has been noted by many historians, collectively as a group, the Mexican Americans earned more Congressional Medals of Honor, the nation's highest award for bravery and valor, than any other: seventeen. In addition to the accounts of unimaginable bravery and hardship are descriptions of the strength of friends and Mexicanidad.[33] The family back home learned of the experiences of their men folk only after the war, due to strict censorship of the mails. Even after the war many veterans preferred to keep silent about their experiences despite their heroism. Oscar Romero and Alfredo Sepulveda are two examples, one a Chicano and the other a Mexicano, who distinguished themselves as heroes during the war and later became community leaders in San Diego, part of the generation that led the civil rights movement after the war.

Oscar Romero was a Chicano who was drafted into the Army in 1942 and was sent to basic training in Little Rock, Arkansas, where they had many volunteers from Mexico. The 76th Infantry Division in particular had many Chicanos from Southern California. Oscar remembered having basic training with Maracario Garcia, who was from Guanajuato, Mexico, who received the Congressional Medal of Honor, and of serving with many other Mexicanos and Chicanos who gave their lives for the U.S. during World War II. Oscar was in the D-Day landing at Normandy and fought to liberate France. Later when crossing the Rhine River, he received the Bronze Star for taking command of his platoon after the lieutenant and sergeant were killed. After the war, Oscar was one of the founders of the all Chicano VFW Don Diego Post in Logan Heights in 1955. He remembers that they formed the post because the local VFW did not want any Mexican or Chicano members. Today Oscar is still active in the post along with his wife Ruth, who was a founder of the woman's auxiliary organizations for the post.

Mexicano immigrants also joined the service and later became activists. Alfredo Sepulveda was born in 1920 in La Paz, Mexico and moved to Los Angeles with his family when he was six. His family was related to the Sepulveda family who had owned a California rancho in the 1840s. He became a professional boxer and got married before volunteering to join the armed services when the war broke out. He remembers being rejected from flight school because he was a Mexican national. He joined the paratroopers, fought at Normandy, and in the Battle of the Bulge, and was wounded three times. Alfredo won the Silver Star and Two Bronze stars, one with clusters for valiant action in WWII. After World War II he worked as a truck driver and later moved to San Diego where he and his wife became leaders in the Don Diego Post of the VFW located in Logan Heights.[34]

Rosita the Riveter

Women too were mobilized during World War II and their experience was crucial for the later struggle for civil rights. In the war hundreds of thousands of Mexican American women had their lives drastically changed by the national emergency of war as they went to work in jobs that had always been reserved for men, in aircraft factories or other war industries. While there is a great diversity of experience arising out of these years, one generalization seems to summarize the importance of this period: the war created new awareness of women's abilities outside of the domestic sphere. In Richard Santillán's words, the war developed among Mexican American women a "political awareness, social independence, grass-roots leadership, and economic self reliance--personal strengths which greatly enhanced the post-war civil rights movement."[35]

It was not always easy for women to enter the work force. Lorinda Flores, a Mexican immigrant to San Diego in the 1930s remembered her experience: "I really enjoyed working... I wanted to grow up and be a buyer and work in a store, but I married a typical Mexican male who said you're not going to work you're going to have kids and stay home. So that was my jale, I was a housewife."[36] Additionally married women usually had small children and growing families to tend care for, and it just was not possible to hold down a full time job in addition to being a mother.   Countering this cultural and economic limit on Mexican American women's working for wages was a long tradition of their working in part time and occasional jobs in order to support the family. This was especially true for migrant farm worker families where the entire family worked to help make ends meet. The experience of Hortencia Carrasco, a farm worker in San Diego during the 1930s was typical: "When I started working I was about 14 or 15 years. I started working at Van Camp in 1943. I went to work to help the family. I had no choice, I had to help my mother, my parents, and the younger kids." [37]

It should be noted that the majority of Mexican American women during World War II were not Rosie the Riveters. They contributed to the war effort in other ways, by raising families and taking care of others. Their prosaic stories have not yet been told--of the difficulties of making ends meet with rationing and scarcity, of the continued discrimination in public services and in education, of the grief over the loss of brothers, uncles, fathers and husbands, of the heroic sacrifices made to keep families together and support the morale of loved ones. All these dimensions of life have yet to be the subject of social historians studying Mexican American women during the war. It was, however, the dominant experience for most adult Mexican American women.

Some of the oral histories gathered about Mexican American women in San Diego illustrate the many themes of their experience. Emma López was a native San Diegan whose parents owned a small barrio restaurant. During the war she quit high school to get good paying jobs, first in the tuna canneries and then at Convair, an aircraft assembly plant.   After the swing shift, there were big band dances: Emma and her friends had enough energy to go almost every week: "I'd go around picking everybody up. We didn't want dates, we wanted to dance with the guys from Texas or New York, New Jersey, New Mexico." She recalled lots of late night parties, going grunion running, and to all-night movies. All this had the blessing of her parents who saw it as part of the war effort.[38]

One factor that dramatically increased young women's freedom and sense of independence was the increased money they had to spend on activities that had been considered frivolous during the depression of the 1930s. Now they had permission to be extravagant. Hortencia Carrasco, another San Diego native with Mexican immigrant parents recalled deciding to quit high school because she "had no clothes to wear." She started working at the tuna canneries rather than at the aircraft factories because she could earn more money through piece rates--up to 100 dollars a week. To get the job she lied about her age, saying she was 18. "A couple of times we worked the whole month without a day off." After lengthy work she felt she earned the right to have fun without the strict supervision of her parents.[39]

Another theme that links the diverse remembrances of Mexican American women during World War II was that of Americanization. In general the war had the effect of stimulating patriotism through the common bond of suffering and sacrifice. Beyond that Mexican Americans along with African Americans felt more justified in asserting their rights as U.S. citizens who had fought and worked for the victory over totalitarianism and fascism. Scores of historians have dated the origins of the Civil Rights Movement to 1945 and the return of black and brown service men. This demand for equal treatment and an end to discrimination gained force because of the common affirmation of loyalty to flag and country.

For Mexican American women this meant voting for the first time during the war. It meant buying war bonds, volunteering for work in the USO and Red Cross. It meant gaining a new awareness of the injustice of unequal treatment. Santillán heard one woman say:

"During the war, there was a lessening of discrimination by some public places only because they needed our money, with so many Anglos in the service. After the war, some restaurants, stores, and taverns again refused to serve us on an equal basis with whites. We knew this was totally unfair because we had worked hard to win the war. My generation realized then that we had to do something to change this condition, not only for ourselves but for the next generation."[40]

Mexican American women encountered the color barrier in employment. In many aircraft assembly plants Whites refused to work with African American women, and the employers assigned Mexican American women to work with them. The result was an education in how racism affected everyone and the formation of cross-ethnic and racial friendships. Many Mexican American women reported that they had formed friendships for the first time with non-Mexicanos, and other women.

Elvira Esparza was born and raised in San Diego of Mexican immigrant parents. During the war she worked at Solar making B24s. She got men's wages because of the quality of her work. She was the first Mexican American woman hired at Solar. She remembered men saying that they liked her but couldn't date her because she was Mexican. "They didn't understand that this person because she had brown skin she had a head just like anyone else, she could do the work, sometimes better."

There were other internal battles to be fought. Then as now Mexican American women had to confront negative stereotypes about themselves. During the 1930s Pachuquismo emerged as a cultural expression of some young people and this added new negative views that young women had to combat. Pachuquismo was a style of dress, talk and behavior that openly flaunted conventional Mexican as well as Anglo-American society. Young men during the late 1930s and war years, young Mexican Americans in the Southwest were usually called "Mexicans." The term "Chicano" was almost exclusively used by barrio residents to refer to recently arrived Mexican immigrants.

In the late 1930s, influenced by African Americans and big band culture, the pachucos created a distinctive youth subculture among younger Mexican Americans who were in the process of rebelling against their parent's conventional values. They adopted their own music, language and dress. For the men, the style was to wear a zoot suit, a flamboyant long coat, with baggy pegged pants, a pork pie hat, a long key chain, and shoes with thick soles. For the women, their style was to wear short skirts, tight sweaters, and padded shouldered jackets. They wore their hair in high style and used lots of make up. They called themselves "pachucos" or "pachucas" a word of uncertain origin, but generally referring to United States-born, Mexican American youth who dressed in the style and spoke Calo, a highly inventive slang composed of English and Spanish.[41]

Many Mexican parents were shocked and outraged by the Pachuco style and were especially critical of the pachucas who were considered to represent sexual deviancy and violence. Needless to say the Anglo American press also publicized the pachuca as a recent reincarnation of the Mexican spitfire stereotype. For older Mexican Americans as well as Anglos, the pachuca represented a threat to the traditional roles of women.[42]

Many Mexican American women who were working in the war industries had neither the time nor the opportunity to affect the pachuca style. In San Diego, Marcy Gastelum, who worked as a riveter at Convair thought that the threat of the pachucos was much exaggerated "...The pachucos use to stand in front of the Cornet Theater, but they were harmless: they never hurt anybody, they just wanted to be the little tough guy, show off their clothing and the way they did their hair do... No one was afraid of them... We never heard of any incidents where there was violence, or killings..."[43] There were also some pachucas who worked in the war industries. During the aftermath of the infamous Zoot Suit Riots, pachucas became scapegoats in the Mexican and Anglo press, accusing them of being pot-smoking prostitutes who were cultural traitors.

San Diego native Marcy Gastellum remembered that "A lot of women preferred to be housewives. But many did work because a lot of them had to. A lot of my friends quit school during my high school years to get married, most of them. The first thing on their mind was leaving school, getting married, raising a family and let the man go to work."[44]

Many Mexican American women were already working when the war began, and the war enabled them to get better paying jobs. Mexican American women continued to be employed outside the home after World War II. The traditional expectations of putting family first and of a woman being a mother and wife first did not change because of their wartime experience. Before the war, working had been seen as an extension of their family responsibility, supplementing the male wage earner. During the war, their work was also seen as supplemental, to help win the war and to fill in for the men while they were in the armed forces. During the war many women reported more independence in their social lives despite very restrictive attitudes of their parents. Indeed Americanization, whether in dress, speech, expectations, or culture progressed faster during the war than before. And pressures for Americanization would continue after the war as well. Part of the Americanization process was to begin to expect equal treatment as a U.S. citizen who had contributed to saving American democracy. The women who worked in industries joined the men after the war to work together for social justice.

Los Braceros

One consequence of the war was to formalize the legal immigration of hundreds of thousands of Mexicano workers in the Bracero Program. This program had two consequences for the struggle for civil rights. First, it increased the numbers of Mexicanos who came to live in San Diego and elsewhere because many braceros did not go back to Mexicano and many more crossed into the U.S. without documents because of the unmet demand for farm laborers. Second, the Bracero Program heightened the awareness of labor union activists and others concerned with labor rights about the injustices and exploitation that the program seemed to encourage. The campaign to eliminate the Bracero Program began with Mexican American activists in the 1950s who saw in it a business controlled effort to keep wages low for all Mexican workers.

The program began during World War II when the United States government signed an agreement with the Mexican government to allow for the temporary migration of contract workers. The Bracero Program was conceived of as an emergency wartime measure but was renewed after the war and continued until 1964, providing a huge stimulus for Mexican immigration to the United States. During the Bracero Program almost five million Mexican workers came to the United States. Some scholars suggest that the Bracero Program established the contours of modern Mexican immigration flows and gave rise to the social, political and cultural issues that dominate discourse over immigration in the present.[45]

California's powerful agribusiness sector was involved early on with the recruitment of Mexican labor. A newspaper article in September 1942 read, "The first contingent of Mexican field workers assigned to alleviate U.S. farm labor shortages will be on route to California beet and cotton fields."[46] Locally, San Diego also faced labor shortages that were alleviated by the Bracero Program. San Diego County farmers filed a request for the importation of three hundred Mexican agricultural workers on January 29, 1943. In Oceanside, Harold E. Person chairman of the Corporation's board and one of the county's largest strawberry growers himself asked for fifty workers. Some experts estimated that the local agricultural industry needed as many as 1500 workers late early in 1943.

Legally, the braceros were to be paid a specified minimum wage, receive basic amenities, and to work only at agricultural jobs. But bracero workers complained of violations of wage agreements, substandard living quarters, exorbitant charges for food and clothing, and racist discrimination. On the other hand, growers liked the Bracero Program and constantly lobbied for its continuance. Growers used braceros to break strikes and to lower wages, and they could dispose of them when they were done.[47]

The bracero camps became a special kind of Mexican community in many rural areas of the Southwest. As a camp they were segregated from whites and even from the Mexican American sections of town. Braceros lived in extreme poverty and worked in dangerous conditions. When they ventured outside the camps on week ends they frequently were the victims of racially inspired beatings and robberies. The wages they were paid were low, in comparison to those paid to Mexican American workers; hence, there was some animosity when braceros were used in the place of local workers, or when they were illegally used to break strikes.

The braceros were not entirely complacent in their acceptance of their role. In May 1944, for example, a group of braceros in Idaho went on strike demanding better wages and talk of a bracero strike spread throughout the Pacific Northwest.[48] After the war the Bracero Program continued to be a thorn in the side of organized labor and an example for many Mexican Americans of how their labor as farm workers was devalued. Criticism of the program based on humanitarian and economic grounds led by Ernesto Galarza during the 1950s eventually helped end the program.

While official data and reports abound on the Bracero Program, there is almost nothing about the perspectives of the braceros themselves. How did they experience World War II in the United States? Amazingly there has not yet been a published collection of bracero stories. The account below tells of how one bracero, known only as Don Jesús, remembered his recruitment in Mexico and of his experience in the United States.

A Bracero Remembers: Don Jesus

When we heard that they were contracting workers to go to the United States we all wanted to go. I, however, could not go because I was a soldier in the Mexican army. I was the chauffeur of a general by the name of Anacleto López. But I really needed to go because I had a son that was ill, and I needed the money for his surgery. So I asked the general for permission to allow me to go. Laughing he said, "sure go try your luck" and so I came. The year was 1942. My compadre José Manuel Sandoval and I went to the stadium in Mexico where we were to gather.

There in the middle of a crowd we found ourselves being sprayed with hoses in order to stop a lice infestation. Boy they gave us quite a shower. The next morning the man in charge of the contracts, his name was Guillermo, came by and I explained my situation. I told him I needed to go to the United States because of the illness in my family. He told me to go ahead and go to the United States and that once I was there to write him and he would send my son to Mexico so that he could receive medical attention.

So that happened and we soon found ourselves on our way to the United States. When we crossed the border at Ciudad Juárez, our hearts pounded wildly. We were afraid because we were in a totally strange country, and I had never really done any other kind of work but mine. They took José Manuel and me to Riverside near Colton. It was a long way from Ciudad Juárez to California. During the trip we entertained ourselves by counting the wagons on the trains that were going by with military equipment and personnel on their way to Europe. Sometimes the soldiers would wave at us and we waved back. The trains passed really closed to each other and sometimes the American soldiers would even give us a cigarette.

Colton was the location for the base of a military squadron but the squadron was not there. The men had been shipped out to Europe to fight in the Second World War, and we were housed there. It was nice and clean there, and we even had a Catholic priest. He saw that most of us were Catholic, and he started to build a small shrine so that we could attend mass on Sundays. However, not everyone attended to mass. On Sundays, five buses would also arrive to take us to town to the movies or to drink wine. There was a lot of drinking, and sometimes-even fancy women would come to take the money from the braceros and things would get very wild.

Buses arrived early in the day to take us to work. There was about twenty of us per bus. They would take us to some groves to pick oranges. There, we had to put one ladder on top of the other to reach one or two oranges that were way on top of the trees. Sometimes, however, they would take us to Japanese groves, and there the trees were really short but falling over full of oranges. We were given cutters to cut the oranges; but some, in order to go faster, would just pull the fruit from the tree. I did everything as I was told, and it helped me get along with my boss, and thus I soon became a driver. That was a lot easier, and I even had a helper.

The end of our contract came in 1944, and Rogelio tried to convince me to go to Canada. Work was good there he said. But I had completed my contract and my son had already received the surgery he needed, so I decided to go back to Mexico. If I had wanted to stay, I could have stayed in the United States. The bosses there wanted me to stay because I was also a mechanic. Nevertheless, I had made my decision; I was worried about my son and wanted to go home. Boy, I remember how the trip to the border seemed endless. The train did not seem to go as fast as when they brought us into the United States. That's the way it always seems when one is coming home. We had some hard times, but we had to better ourselves. What could we do? But I had no desire to go back. That was my luck.[49]

Don Jesús did not return to work in the United States after the war but he did return in 1997 to live with his daughter in San Diego where he died on January 2001. A large number of braceros "skipped" their contract and remained in the United States after World War II. Here they married, had families and their children, Mexican Americans and Chicanos became part of an expanding Mexican heritage population in the U.S.

A New Identity
World War II changed the Mexican American people's perception of themselves. George Sánchez, author of Becoming Mexican American, believes that the war resulted in a shift of leadership. Moreover, that there was a "transition from a Mexico-centered leadership to one focused on political and social advancement in American society."[50] Throughout the 1930s, the children of Mexican immigrants matured and came of age. They were citizens of the United States and prophetically in 1940 the U.S. Census

showed that the native born Mexican Americans outnumbered Mexican immigrants. Their new majority was emphasized by World War II where, on both the home front and in battle, Mexican Americans "proved" their patriotism and broke with their immigrant identity. Increasingly they thought of themselves as Americans not Mexicans, at least in a political sense. During and after the war these Mexican Americans were targets of discrimination and racism, and this provoked among their new leadership a renewed commitment to work for civil rights. Ultimately the war changed the larger society too, making the American public more sensitive to the evils of racism. This made it possible for there to be more positive gains in terms of social justice.

Notes

1. The following is taken from a more detailed discussion in Carlos Larralde and Richard Griswold del Castillo, "Luisa Moreno: A Hispanic Civil Rights Leader in San Diego," Journal of San Diego History, Vol. 41, no. 4 (Fall 1995).

2. Interview with Luisa Moreno, April 17, 1971. California's port cities have had a long tradition of canary industries. While in San Francisco, "We visited one of the large canning establishments where California fruits are put up in immense quantities, and where hundreds of hands are employed in the business," wrote D.B. Bennett, A Truth Seeker Around the World: From Hong Kong to New York (New York: D.M. Bennett, Liberal Publishers, 1882), p. 458.

3. Letter of S. Dewberry to C. Larralde, November 22, 1995. Petroleum Administration for War Records, National Federal Archives Pacific Southwest Region, Laguna Nigeul, California. We thank the archivist Suzanne Dewberry for pointing out this source.

4. Ironically, the same conclusion was reported by James Bornemeier, "Study Paints Positive Picture of Immigration," Los Angeles Times, December 11, 1995, p. A 3.

5. McWilliams, The Education of Carey McWilliams (New York: Simon and Schuster, 1978), p 109.

6. Interview with Luisa Moreno, April 17, 1971.

7. Interview with Luisa Moreno, June 2, 1971. See also Carey McWilliams, The New Republic, January 18, 1943.

8. See John Celardo, "Shifting Seas: Racial Integration in the United States Navy, 1941-1945," in Prologue: Quarterly of the National Archives, Fall 1991, pp 230-235.

9. Carey McWilliams, North from Mexico: The Spanish-Speaking People of the United States (New York: Greenwood Press, 1968), p 242.

10. McWilliams, North from Mexico, p 245.

11. McWilliams, North from Mexico, p 246.

12. Interview with Moreno, April 20, 1971.

13. McWilliams, North from Mexico, p 246.

14. McWilliams, The Education of Carey McWilliams, p 113.

15. Garcia, Memories of Chicano History, p 143. For more information about the Zoot Suit riots, see Mauricio Mazon, The Zoot Suit Riots: The Psychology of Symbolic Annihilation (Austin: University of Texas Press, 1984).

16. See also the Los Angeles Times, May 25, June 16, 18, 1943.

17. Port Director Routing Slip, October 23, 1942, Records of Shore Establishments and Naval Districts: Eleventh Naval District, Records of the Commandant's Office, General Correspondence, 1924-1955, National Federal Archives Pacific Southwest Region, Laguna Niguel, California, Box No., 296,

File No., P 8-5, 1942 [2/2]. All other following citations to this source will be cited as only Federal Archives with its dates.

18. Statement of Provost Marshal John E. Hudson regarding La Reine Cafe, August 10, 1942, Federal Archives, Box No., 296, File No., P 8-5, 1942 [1/2].

19. Dan Buckly, Adjutant San Diego Council to Commander 11th Naval District, June 29, 1942, Federal Archives, Box No., 295, File No., P 8-5, 1942 [1/2].

20. "Zoot-Suiters Hunted in S.D.," San Diego Union, June 10, 1943, p. 1.

21. "Zoot-Suiters Hunted in S.D," San Diego Union, June 10, 1943, p 1.

22. Letter from Councilman Charles C. Dail to Admiral David W. Bagley, June 10, 1943, Federal Archives, Box No., 296, File No., P 8-5 [Zoot Suit Gang] 1943, 296.

23. Interview with Moreno, April 20, 1971.

24. Routine slip, January 27, 1994; T. M. Leovy, District Patrol Officer, to Chief of Staff, May 1, 1944, Federal Archives, Box 297, File No., P 8-5 [Zoot Suit Gang] 1944 [½].

25. Interview with Moreno, April 20, 1971.

26. Interview with Luisa Moreno, April 20, 1971.

27. Luisa Moreno to Robert Morris, December 1, 1950, Folder 56, Robert Kenny Collection. Moreno and her husband, Gray Bemis, first went to Chihuahua, Mexico and slowly drove down in their Studebaker to the interior of the country. Later they went to Guatemala to see her family. Again in Folder 56, see the correspondence of Moreno to Kenny.

28. W.F. Kelly, Department of Justice, Immigration and Naturalization Service, Assistant Commissioner, to Robert Kenny, November 1, 1950; Luisa Moreno, "Application for Voluntary Departure," November 1, 1950, Folder 55, Robert Kenny Collection.

29. H.R. Landon, U.S. Department of Justice, Immigration and Naturalization Service, District Director, Los Angeles, Folder 54, Robert Kenny Collection.

30. Rudolfo Acuña, Occupied America: A History of Chicanos, 4th ed. (New York: Longman, 2000), p. 264.

31. Raul Morin, Among the Valiant: Mexican Americans in World War II and Korea (Alhambra, Ca.; Borden Publishing Co., 1966), p. 24.

32. Every community has its aging veterans, but those of World War II are dying off quickly. It is very important that historians collect their stories and histories so that later generations can understand the sacrifices that were made. Professor Maggie Rivas Rodríguez at the University of Texas has organized a project to collect the oral histories of the Latinos and Latinas who lived through World War II many of these stories are available on line at http://

www.utexas.edu/projects/latinoarchives/. See the most recent scholarship on aspects of the war experience in Rivas-Rodriguez, Maggie, ed., Mexican Americans & World War II (Austin: University of Texas Press, 2005).

33. The University of Texas at Austin is attempting to collect the stories of the veterans of World War II in a project directed by Maggie Rivas Rodgriguez, UT School of Journalism. In June of 2000 they sponsored the first ever national conference to bring together veterans and scholars to begin to assemble the national story of Mexican Americans during World War II. For additional information on this project visit the web site http://www.utexas. edu/projects/latinoarchives/. At this site you can also read their Narratives publication which contains stories of Mexican American G.I.s during the war.

34. Oral interviews by Richard Griswold del Castillo, February 23, 1993.

35. Richard Santillan, Rosita the Riveter: Midwest Mexican American Women During World War II, 1941-1945, Perspectives in Mexican American Studies, Vol. 2 (1989), p. 138.

36. Solis Interviews, p. 55.

37. Solis Interviews, p. 70.

38. Santiago Solis interviews, SDSU Special Collections, Rosita the Riveter.

39. Solis interviews.

40. Santillan, p. 137.

41. The classic critique of the Pachuqismo appears in Octavio Paz, The Lambrynth of Solitude: Life and Thought in Mexico (New York, 1961), Ch. 1; For contemporary interpretations of this phenomenon see Beatrice Griffith, American Me (Boston, 1948), 15-28; George I. Sanchez, "Pachucos in the Making," Common Ground, IV, (Autumn, 1943), 13-20; Ruth D. Tuck, Not With the Fist: Mexican-Americans in a Southwest City (New York, 1974); also Ralph H. Turner and Samuel J. Surace, "Zoot-Suiters and Mexicans: Symbols in Crowd Behavior," American Journal of Sociology, 62, (1956), 14-24.

42. See Elizabeth Escovedo's discussion of this pp. 34-35.

43. Solis, p. 64.

44. Solis, p. 61.

45. David Gutierrez, Between Two Worlds Mexican Immigrants in the United States. (Scholarly Resources Inc. 1996), p. I.

46. "Mexican Labor Due Soon in California," San Diego Union Tribune, September 18, 1942, p.10.

47. "Farmers to ask for 300 Mexicans" San Diego Union Tribune, Jan 29, 1943, p. 10.; Ronald Takaki, Double Victory: Multicultural History of America in World War II (New York: Little, Brown and Co., 2000), p. 96.

48. Ronald Takaki, Double Victory: Multicultural History of America in World War II (New York: Little, Brown and Co., 2000), p. 96.

49. Oral interview courtesy of Rodolfo Jacobo, SDSU.

50. George I. Sanchez, Becoming Mexican American: Ethnicity, Culture, and Identity in Chicano Los Angeles, 1900-1945 (New York: Oxford University Press, 1993), p. 274.

10

A Brief History of Labor, Immigration, and Anti-Immigrant Municipal Policies in San Diego's North County

Henry Lesperance

October 29, Escondido, California, 2017. The feelings in the Latino community in North County are one of great uncertainty. The change in the rhetoric of the president that now has rescinded the DACA program coupled with the building of a bigger U.S./MEX. Border, continues to perpetuate an atmosphere of fear for many. Political tensions are reverberating through the social atmosphere that manifests every day in grocery stores, classrooms, and work. Racist comments are more commonplace in this anti-immigrant politics and society. The manifestations of the anti-immigrant rhetoric that travels not only through the mass media but through history continue to influence our present. As we will explore in this paper, these fears and uncertainties are not particular to the present we live, but have past trajectories that continue to influence people and ideas today. Examining some of the forces that have shaped how we see our present today is the first step in exploring strategies and thinking of alliances to change the course of our future, as we attempt to spark these conversations with this paper. However, conceptualizing the influence of the past in the present is more than just an intellectual exercise but should also be an exercise of the heart, and learning how to better communicate with each other in order to work in unity. In this paper we focus in large part on a city in North Country San Diego as a case study of all these forces coming together.

Escondido in Spanish means hidden. But over the past decades the 'hidden' City located in northern San Diego County has captured national attention by contributing through its municipal policies to the national immigration debate. In 2006, Escondido, along with several other cities in the nation, stepped into the spotlight by passing legislation to ban home and apartment rentals to undocumented immigrants.

Additionally, Escondido has also developed unprecedented partnerships with federal immigration and custom enforcement officials who now collaborate in the arrests of illegal immigrants with past criminal records. This paper identifies the different ways in which Escondido has fueled the current national immigration debate by enacting legislation aimed to deter immigration and/or expel those already living in the city.

Historically anti-immigration sentiment has been present throughout different regions of San Diego County, influencing municipal legislation. This paper will identify some of these surges of anti-immigrant sentiment in San Diego and will seek to reveal some of the forces driving them.

The City of Escondido is located forty-five miles north of the U.S. /MEX border and eighteen miles east of the California coast. Located twenty-two miles north of San Diego, Escondido was first settled in 1890 and was developed around the agricultural sector. Due to a dearth of water in the region during the early part of the 20th century grapes became the crop of preference. As water gradually became supplied to the region, citrus and avocados replaced the vineyards.

The continuous economic development of the region brought about a steady population growth. From 1890 to 1950 the city went from having 541 residents to 6,540. During the second half of the 20th century citrus production declined and industry and retail gained importance. During the 1950s Escondido's population amounted to 6,540 and a decade later in 1960 this would rise to 18,107. The linking of Escondido to San Diego through new highway 395 coupled with a growing industry made the city more noticeable and appealing for people looking for a place to call home.[1] Today the population of Escondido is approximately 144,000 with half of the population of Hispanic descent. (Figure 1.1)

Escondido like other neighboring cities in the county of San

Diego historically attracted many immigrant laborers looking for work. The demand for cheap labor lured many Mexican immigrants that settled throughout different pockets of San Diego County. This

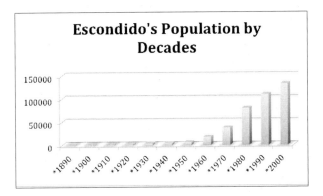

Figure 1.1

often resulted in cultural collision. The resentment that started to take place between Mexicans and Anglos can be traced back to the 1830s when Anglos doing commerce off the coast of California viewed Mexicans living there as lazy, dirty, and Catholic.

The U.S. incorporation of the southwestern states in 1848 through the Treaty of Guadalupe Hidalgo meant these feelings of racial superiority would continue and clash with Native American and Mexican communities already settled in the region.[2] As time progressed, so did racial tension. In the case of San Diego, the 1920s witnessed an emergence of the Ku Klux Klan, which was an organization that in the nineteenth century targeted newly freed slaves in the South.

Now the Klan found a new enemy in the southwestern United States. A Klan member declared that the organization never intimidated any ethnic groups while at the same time admitting that their main purpose was "chasing the wetbacks across the border."[3] The Klan presented themselves as defenders of Christian morality and law enforcement. They also were chosen to be members of grand juries where they were able to influence district attorneys.[4] Many of the cases involved great injustices against minorities.

Tensions in San Diego County reached an all-time high during the 1930s with the onset of the Great Depression. Mercedes Acasan

Garcia an expatriate of the Mexican revolution living in San Diego witnessed Mexicans being lynched, dragged, whipped, and burned.[5] Victims testimonies reveal that Mexican bodies were occasionally discovered dead, sometimes disfigured by torture among the citrus orchards in suburban San Diego and in its rural areas.[6]

During this same time period the school board in the neighboring of Lemon Grove enacted an ordinance to segregate Mexican children from attending school with Anglo children. The deliberations to segregate the Mexican children revealed racial tensions between Anglos and Mexicans. The school board based its decision on testimony from the Anglo community that promoted the premises that Mexican children held back the Anglo children, started trouble, had language problems and spread diseases. They also concluded that they were probably illegal anyway. In the now well-known court decision, *Roberto Alvarez v. The Board of Trustees of the Lemon Grove School District*, the segregation order was ruled unconstitutional.

Despite the hostile environment immigrants faced upon their arrival in San Diego, many were lured to work in California's powerful agribusiness sector. The scarcity of labor and low wages during World War II threatened the stability of several economic sectors in the United States.

The agricultural sector came to suffer significant labor shortage as a consequence of Americans joining the Armed Forces, Japanese-Americans being placed into internment camps, and more attractive occupations in urban manufacturing plants. But Agricultural growers became alarmed by the political leverage that union organizers could gain so they turned to Mexico and discussed the possibility of importing laborers.[7] The solution reached by Mexico, the United States and growers was temporary labor in the form of the Bracero Program.

Locally, San Diego also faced labor shortages that were alleviated by the Bracero Program. Early in the program on January 29, 1943 San Diego County farmers filed a request for the importation of three hundred Mexican agricultural workers to alleviate the labor shortages.

Anti-immigrant sentiment evolved in conjunction with, and in opposition to, the need for cheap immigrant manual labor. For some it was through fear tactics that cheap manual labor was vilified in value in order to help California's growing agriculture.

In the 1980s Louis Hock, Professor of Visual Arts at UCSD, directed a documentary, The Mexican Tapes, in which he intimately records the lives of two undocumented families living in Solana Beach. The film explored the different impacts that living outside the law had on these Mexican families. Within the film one can find a sequence in which a dozen young kids are running and playing in a parking lot of an apartment complex. What appears to be an everyday scene of kids playing and having fun reveals to us instead a much more complex and somber social phenomena unfolding.

The kids are playing a game called 'la migra.' The game consisted of choosing certain kids to act as border patrol agents while the others hide and escape desperately from them. This game was more than a kid's game; the kids were subconsciously re-enacting the fears that their parents live every day when the 'migra' arrived to the apartment complex checking for identifications.

The anti-immigrant sentiment we hear resonate in the voices of San Diegans today embodies in part the historical legacy that has shaped it; a legacy that has depicted immigrants as unassimilable, dirty, disease-carrying, and culturally and biologically unsuitable, and more recently a burden to the state. Escondido, carrying that lingering historical baggage,[8] passed a City ordinance to ban property rental to any suspected undocumented immigrant in 2006.

Escondido's Councilwoman Waldron explained that immigrants hurt the community in many ways, including by exposing school children to diseases like tuberculosis and leprosy.[9] Under Escondido's ordinance persons and businesses that owned dwelling units were prohibited from "harbor[ing] an illegal alien in the dwelling unit, known or in reckless disregard of the fact that an alien has come, entered, or remains in the United States in violation of law."

The city enabled city officials, businesses, and even individual residents to enforce the ordinance by filling a written complaint form. In this sense it promoted a form of vigilantism that would help greatly discredit the city of Escondido. The content of the ordinance was predominantly based on a report by City Attorney Jeffrey Epp, which cited the presence of undocumented immigrants as a significant cause in the deterioration of the "overall appearance and living conditions in neighborhoods" in the City. The ordinance started with a list of findings:

> "The harboring of illegal aliens in dwelling units in the City, and crime committed by illegal aliens harm the health, safety, and welfare of legal residents in the City.....The regulations of the city regarding housing...often depend on reporting by residents and neighbors [of]...unlawful conditions....Because illegal aliens do not wish to call to their attention to their presence, such individuals are less likely to report such conditions."[10]

The ordinance also echoed a growing dissatisfaction by many leaders of small cities toward the federal government and it called for municipal policies that would be enforced by vigilantes in order to deter the flow of undocumented immigrants into the City. As one Pennsylvania mayor lamented, "Small cities can no longer sit back and wait for the federal government do something."[11]

Adding to this feeling, Escondido's ordinance stated "The state and federal government lack the resources to properly protect the citizens of the City of Escondido from the adverse effects of the harboring of illegal aliens, and the criminal activities of some illegal aliens." Through its ordinance Escondido sought to remedy the concerns many Americans felt over the federal government's inability to keep illegal immigrants out;[12] concerns that circulated at a national and municipal level over a misconception that the federal government was not doing enough to keep immigrants out.[13] However when analyzed more closely one can see the federal government has been doing "its job."

Since 1993 the U.S. government has been seriously committed to reducing the flow of unauthorized immigration from Mexico through border enforcement. In San Diego's border sector operation

"Gatekeeper" was implemented in 1994. As a result of this heightened federal security 75 miles of sturdy metal fencing were erected to prevent crossings in urban areas where illegal entry was most visible.

In addition, there was a remarkable increase in the sophistication of surveillance and apprehension technology, including remote video surveillance systems, infrared monitors, seismic sensors that can detect footsteps, helicopters, unmanned aerial vehicles (drones), and computerized databases. The number of Border Patrol agents in the U.S./MEX border rose from 3,965 in September 1993 to 11,106 in September 2005, and total spending on border enforcement grew six-fold during this period.[14]

Assuming the federal government is at fault for the unprecedented influx of migrants to the United States, why are the push-factors influencing immigrants to make the decision to come to the United States even in light of the risks? For many, what needs to be challenged is not whether the federal government is doing enough but whether their strategy is effective to begin with.

The rental bans would meet swift legal challenges by local landlords, immigrants, and civil rights groups who claimed the ban was unconstitutional and in violation of various state and federal laws. Primarily the plaintiffs argued that regulating immigration is a federal duty, not a state or municipal responsibility. According to Kai Bartolomeo, an attorney that studied this case, "under mounting fiscal pressure and faced with the dim hope of success, Escondido stipulated to a permanent injunction of the rental ban, thereby ending its stint in local legislative activism."[15]

Yet, the end of the rental ban would not mean the end of the community's anti-immigrant sentiment, a sentiment that has become institutionalized through law enforcement activities that for many seek to intimidate Hispanic/Latino immigrants living in San Diego's north county.

Over the years local and federal law enforcement agencies in San Diego have become more sophisticated and skilled at circumventing these legal strictures in order to carry out their own agendas. A clear example of this can be seen in America's internal checkpoints.

Over the years internal checkpoints through highly transited highways have become a common sight for many residents of San Diego. Administered by (CBS) the U.S. Customs and Border Protection agency, these checkpoints operate inside U.S. territory.[16]

San Diego is controlled by the Border Patrol at two main interior traffic checkpoints, Temecula and San Clemente, in addition to tactical checkpoints on different highways close to the border's main ports of entry, on the U.S. /MEX San Diego border sector.[17]

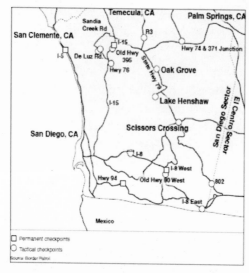

Figure 1.2

What is troubling is that these internal checkpoints can be placed up to 100 miles north of the border ultimately affecting two-thirds of the U.S. population.[18] In San Diego these internal checkpoints are meeting legal challenges by concerned citizens that feel their Fourth Amendment rights are being violated. (Figure 1.2)

Such was the case of San Diegan resident Pastor Steven Anderson who was stopped at a checkpoint where he declined to cooperate leading to his violent detention. Following the footsteps of Pastor Steven there has been a steady rise of anti-checkpoint activism on YouTube that seeks to challenge the constitutionality of these checkpoints.[19]

In the court case Martinez-Fuerte, the court declared, "We have held that checkpoint searches constitutional only if justified

by consent or probable cause to search."[20] Many commuters in
San Diego are still unaware they do not have to comply with the
Border Patrol's questioning. Yet, in spite of this growing checkpoint
activism there are still mixed feelings in the community about these
internal practices.

In a survey conducted as part of this project at Palomar College
in San Marcos (2014), half of the sample, 42 of 87 people, did not
find a problem with the current internal immigrant checkpoints
nor an increase in their operations, like the case of San Clemente.
This divide suggests that tensions over the legitimacy of internal
checkpoints are still being debated, negotiated, and challenged
in San Diego. (Figure 1.3) It should be noted that current policy
heavily relies on profiling.

In 2010 Escondido's Police Department initiated partnerships
with Immigration and Customs Enforcement officials. Escondido
Police Chief Jim Maher saw this collaboration by his department
with federal officials as a national model for law enforcement

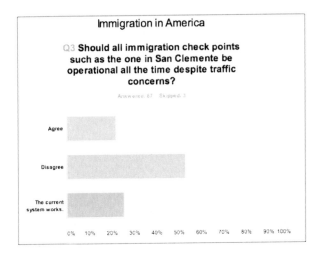

Figure 1.3

agencies. As a result, Escondido implemented several random
daytime blockades on the grounds of verifying driver's licenses and
auto insurance.

These police checkpoints have been highly criticized for

intimidating and targeting undocumented migrants. However, Escondido's Chief argues these allegations are incorrect. He states, "America has enough of its own criminals; we really don't need criminals from another country..." And he went on to explain that, "most of the tips they get about criminal activity come from members of those immigrant communities."[21] He further suggested that Latinos tend to accept and aid police enforcement on these matters.

Our survey indicates some level of truth to that comment. As mentioned before on the issue of internal checkpoints, the concerns on the topics are divided. One lesson learned in this study is contrary to the hypothesis that local Latinos/or Hispanics share similar political views on immigration policy. Historically, many Latinos oppose illegal immigration seeing it as the root of discrimination affecting them. This appears to be the case in San Diego.

Needless to say, there is a concern by local activist who argue these checkpoints constitute a form of racial profiling since they disproportionately affect illegal immigrants that happen to be of Latino/Hispanic origin, many of whom are barred from the state from obtaining driver's licenses.[22]

Moreover, many of these law enforcement operations in north county target regions with a higher propensity of Latino inhabitants, which people in North County identify as a form of racial profiling. (Figure 1.4) In addition, Escondido's checkpoints alone garnered more than $1 million a year, which creates suspicion on whether these checkpoints are being implemented for the money they are able to generate.[23]

In conclusion, historically anti-immigrant municipal policies in San Diego's North County have originated simultaneously with the demand for cheap immigrant labor to the United States. This appears to be particularly true in San Diego County. This anti-immigrant sentiment has fueled polices meant to deter immigration by projecting fear onto these immigrants.

This historical resentment has materialized in federal and municipal policies meant to regulate the influx of migrants to the United States creating tension in these communities. With the recent

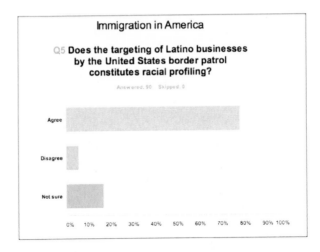

Figure 1.4

influx of Central American immigration, tensions have increased. Protest in local towns such a Murrieta, California some thirty miles from Escondido in Riverside County have made the national news. There is now talk about the Minutemen group patrolling the border as they have in the past when similar tension arose.

Notes

1. http://www.escondidohistory.org/history_center_009.htm.

2. Mexicanos, Second Edition: A History of Mexicans in the United States, Manuel G. Gonzales.

3. The K.K.K. in San Diego was formed about 1922. See Constitution and Rituals, 1927-1928, Mss 203, V. Wayne Kenaston Papers, San Diego Historical Society, Research Archives, Box 1, File 1, Item 3, hereafter KKK, SDHC. For California Klan activities see, Ed Cray, Chief Justice: A Biography of Earl Warren (New York: Simon and Schuster, 1997), 52-54, 56-57.

4. The Klan and other radical groups flourished in Southern California. See the Los Angeles Times, April 23, 30, 1922; Santa Ana Register, May 1, 1922; Anaheim Bulletin, December 31, 1924, June 4 and November 16, 1925; La Habra Star, July 2, 1924; Balboa Times, January 27, 1927.

5. Garcia Interview, June 14, 1979. In F 1, Garcia Papers, there is a thank you note from Mrs. Hamilton "for Coming." Apparently, Garcia did some extra chores for her.

6. Kenaston, Jr., 8.

7. Deborah Cohen, Braceros: Migrant Citizens and Transnational Subjects in the Postwar United States and Mexico (University of North Carolina Press, 2011), 22.

8. A City that has only elected two Latinos to the City Council in its 124 years.

9. Targeting Landlords Who Rent to Illegal Immigrants by Amy Isackson October 21, 2006.

10. Immigration and The Constitutionality of Local Self-Help: Escondido's Undocumented Immigrant Rental Ban. Kai Bartolomeo.

11. Bartolomeo, 866.

12. In 2006 Time Magazine poll, 82% of those surveyed felt that the federal government was not doing enough along its boarders to keep illegal immigrants out.

14. Impacts of Border Enforcement on Mexican Migration The View From Sending Communities. Edited by Wayne A. Cornelius and Jessica M. Lewis.

15. Bartolomeo, 856.

16. America's Internal Checkpoints, Wes Kimbell, Dec 28, 2013.

18. America's Internal Checkpoints, Wes Kimbell, Dec 28, 2013.

19. Through thousands of uploaded videos can be found on YouTube.

20. Kimbell, 9.

21. Escondido Chief Explains City's Illegal Immigration Policy, by Mathew T Hall. June 26, 2012.

22. Vista: Trial For Two Men Arrested at Escondido Checkpoint Will go Forward, By Edward Sifuentes, July 8, 2011.

23. Escondido Checkpoint Story by The Numbers, By Logan Jenkins
March 13, 2012.

11

Examining the Experiences of Undocumented College Students: Walking the Known and Unknown Lived Spaces

Rodolfo Jacobo & Alberto M. Ochoa

Abstract

This article examines the experiences of undocumented students attending college, and the trauma they live on a daily basis. A conceptual framework is provided for examining the tensions experienced by undocumented students. Using qualitative mixed methods, as an exploratory study, undocumented college students identified eight themes that uncover the journey they travel in their desire to improve their life possibilities in unauthorized societal space.

Introduction

The criminalization and virtual internment of undocumented youth in the United States is the result of historical prejudice and a failed immigration policy that condemns youth into a lifetime of uncertainty (Chavez, 1991; Pizarro, 2005, Acuña, 2007). The impact of past injustices and a failed immigration policy is painfully clear in K-12 schools and colleges where undocumented students live in constant fear of their status been disclosed and where despite their educational success, their dreams and professional objectives are currently futureless (Olivas, 2004; Rincon, 2008).

Sources estimate that there are some two million undocumented children in schools in the United States with an estimated 65,000 graduating from high school every year with no more than 5%

attending college (Horwedel, 2006; CNNU.S., 2009). Existing law established by the Supreme Court case Plyler vs. Doe in 1982 gives undocumented immigrant students the right to a K-12 education under the 14th amendment. The court, however, never extended that right to higher levels of education (Olivas, 2004; Horwedel, 2006).

Over the years both federal and state court's decisions have not only limited the undocumented students by capping their education but also produced a bitter debate throughout the United States on the issue of access to higher education and undocumented students. Horwedel (2006) and the UCLA Center for Labor Research and Education (2007) have estimated that there are some 50,000 undocumented college age students in United States colleges, with over one-third living in California. Given the data, we may deduce that Mexican youth are highly represented in this group (Diaz-Strong, Luna-Duarte, Meiners, & Valentin, 2010). For undocumented students the main issues of access to higher education are both legal and financial. Passel and Cohn (2009) also documents that at least 39% of undocumented students live below the federal poverty line and 40% lower than legal immigrant families.

Overview of the Literature

The debate over the rights of immigrants, especially from Mexico is not new. The educational rights of Mexican origin children in general, and of the undocumented in particular have historically been at the center of the debate (Chavez, 1991; Zinn, 2003). A clear pattern of discrimination against the Mexican origin population and the marginalization of their children are historically evident (Zinn, 2003; Acuña, 2007). Thus, important questions for understanding the present conditions facing undocumented Latino immigrants are: What has been the historical anti-Mexican sentiment and U.S. immigration policy? and, how have immigration policies hinder undocumented college age (UCA) students' access to higher education?

The vast majority of UCA students did not make the personal choice to enter illicitly into the country (Chavez, 1991; Zinn, 2003). Instead, they were caught in the historically complex web of American immigration policy. Legal and undocumented immigration from Mexico to the United States has been constant for over one hundred years, recurrently triggered by American appetite for inexpensive labor. Along with the demand for labor came a failure to implement a viable and just immigration policy that meets the labor demands of the nation and in providing post secondary education, while keeping immigrants and their families together (Jacobo, 2006; Acuña, 2007; Diaz-Strong, et al. 2010).

More recently the Amnesty Act of 1986, known as the Immigration Reform and Control Act of 1986 (IRCA), not only proved the need to secure foreign labor but also created much of the turmoil we are currently experiencing (Diaz-Strong, et al., 2010). The law granted amnesty to undocumented immigrants who entered the U.S before January 1st 1982, and resided here. While the law placed some two million people on a path to citizenship it did little to rapidly unite families, thus creating a wave of unauthorized children into the United States. These children eventually went to school and were the target of Proposition 187 in California. The goal of Proposition 187 was to bar undocumented immigrants from receiving social services, health care and public education, under the SAVE OUR STATE initiative. The law was overturned by federal courts but not without adding to the legacy of anti-immigrant sentiment in the United States (Acuña, 2007). A consequence of the Amnesty Act was the influx of undocumented children to the United States to be with their families with the hope that one day the laws would change (Diaz-Strong, et al., 2010). In this regard the present continues like the past.

Today, when undocumented children enter school, they face a world of uncertainty and fear. During their high school years as they apply for work and college they must confront the reality that they are unauthorized in the United States and could very well be detained and deported. For many UCA students the years can go by without ever being detained. Nevertheless, they consistently struggle having to negotiate their living spaces and schooling (Soja, 2007). They live shadowed lives.

While studies on undocumented youth, data suggest that they

are under severe emotional strain and trauma (Capps, Chundy, & Santos, 2007). They suffer from extreme isolation, are vulnerable, and easily exploited. Students tend to live in fear and shame, feelings that are often fueled by political discourse and biased media in the United States (Diaz-Strong, et al., 2010; Jacobo, 2010). The psychological stress experienced by undocumented youth builds up as they enter high school and college. The recent defeat of immigration reform at the federal level, including the Dream Act in 2010, further alienated UCA students as their legal and academic status continues to be unresolved. The proposed Dream Act of 2010 was proposed federal legislation that would grant high school students with good academic standing legal status in the United States. Legal status would also be extended to undocumented immigrants of good moral character who wanted to serve in the armed forces or attend college.

The support and resistance toward accessing higher education for UCA students can be seen in the conditions placed upon them by states in our nation. Since 2001, 11 states have passed laws that allow undocumented students to qualify for in-state tuition in public universities in their state of residence (California, Illinois, Kansas, Nebraska, New Mexico, New York, Oklahoma, Texas, Utah, Washington, and Wisconsin) under the criteria that they need to have attended for at least three years and graduated from a high school in their state of residence. This has created uproar in many American communities who see such laws as pandering to undocumented students. Against such access, since 2006, Arizona, Alabama, Colorado, Georgia, Missouri, and Oklahoma, North and South Carolina, have voted against in-state tuition for undocumented students or banning undocumented students from attending (Frum, 2007; Diaz, et al., 2010). More recent studies of UCA students have began to document the path and challenges faced by UCA students, specifically with regard to college persistence (Muñoz & Maldonado, 2010), their resiliency (Perez, Espinoza, Ramos, Coronado & Cortez, 2009), their struggle for opportunity (Perez-Huber, Malagon & Solorzano, 2009), and the barriers of ideological divide in human dignity and equality (Rincon, 2008).

Framework for Framing the Experiences of Undocumented College Students

To examine the pressures and social-psychological forces that shape the daily-lived experiences and negotiated spaces of UCA students pursuing higher education, a conceptual framework developed by Jacobo and Ochoa (Jacobo, 2010) is provided. The framework in Figure 1 emerged from our work with K-12 Southwest school districts near the Mexican border, living the presence of the Border Patrol in border communities, through our engagement in higher education institutions and direct interaction with college aged undocumented students in our courses. Also supporting the framework is critical theory (McLaren, 1997; Kincheloe, 2008) that is concerned with issues of power, justice, and specifically diverse forms of oppression. Critical theory as a perspective searches for new theoretical insights and interconnected ways of understanding power and oppression and the way they shape everyday life and human experience (Kincholoe, 2008, p. 49). In the context of one's legal status in a global economy the struggle of contesting one's residency is both a political, psychological, and social struggle (Aronowitz, 2003). Figure 1 illustrates two dimensions and four quadrants that allows one to reflect on how undocumented college students navigate their lived spaces on a daily basis. The first dimension (vertical) consists of explicit and implicit modes of behavior—behaviors that are seen by others who interact with the individual (explicit) and behaviors that are not see by others (implicit). The second dimension (horizontal) is the legal status of the individual or the unauthorized status of the person living in the United States. The legal dimension is expressed from a legal continuum—at one end are unauthorized and unregulated social policies where the individual is able to negotiate his/her lived space by being very familiar of his/her surroundings. At the other end are unauthorized and regulated social policies, where the individual in public spaces runs the risk of being apprehended for not having legal documentation.

To examine the lived spaces of undocumented youth/students living in the U.S., the framework offers four quadrants of analysis. In the *quadrant I Ambivalence* (unauthorized and unregulated legal social policy and explicit lived space) the undocumented youth experiences incomprehension, a state of living in a part of the community where s/he feels familiar and has a high degree of awareness of civic behavior while understanding his/her legal status and interacting in low risk social activities that are part of the daily social dynamics of the community. S/he while experiencing a sense of "zone of comfort" in the community, nevertheless has the constant worry or trauma of not being "legal" and living under stress. Involvement in church activities or family gatherings at a park are enjoyed but not without the fear of legal ramifications. S/he lives in a space of ambivalence (Miao, Esses, & Bell, 2000).

Under the *quadrant II Encapsulated* (unauthorized and unregulated legal social policy and implicit lived space) the undocumented youth experiences encapsulation, a state of constant fear only known to him/her or an intimate other. The youth is constantly aware that s/he must always be on the lookout and negotiating the lived spaces that offer him/her a sense of control. Trauma under quadrant II is expressed as an emotional distress. Teachers and peers are unaware of a student's legal status in an implicit lived space. Therefore, a school field-trip designed to be educational and fun can elicit feelings of fear and apprehension in the unauthorized student as legal and physical barriers may be present. S/he lives in a space of encapsulation (Clark, Aaron, & Beck 2009).

Under *quadrant III Dissonance* (unauthorized and regulated legal social policy and implicit lived space) the undocumented youth experiences dissonance, a state of living in trauma and out of harmony within the community and within the self. The inability to share the legal status with others creates conflict, a feeling of helplessness, and depression. A simple college night out with friends to establishments that require a driver's license for identification becomes an emotional test for unauthorized individuals. S/he lives in a space of dissonance (Goldsmith, Barlow, & Freyd, 2004).

Under *quadrant IV Rejection* (unauthorized and regulated legal social policy and explicit lived space) the undocumented youth experiences rejection, a state of living outside of the community where he/she feels excluded from civic participation. In this quadrant, the individual suffers the trauma of having no legal assurance and exclusion from social integration and civil social identity. Not being able to take part in the political process during this historic period serves as an example of such exclusion from social and civic integration. S/he lives in a space of rejection (Pehrson, Brown, & Zagefka, 2009).

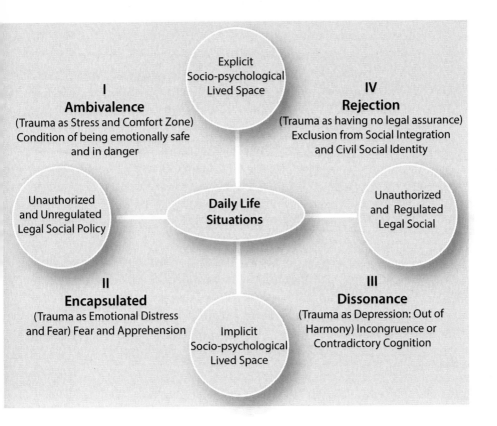

Figure 1. Framework for understanding the lived spaces of unauthorized youth.

Approach

Qualitative mixed methods were used in ascertaining the concerns and issues faced by UCA students (Denzin & Lincoln, 2000). Specifically a three-phase approach was taken. The first phase consisted of submitting an Institutional Research Board (IRB) proposal to a CSU university to identify a pool of UCA students enrolled in a college education in the community college and/or the CSU systems of California. Upon receiving IRB approval that involved participant consent, recruitment process, structured interview processes, protocols on data collection, a pool of over 30 candidates were identified and four selected for this exploratory study. All were from Mexico, one male (Roque) and three females (Maria & Brenda, & Norma), two attending a community college and two in a four-year college (CSU). All four entered the U.S. unauthorized between the ages of 2 to 5 years old. The second phase consisted of using case study methodology that included interviews, autobiographies, and face-to-face meetings using a focus group approach. Four undocumented college students were invited to participate in an open-ended discussion on their lived experiences as UCA students. A three-hour discussion was recorded with their permission for coding their opinions and perspectives and in the focus group used a fictitious nickname. The conversations with the four participants were analyzed to identify salient themes. The themes were shared with the UCA students on different dates for accuracy and content validity. The third phase was an interactive process of data analysis consisting of data content analysis, data display, data coding, data reduction, and generation of themes and thematic interpretation.

Examining the Experiences of Unauthorized College Aged Students

Eight themes were derived from the interviews and focus group discussion, with each pointing to a social-psychological force that shape the daily-lived experiences of UCA students. These themes are: Identity, Membership, Micro-Aggressions, Trauma, Adaptability, Pragmatism - Resiliency, Agency, Family, and Structural Violence.

In some direct or indirect form the themes correlated with all of the four concepts that described the psychological feelings of the participants as they described how they navigate their regulated and unregulated lived space, namely living in Ambivalence, Encapsulation, Dissonance, and Rejection. A brief discussion of each theme as expressed by selected UCA students provides a glimpse of their identified thematic tensions (ambivalence, encapsulation, dissonance, rejection) that they negotiate on a daily basis:

1. In reference to the Identity theme, consider not having any legal form of identification granting access to credit, travel, or simply driving from point A to B. Travel and driving has become heavily politicized in the United States in recent years with numerous states denying the unauthorized population a driver's license and check points on the road. The impact of not having a driver's license goes far beyond not being able to drive a vehicle. In a culture were a driver's license has become consistent with identity, to be denied one is analogous to one's legal existence.

Maria tells of her ordeal with identity and belonging after experiencing a traumatizing event that involved the San Diego police department. While she negotiated her legal status throughout her life it was a specific episode with police and the lack of a driver's license that made her confront the reality of regulated social policy and the issue of identity.

I had never been treated like a criminal. This incident was a huge wakeup call for me. Yes, I did come to this country illegally but I was never treated like I was. For the first time in my life, I felt what it's like to be seen different in someone else's eyes because I was not born in the United States.

The issues of legality and identity can have more perverse effects. Brenda commented of the recurrent reminder of her legal status and identity at work by her boss:

I decided to confront the owner one day and ask him why I was not getting paid all the hours that I had worked. He replied, "You have no right to tell me what to pay you because you are an illegal immigrant and if you don't like it I can fire you." I felt so terrible that day and I went home crying, but I did not let my mom see me or know why I was crying.

2. Membership was not only described at the macro-level as having no voice in the society, but also at the micro-level. The impact of not having a legal document prevents UCA students from a fundamental component of the American economy such as obtaining credit, having a passport to travel or a driver's license, or simply accessing a gym membership. While the denial of membership to a gym might appear to some as insignificant. Such rejection, however, goes beyond the seeking of fitness. Membership denial to a gym based on the lack of valid forms of identification transcends into the realms of inclusive and exclusionary policy in a society. In other words, who can become a member of a group, and how can the privilege of membership be proven resides in one's ability to have legal identification. In the United States a social security number or the preferred form of identification of membership is a requirement that UCA students do not possess. In the case of Roque, he states:

I was able to get a part-time job when I graduated high school. The interview was one of the most nerve-racking situations I have ever been in since I had no legal documentation. While I worked I was always scared to mess up on the job in any way, because I thought that would be enough reason to review my background and possibly discover that I'm illegal. Fortunately I was able to work and save money for college.

3. Micro-aggressions as a theme was expressed as being consistently on the alert at every hour of the day given one's unauthorized status in the United States. Micro-aggressions are psychological, social, political, economic acts that go unrecognized by the general public. UCA student's alertness, however, is not without consequences. The reality of living always vigilant of

their surroundings, negotiating acts of disrespect and aggression, adapting to restrictions by legal conditions, and negotiating the conflict produced by their legal status generates trauma, fear, and emotional stress (dissonance, rejection). To respond to the daily psychological trauma (ambivalence, encapsulation, dissonance, rejection) Latino UCA students create an array of coping skills that positively or negatively confronts complex situations produced by their unauthorized status. Brenda personalizes the issues of micro-aggressions in her own social circle. She survives by being silent while enduring the emotional pain.

All my life I have heard people use words that caused me to feel uncomfortable and have reduced my humanity. At work for example, when I worked at a restaurant or even with the family members of my ex-boyfriend I would hear people use the word "wetback" when they talked about Mexican immigrants. I felt anger but also helpless unable to say anything.

The exposure to micro aggressions, in a society that while seeing itself as humanitarian and the product of an immigrant experience is nativist and detached. Prejudice and fear permeate and are diluted through public commentary and the local and national media.

4. Trauma, described as living always wary of one's surroundings, can be emotionally draining and psychologically distressing. Various types of psychological trauma impact how undocumented youth negotiate their daily-lived situations. Trauma is defined from a psychological perspective as the feeling of fear, stress, depression, exclusion and apprehension as a result of having unauthorized legal status.

In the case of Norma, apprehension, deportation, and family separation by immigration authorities generated conditions of trauma or post-traumatic disorder syndrome. Norma recalls the emotional depression she suffered when her mother was taken to a women's prison. Norma's grades in college dropped, as did her overall health when ICE arrested her mother. She recounts.

> In January of 2007 my mother received a letter from the district attorney's office stating she was being charged with three felonies because she used false documentation to obtain a job. Thereafter a series of never-ending court appearances proceeded. We had to get a lawyer, who ended up taking advantage of us. He did nothing to help my mother instead his actions landed her in jail one more time, but this time for nearly a month in late August of this year. It has been a horrible nightmare.

The participants in the focus group expressed how they all had been impacted emotionally by their legal status in the United States. At one time or another all have experienced the fear of being apprehended and deported. Two had vivid memories of crossing the border (ages 4 and 5) and of loved ones being apprehended. Deportation for them would mean the end of all their hard work, dreams and aspirations. It would mean the separation from their family and forceful adaptation to a country that while they were born there, they know little about.

5. Adaptability was identified as negotiating unauthorized environments. The UCA students pointed out the irony that while expressing love for their country of birth if deported would feel "alien" in Mexico. Their lives since childhood have been formed in the United States. To think that they can be exiled from the place they have always known as home causes fear and depression. Participants in the study reported lack of sleep and concentration when confronted with the possibility of deportation. Maria highlights this point when she comments on her ordeal with police and what she would consider doing to negotiate her status.

> I have never really thought about getting married to get my citizenship, but this incident really traumatized me. It

has been something that I have been thinking about doing because I really want to be legal. I want to be able to drive a car with a license, and be insured. I have not been able to get behind the wheel again because of my fear of getting pulled over and/or getting the car impounded and/or getting a ticket. I am also stressed out about choosing a major and a career because of my current situation. I want to be able to choose a career that I really want and not because I think I will be able to cheat the system.

6. Under the theme of Pragmatism, Latino UCA students described the psychological trauma that they experience often with pragmatism and resiliency. Confronted with legal, financial, and other social obstacles they are consistently constructing ways to create support systems and find avenues and spaces where not only can they exist but thrive. The very fact that they are enrolled in colleges and universities speaks volumes about the resiliency of these UCA students. Finding ways to earn money for college, arranging transportation, taking care of their health, and learning whom to trust are but a few of pragmatic ways the unauthorized youth cope with their reality.

Finding a way to negotiating unauthorized environments including employment is highly problematic and the risk taking emotionally stressful as in the case of Norma.

Someone gave me the idea of erasing the "NOT VALID FOR EMPLOYMENT" of my real government card, I did that and it worked! I worked for Mickey Mouse at the happiest place on earth for 5 years. I worked there my senior year of high school and all the way through community college. I am still employed using that same card.

7. Referring the theme of Family, UCA students identified family and friends a source of strength and the basis from which their quest for higher education emanates. The family nucleus appears to be the centerpiece in many of these otherwise "American"

success stories. Sadly, family values as the centerpiece of American and Christian ideals in this country are overlooked when legal status is concerned. Roque spoke of the importance of family.

> I was too young to understand the legal system, but my parents would always tell me to get good grades, go to college, and nothing was ever going to stop me from doing what I wanted to do. Over the years I have been able to study and be motivated in pursuing my education because of family support and sacrifice.

8. Structural violence as a theme was expressed as facing institutional barriers that limit the opportunity to fully participate and access their education. Brenda lamented the labeling of her legal status:

> Everywhere I go, anything I see and everything is I do, is controlled by being illegal in the United States. On television, in the streets and even in my dreams that word "Illegal" terrorizes me, even in a college class or in high school with my counselor the word is mentioned, I feel as if there was something wrong with me, as if I was guilty always guilty of something I had no control over.

Despite the many obstacles and tensions faced by UCA students, their personal fears, sense of belonging, identity, and the psychological and social traumas, one finds them resilient and unwilling to be denied their future and very determined to succeed. They understand the value of higher education and are hopeful that the laws of this country will allow them to live out of the shadows of the law. Waiting for change, UCA students navigate the parameters constructed by the legal and explicit and implicit lived space dimensions of society. The constant navigation of lived spaces creates experiences that correlate with feelings of ambivalence, encapsulation, dissonance, and rejection.

Discussion

In synthesis, the Jacobo and Ochoa conceptual framework is useful to examine the lived spaces of UCA students and as a tool to analyze the explicit and implicit lived spaces of UCA Latino youth living in the United States and how they negotiate their tensions as illustrated by the eight themes derived from interviews and dialogue in this exploratory study, namely: Identity, Membership, Micro-Aggressions, Trauma, Adaptability, Pragmatism - Resiliency, Agency, Family, and Structural Violence.

The voices of UCA students reminds us that under federal policy they have a right to access a free public K-12 education, yet, once they reach college age they are abandoned by the public educational system (Passel, 2006). Given the size of the undocumented immigrant population in the United States, now estimated to number some 11 million (Passel & Cohn, 2009) a significant public policy debate exits that centers on whether (1) undocumented students should be entitled to attend public postsecondary institutions, (2) whether they should be eligible for resident or in-state tuition, (3) who should have the authority to determine this, and (4) what are the economic and social returns from investing in undocumented immigrants' higher education.

Frum (2007) further asserts that passage of the federal DREAM Act is the best solution currently on the table, since it would allow access to federal student loans and enable eligible students to obtain legal permanent residence. Yet, the reality is that neither higher education nor immigration policies are made in a political vacuum, and what may be good in the long term from a public policy perspective may not be possible as a political position due to the politics of the next election cycle.

Lastly, Rincon (2008) points to the ideological challenges of educational access by proposing that collectively we reframe the debate on the rights of undocumented immigrants from a lens focused on economics and assimilation to one that emphasizes the struggle for human dignity and equality. Such dialogue may help close the deep ideological divides in the existing immigration debate and advance educational policies that reduce inequality in our nation.

REFERENCES

Acuña, R. (2007). Occupied America: A history of Chicanos (5th ed.). London: Pearson.

Aronowitz, S. (2003). How class works: Power and social movement. New Haven, CT: Yale University Press.

California Proposition 227 (June 2, 1998). English Language in Public Schools Statute, in California as an initiated state statute.

Capps, R., M. C., Chundy, A., & Santos, R. (2007). Paying the price: The impact of immigration raids on America's children. The National Council of La Raza

Chavez, R. L. (1991). Shadowed Lives: Undocumented immigrants in American society. Stanford: Stanford Press.

Clark, D. A., & Aaron T. Beck, A.T. (2009). Cognitive therapy of anxiety disorders: Science and practice. New York, NY: Guilford Publication.

CNNU.S. (April 22, 2009). Report finds undocumented students face college roadblocks. Retrieved 2/28/2011 from http://articles.cnn.com/2009-04-22/us/undocumented.students_1_undocumented-s

Denzin, N. K., & Lincoln, Y. S. (2000). Handbook of qualitative research (2nd ed.). Thousand Oaks, Calif.: Sage Publications.

Diaz-Strong, D., Luna-Duarte M., E. Meiners, E., & Valentin,, L. (2010, May-June). Undocumented youth and community colleges. Academe Magazine, volume 96, no. 3.

Frum, J. (January 2007). Postsecondary educational access for undocumented students: Opportunities and Constraints, American Federation of Teacher, pp.83-108.

Goldsmith, R. E., Barlow, M. R., & Freyd, J. J. (2004,Winter). Knowing and not knowing about trauma: Implications for therapy. Psychotherapy: Theory, Research, Practice, Training, Vol 41(4), Win 2004, 448-463.

Horwedel, M. D. (2006). For illegal college students, an uncertain future. Retrieved 4/22/08, from www.diverseeducation.com/artman/publish/printer_5815.shtml

Jacobo, J. R. (2006). Frontera del norte : readings in Chicano and border history ([3rd] ed.). San Diego, CA: Southern Border Press.

Jacobo, R. (2010). The negotiation of lived spaces by unauthorized college aged youth. Unpublished Dissertation, Claremont Graduate University and San Diego State University.

Kincholoe, J. (2008). Critical pedagogy. New York, NY: Peter Lang.

Miao, G.R., Esses, V.M. & Bell, D.W. (April 2000). Examining conflict between components of attitudes: Ambivalence and inconsistency are distinct constructs. Canadian Journal of Behavioural Science, 32, 58-70.

McLaren P. (1997). Revolutionary multiculturalism: Pedagogies of dissent for the new millennium. Boulder, CO: Westview.

Muñoz, S.M & Maldonado, M.M. (2011, February). Counterstories of college persistence by undocumented Mexicana students: navigating race, class, gender, and legal status. Department of Educational Leadership and Policy Studies, Iowa State University, Ames, IA, USA.

Orfield, G. & Lee C. (August 2007). Historic reversals, accelerating resegregation, and the need for new integration strategies. A report of the Civil Rights Project/Proyecto Derechos Civiles, UCLA., pp. 1-49.

Passel, J. S. & Cohn, D. (2009). A portrait of unauthorized immigrants in the United States. Washington, DC: Pew Hispanic Center, April.

Pehrson S, Brown R, Zagefka H. (2009, March). When does national identification lead to the rejection of immigrants? Cross-sectional and longitudinal evidence for the role of essentialist in-group definitions, British Journal of Social, 48 (Pt 1): 61-76.

Perez Huber, L., Malagon, M.C., & Solorzano, D.G. (2009). Struggling for opportunity: Undocumented AB 540 students in the Latino education pipeline. CSRC Research Report No. 13. Los Angeles, CA: UCLA Chicano Studies Research Center. Perez, W., Espinoza, R., Ramos, K., Coronado, H.M., & Cortes, R. (2009). Academic resilience among undocumented Latino students. Hispanic Journal of Behavioral Sciences 31(2): 149-181.

Plyer v Doe 457 US 202 (1982).

Rincon, A. (2008). Undocumented Immigrants and Higher Education. New York: LFB Scholarly Publishing.

Soja, W.E. (2007). Journey to Los Angeles and other real and imagined laces. Maryland: Blackwell.

UCLA Center for Labor Research and Education (2007). Undocumented students: Unfulfilled dreams. University of California Los Angeles, www.labor.ucla.edu.

Zinn, H. (2003). A Peoples History of the United States: Volume II, The Civil War to the Present. New York: The New Press.

Contributors

Carlos M. Larralde is an independent scholar who has written several monographs and articles in Mexican American studies. He has a Ph.D. in sociology from the University of California, Los Angeles. Dr. Larralde is the author of Mexican American Movements and Leaders (1976)

Richard Griswold del Castillo is Professor of Mexican American Studies at San Diego State University. He received his Ph.D. in history from the University of California, Los Angeles. Dr. Griswold is the author of The Treaty of Guadalupe Hidalgo (1990) and with Richard Garcia, Cesar Chavez: A Triumph of the Spirit (1995).

Henry Lesperance is a doctoral candidate at Claremont Graduate University and an adjunct professor at Palomar College. He is a director and Producer of documentary film. His latest production is entitled "Pies Ligeros" Ojo de Venado Cinema (2014).

Raymund A. Paredes spent most of his academic career at UCLA where for 30 years he taught as an English professor and served for ten years as vice chancellor for Academic Development. In addition, he served as special assistant to the president of the University of California System in outreach efforts to improve access to higher education for students from educationally disadvantaged communities.

Michael Ornelas has been a professor of Chicano/a Studies at Mesa College in San Diego for over forty years. He is also the editor of several books on the early and modern Chicano Historical experience, including Between the Conquests and Beyond 1848. He is also the author of The Sons of Guadalupe: Voices of the Vietnam Generation and Their Journey Home. He received his academic degrees from the University of California at Santa Barbara and has been awarded two National Endowment for the Humanities fellowships for summer study and research at the Library of Congress in Washington, D.C. and the University of Arizona.

Treaty of Guadalupe Hidalgo; February 2, 1848

Treaty of peace, friendship, limits, and settlement between the United States of America and the United Mexican States concluded at Guadalupe Hidalgo, February 2, 1848; ratification advised by senate, with amendments, March 10, 1848; ratified by president, March 16, 1848; ratifications exchanged at Queretaro, May 30, 1848; proclaimed, July 4, 1848

IN THE NAME OF ALMIGHTY GOD

The United States of America and the United Mexican States animated by a sincere desire to put an end to the calamities of the war which unhappily exists between the two Republics and to establish Upon a solid basis relations of peace and friendship, which shall confer reciprocal benefits upon the citizens of both, and assure the concord, harmony, and mutual confidence wherein the two people should live, as good neighbors have for that purpose appointed their respective plenipotentiaries, that is to say: The President of the United States has appointed Nicholas P. Trist, a citizen of the United States, and the President of the Mexican Republic has appointed Don Luis Gonzaga Cuevas, Don Bernardo Couto, and Don Miguel Atristain, citizens of the said Republic; Who, after a reciprocal communication of their respective full powers, have, under the protection of Almighty God, the author of peace, arranged, agreed upon, and signed the following: Treaty of Peace, Friendship, Limits, and Settlement between the United States of America and the Mexican Republic.

ARTICLE I

There shall be firm and universal peace between the United States of America and the Mexican Republic, and between their respective countries, territories, cities, towns, and people, without exception of places or persons.

ARTICLE II

Immediately upon the signature of this treaty, a convention shall be entered into between a commissioner or commissioners appointed by the General-in-chief of the forces of the United States, and such as may be appointed by the Mexican Government, to the end that a provisional suspension of hostilities shall take place, and that, in the places occupied by the said forces, constitutional order may be reestablished, as regards the political, administrative, and judicial branches, so far as this shall be permitted by the circumstances of military occupation.

ARTICLE III

Immediately upon the ratification of the present treaty by the Government of the United States, orders shall be transmitted to the commanders of their land and naval forces, requiring the latter (provided this treaty shall then have been ratified by the Government of the Mexican Republic, and the ratifications exchanged) immediately to desist from blockading any Mexican ports and requiring the former (under the same condition) to commence, at the earliest moment practicable, withdrawing all troops of the United States then in the interior of the Mexican Republic, to points that shall be selected by common agreement, at a distance from the seaports not exceeding thirty leagues; and such evacuation of the interior of the Republic shall be completed with the least possible delay; the Mexican Government hereby binding itself to afford every facility in its power for rendering the same convenient to the troops, on their march and in their new positions, and for promoting a good understanding between them and the inhabitants. In like manner orders shall be dispatched to the persons in charge of the custom houses at all ports occupied by the forces of the United States, requiring them (under the same condition) immediately to deliver possession of the same to the persons authorized by the Mexican Government to receive it, together with all bonds and evidences of debt for duties on importations and on exportations, not yet fallen due. Moreover, a faithful and exact account shall be made out, showing the entire amount of all duties on imports and on exports, collected at such custom-houses, or elsewhere in Mexico, by authority of the United States, from and after the day of ratification of this treaty by the Government of the Mexican Republic; and also an account of the cost of collection; and such entire amount, deducting only the cost of collection, shall be delivered to the Mexican Government, at the city of Mexico, within three months after the exchange of ratifications.

The evacuation of the capital of the Mexican Republic by the troops of the United States, in virtue of the above stipulation, shall be completed in one month after the orders there stipulated for shall have been received by the commander of said troops, or sooner if possible.

ARTICLE IV

Immediately after the exchange of ratifications of the present treaty all castles, forts, territories, places, and possessions, which have been taken or occupied by the forces of the United States during the present war, within the limits of the Mexican Republic, as about to be established by the following article, shall be definitely restored to the said Republic, together with all the artillery, arms, apparatus of war, munitions, and other public property, which were in the said castles and forts when captured, and which shall remain there at the time when this treaty shall be duly ratified by the Government of the Mexican Republic. To this end, immediately upon the signature of this treaty, orders shall be dispatched to the American officers commanding such castles and forts, securing against the removal or destruction of any such artillery, arms, apparatus of war, munitions, or other public property. The city of Mexico, within the inner line of entrenchments surrounding the said city, is comprehended in the above stipulation, as regards the restoration of artillery, apparatus of war, & c.

The final evacuation of the territory of the Mexican Republic, by the forces of the United States, shall be completed in three months from the said exchange of ratifications, or sooner if possible; the Mexican Government hereby engaging, as in the foregoing article to use all means in its power for facilitating such evacuation, and rendering it convenient to the troops, and for promoting a good understanding between them and the inhabitants.

If, however, the ratification of this treaty by both parties should not take place in time to allow the embarkation of the troops of the United States to be completed before the commencement of the sickly season, at the Mexican ports on the Gulf of Mexico, in such case a friendly arrangement shall be entered into between the General-in-Chief of the said troops and the Mexican Government, whereby healthy and otherwise suitable places, at a distance from the ports not exceeding thirty leagues, shall be designated for the residence of such troops as may not yet have embarked, until the return of the healthy season. And the space of time here referred to as, comprehending the sickly season shall be understood to extend from the first day of May to the first day of November.

All prisoners of war taken on either side, on land or on sea, shall be restored as soon as practicable after the exchange of ratifications of this treaty. It is also agreed that if any Mexicans should now be held as captives by any savage tribe within the limits of the United States, as about to be established by the following article, the Government of the said United States will exact the release of such captives and cause them to be restored to their country.

ARTICLE V

The boundary line between the two Republics shall commence in the Gulf of Mexico, three leagues from land, opposite the mouth of the Rio Grande, otherwise called Rio Bravo del Norte, or Opposite the mouth of its deepest branch, if it should have more than one branch emptying directly into the sea; from thence up the middle of that river, following the deepest channel, where it has more than one, to the point where it strikes the southern boundary of New Mexico; thence, westwardly, along the whole southern boundary of New Mexico (which runs north of the town called Paso) to its western termination; thence, northward, along the western line of New Mexico, until it intersects the first branch of the river Gila; (or if it should not intersect any branch of that river, then to the point on the said line nearest to such branch, and thence in a direct line to the same); thence down the middle of the said branch and of the said river, until it empties into the Rio Colorado; thence across the Rio Colorado, following the division line between Upper and Lower California, to the Pacific Ocean.

The southern and western limits of New Mexico, mentioned in the article, are those laid down in the map entitled "Map of the United Mexican States, as organized and defined by various acts of the Congress of said republic, and constructed according to the best authorities. Revised edition. Published at New York, in 1847, by J. Disturnell," of which map a copy is added to this treaty, bearing the signatures and seals of the undersigned Plenipotentiaries. And, in order to preclude all difficulty in tracing upon the ground the limit separating Upper from Lower California, it is agreed that the said limit shall consist of a straight line drawn from the middle of the Rio Gila, where it unites with the Colorado, to a point on the coast of the Pacific Ocean, distant one marine league due south of the southernmost point of the port of San Diego, according to the plan of said port made in the year 1782 by Don Juan Pantoja, second sailing-master of the Spanish fleet, and published at Madrid in the year 1802, in the atlas to the voyage of the schooners Sutil and Mexicana; of which plan a copy is hereunto added, signed and sealed by the respective Plenipotentiaries.

In order to designate the boundary line with due precision, upon authoritative maps, and to establish upon the ground landmarks which shall show the limits of both republics, as described in the present article, the two Governments shall each appoint a commissioner and a surveyor, who, before the expiration of one year from the date of the exchange of ratifications of this treaty, shall meet at the port of San Diego, and proceed to run and mark the said boundary in its whole course to the mouth of the Rio Bravo del Norte. They shall keep journals and make out plans of their operations; and the result agreed upon by them shall be deemed a part of this treaty, and shall have the same force as if it were inserted therein. The two Governments will amicably agree regarding what may be necessary to these persons, and also as to their respective escorts, should such be necessary.

The boundary line established by this article shall be religiously respected by each of the two republics, and no change shall ever be made therein, except by the express and free consent of both nations, lawfully given by the General Government of each, in conformity with its own constitution.

ARTICLE VI 6

The vessels and citizens of the United States shall, in all time, have a free and uninterrupted passage by the Gulf of California, and by the river Colorado below its confluence with the Gila, to and from their possessions situated north of the boundary line defined in the preceding article; it being understood that this passage is to be by navigating the Gulf of California and the river Colorado, and not by land, without the express consent of the Mexican Government.

If, by the examinations which may be made, it should be ascertained to be practicable and advantageous to construct a road, canal, or railway, which should in whole or in part run upon the river Gila, or upon its right or its left bank, within the space of one marine league from either margin of the river, the Governments of both republics will form an agreement regarding its construction, in order that it may serve equally for the use and advantage of both countries.

ARTICLE VII 7

The river Gila, and the part of the Rio Bravo del Norte lying below the southern boundary of New Mexico, being, agreeably to the fifth article, divided in the middle between the two republics, the navigation of the Gila and of the Bravo below said boundary shall be free and common to the vessels and citizens of both countries; and neither shall, without the consent of the other, construct any work that may impede or interrupt, in whole or in part, the exercise of this right; not even for the purpose of favoring new methods of navigation. Nor shall any tax or contribution, under any denomination or title, be levied upon vessels or persons navigating the same or upon merchandise or effects transported thereon, except in the case of landing upon one of their shores. If, for the purpose of making the said rivers navigable, or for maintaining them in such state, it should be necessary or advantageous to establish any tax or contribution, this shall not be done without the consent of both Governments.

The stipulations contained in the present article shall not impair the territorial rights of either republic within its established limits.

ARTICLE VIII

Mexicans now established in territories previously belonging to Mexico, and which remain for the future within the limits of the United States, as defined by the present treaty, shall be free to continue where they now reside, or to remove at any time to the Mexican Republic, retaining the property which they possess in the said territories, or disposing thereof, and removing the proceeds wherever they please, without their being subjected, on this account, to any contribution, tax, or charge whatever.

Those who shall prefer to remain in the said territories may either retain the title and rights of Mexican citizens, or acquire those of citizens of the United States. But they shall be under the obligation to make their election within one year from the date of the exchange of ratifications of this treaty; and those who shall remain in the said territories after the expiration of that year, without having declared their intention to retain the character of Mexicans, shall be considered to have elected to become citizens of the United States.

In the said territories, property of every kind, now belonging to Mexicans not established there, shall be inviolably respected. The present owners, the heirs of these, and all Mexicans who may hereafter acquire said property by contract, shall enjoy with respect to it guarantees equally ample as if the same belonged to citizens of the United States.

ARTICLE IX

The Mexicans who, in the territories aforesaid, shall not preserve the character of citizens of the Mexican Republic, conformably with what is stipulated in the preceding article, shall be incorporated into the Union of the United States. and be admitted at the proper time (to be judged of by the Congress of the United States) to the enjoyment of all the rights of citizens of the United States, according to the principles of the Constitution; and in the meantime, shall be maintained and protected in the free enjoyment of their liberty and property, and secured in the free exercise of their religion without; restriction.

ARTICLE X

[Stricken out]

ARTICLE XI

Considering that a great part of the territories, which, by the present treaty, are to be comprehended for the future within the limits of the United States, is now occupied by savage tribes, who will hereafter be under the exclusive control of the Government of the United States, and whose incursions within the territory of Mexico would be prejudicial in the extreme, it is solemnly agreed that all such incursions shall be forcibly restrained by the Government of the United States whensoever this may be necessary; and that when they cannot be prevented, they shall be punished by the said Government, and satisfaction for the same shall be exactedall in the same way, and with equal diligence and energy, as if the same incursions were meditated or committed within its own territory, against its own citizens.

It shall not be lawful, under any pretext whatever, for any inhabitant of the United States to purchase or acquire any Mexican, or any foreigner residing in Mexico, who may have been captured by Indians inhabiting the territory of either of the two republics; nor to purchase or acquire horses, mules, cattle, or property of any kind, stolen within Mexican territory by such Indians.

And in the event of any person or persons, captured within

Mexican territory by Indians, being carried into the territory of the United States, the Government of the latter engages and binds itself, in the most solemn manner, so soon as it shall know of such captives being within its territory, and shall be able so to do, through the faithful exercise of its influence and power, to rescue them and return them to their country. or deliver them to the agent or representative of the Mexican Government. The Mexican authorities will, as far as practicable, give to the Government of the United States notice of such captures; and its agents shall pay the expenses incurred in the maintenance and transmission of the rescued captives; who, in the meantime, shall be treated with the utmost hospitality by the American authorities at the place where they may be. But if the Government of the United States, before receiving such notice from Mexico, should obtain intelligence, through any other channel, of the existence of Mexican captives within its territory, it will proceed forthwith to affect their release and delivery to the Mexican agent, as above stipulated.

For the purpose of giving to these stipulations the fullest possible efficacy, thereby affording the security and redress demanded by their true spirit and intent, the Government of the United States will now and hereafter pass, without unnecessary delay, and always vigilantly enforce, such laws as the nature of the subject may require. And, finally, the sacredness of this obligation shall never be lost sight of by the said Government, when providing for the removal of the Indians from any portion of the said territories, or for its being settled by citizens of the United States; but, on the contrary, special care shall then be taken not to place its Indian occupants under the necessity of seeking new homes, by committing those invasions which the United States have solemnly obliged themselves to restrain.

ARTICLE XII

In consideration of the extension acquired by the boundaries of the United States, as defined in the fifth article of the present treaty, the Government of the United States engages to pay to that of the Mexican Republic the sum of fifteen millions of dollars.

Immediately after the treaty shall have been duly ratified by the

Government of the Mexican Republic, the sum of three millions of dollars shall be paid to the said Government by that of the United States, at the city of Mexico, in the gold or silver coin of Mexico The remaining twelve millions of dollars shall be paid at the same place, and in the same coin, in annual installments of three millions of dollars each, together with interest on the same at the rate of six per centum per annum. This interest shall begin to run upon the whole sum of twelve millions from the day of the ratification of the present treaty by--the Mexican Government, and the first of the installments shall be paid-at the expiration of one year from the same day. Together with each annual installment, as it falls due, the whole interest accruing on such installment from the beginning shall also be paid.

ARTICLE XIII

The United States engage, moreover, to assume and pay to the claimants all the amounts now due them, and those hereafter to become due, by reason of the claims already liquidated and decided against the Mexican Republic, under the conventions between the two republics severally concluded on the eleventh day of April, eighteen hundred and thirty-nine, and on the thirtieth day of January, eighteen hundred and forty-three; so that the Mexican Republic shall be absolutely exempt, for the future, from all expense whatever on account of the said claims.

ARTICLE XIV

The United States do furthermore discharge the Mexican Republic from all claims of citizens of the United States, not heretofore decided against the Mexican Government, which may have arisen previously to the date of the signature of this treaty; which discharge shall be final and perpetual, whether the said claims be rejected or be allowed by the board of commissioners provided for in the following article, and whatever shall be the total amount of those allowed.

ARTICLE XV

The United States, exonerating Mexico from all demands on account of the claims of their citizens mentioned in the preceding article, and considering them entirely and forever canceled, whatever their amount may be, undertake to make satisfaction for the same, to an amount not exceeding three and one-quarter millions of dollars. To ascertain the validity and amount of those claims, a board of commissioners shall be established by the Government of the United States, whose awards shall be final and conclusive; provided that, in deciding upon the validity of each claim, the boa shall be guided and governed by the principles and rules of decision prescribed by the first and fifth articles of the unratified convention, concluded at the city of Mexico on the twentieth day of November, one thousand eight hundred and forty-three; and in no case shall an award be made in favour of any claim not embraced by these principles and rules.

If, in the opinion of the said board of commissioners or of the claimants, any books, records, or documents, in the possession or power of the Government of the Mexican Republic, shall be deemed necessary to the just decision of any claim, the commissioners, or the claimants through them, shall, within such period as Congress may designate, make an application in writing for the same, addressed to the Mexican Minister of Foreign Affairs, to be transmitted by the Secretary of State of the United States; and the Mexican Government engages, at the earliest possible moment after the receipt of such demand, to cause any of the books, records, or documents so specified, which shall be in their possession or power (or authenticated copies or extracts of the same), to be transmitted to the said Secretary of State, who shall immediately deliver them over to the said board of commissioners; provided that no such application shall be made by or at the instance of any claimant, until the facts which it is expected to prove by such books, records, or documents, shall have been stated under oath or affirmation.

ARTICLE XVI

Each of the contracting parties reserves to itself the entire right to fortify whatever point within its territory it may judge proper so to fortify for its security.

ARTICLE XVII

The treaty of amity, commerce, and navigation, concluded at the city of Mexico, on the fifth day of April, A. D. 1831, between the United States of America and the United Mexican States, except the additional article, and except so far as the stipulations of the said treaty may be incompatible with any stipulation contained in the present treaty, is hereby revived for the period of eight years from the day of the exchange of ratifications of this treaty, with the same force and virtue as if incorporated therein; it being understood that each of the contracting parties reserves to itself the right, at any time after the said period of eight years shall have expired, to terminate the same by giving one year's notice of such intention to the other party.

ARTICLE XVIII

All supplies whatever for troops of the United States in Mexico, arriving at ports in the occupation of such troops previous to the final evacuation thereof, although subsequently to the restoration of the custom-houses at such ports, shall be entirely exempt from duties and charges of any kind; the Government of the United States hereby engaging and pledging its faith to establish and vigilantly to enforce, all possible guards for securing the revenue of Mexico, by preventing the importation, under cover of this stipulation, of any articles other than such, both in kind and in quantity, as shall really be wanted for the use and consumption of the forces of the United States during the time they may remain in Mexico. To this end it shall be the duty of all officers and agents of the United States to denounce to the Mexican authorities at the respective ports any attempts at a fraudulent abuse of this stipulation, which they may know of, or may have reason to suspect, and to give to such authorities all the aid in their power with regard thereto; and every such attempt, when duly proved and established by sentence of a competent tribunal, They shall be punished by the confiscation of the property so attempted to be fraudulently introduced.

ARTICLE XIX

With respect to all merchandise, effects, and property whatsoever, imported into ports of Mexico, whilst in the occupation of the forces of the United States, whether by citizens of either republic, or by citizens or subjects of any neutral nation, the following rules shall be observed:

(1) All such merchandise, effects, and property, if imported previously to the restoration of the custom-houses to the Mexican authorities, as stipulated for in the third article of this treaty, shall be exempt from confiscation, although the importation of the same be prohibited by the Mexican tariff.

(2) The same perfect exemption shall be enjoyed by all such merchandise, effects, and property, imported subsequently to the restoration of the custom-houses, and previously to the sixty days fixed in the following article for the coming into force of the Mexican tariff at such ports respectively; the said merchandise, effects, and property being, however, at the time of their importation, subject to the payment of duties, as provided for in the said following article.

(3) All merchandise, effects, and property described in the two rules foregoing shall, during their continuance at the place of importation, and upon their leaving such place for the interior, be exempt from all duty, tax, or imposts of every kind, under whatsoever title or denomination. Nor shall they be there subject to any charge whatsoever upon the sale thereof.

(4) All merchandise, effects, and property, described in the first and second rules, which shall have been removed to any place in the interior, whilst such place was in the occupation of the forces of the United States, shall, during their continuance therein, be exempt from all tax upon the sale or consumption thereof, and from every kind of impost or contribution, under whatsoever title or denomination.

(5) But if any merchandise, effects, or property, described in the first and second rules, shall be removed to any place not occupied

at the time by the forces of the United States, they shall, upon their introduction into such place, or upon their sale or consumption there, be subject to the same duties which, under the Mexican laws, they would be required to pay in such cases if they had been imported in time of peace, through the maritime custom-houses, and had there paid the duties conformably with the Mexican tariff.

(6) The owners of all merchandise, effects, or property, described in the first and second rules, and existing in any port of Mexico, shall have the right to reship the same, exempt from all tax, impost, or contribution whatever.

With respect to the metals, or other property, exported from any Mexican port whilst in the occupation of the forces of the United States, and previously to the restoration of the custom-house at such port, no person shall be required by the Mexican authorities, whether general or state, to pay any tax, duty, or contribution upon any such exportation, or in any manner to account for the same to the said authorities.

ARTICLE XX

Through consideration for the interests of commerce generally, it is agreed, that if less than sixty days should elapse between the date of the signature of this treaty and the restoration of the custom houses, conformably with the stipulation in the third article, in such case all merchandise, effects and property whatsoever, arriving at the Mexican ports after the restoration of the said custom-houses, and previously to the expiration of sixty days after the day of signature of this treaty, shall be admitted to entry; and no other duties shall be levied thereon than the duties established by the tariff found in force at such custom-houses at the time of the restoration of the same. And to all such merchandise, effects, and property, the rules established by the preceding article shall apply.

ARTICLE XXI

If unhappily any disagreement should hereafter arise between the Governments of the two republics, whether with respect to the interpretation of any stipulation in this treaty, or with respect to any other particular concerning the political or commercial relations of the two nations, the said Governments, in the name of those nations, do promise to each other that they will endeavour, in the most sincere and earnest manner, to settle the differences so arising, and to preserve the state of peace and friendship in which the two countries are now placing themselves, using, for this end, mutual representations and pacific negotiations. And if, by these means, they should not be enabled to come to an agreement, a resort shall not, on this account, be had to reprisals, aggression, or hostility of any kind, by the one republic against the other, until the Government of that which deems itself aggrieved shall have maturely considered, in the spirit of peace and good neighbourship, whether it would not be better that such difference should be settled by the arbitration of commissioners appointed on each side, or by that of a friendly nation. And should such course be proposed by either party, it shall be acceded to by the other, unless deemed by it altogether incompatible with the nature of the difference, or the circumstances of the case.

ARTICLE XXII

If (which is not to be expected, and which God forbid) war should unhappily break out between the two republics, they do now, with a view to such calamity, solemnly pledge themselves to each other and to the world to observe the following rules; absolutely where the nature of the subject permits, and as closely as possible in all cases where such absolute observance shall be impossible:

(1) The merchants of either republic then residing in the other shall be allowed to remain twelve months (for those dwelling in the interior), and six months (for those dwelling at the seaports) to collect their debts and settle their affairs; during which periods they shall enjoy the same protection, and be on the same footing, in all respects, as the citizens or subjects of the most friendly nations; and, at the expiration thereof, or at any time before, they shall have full liberty to depart, carrying off all their effects without molestation or hindrance, conforming therein to the same laws which the citizens or subjects of the most friendly nations are required to conform to. Upon the entrance of the armies of either nation into the territories

of the other, women and children, ecclesiastics, scholars of every faculty, cultivators of the earth, merchants, artisans, manufacturers, and fishermen, unarmed and inhabiting unfortified towns, villages, or places, and in general all persons whose occupations are for the common subsistence and benefit of mankind, shall be allowed to continue their respective employments, unmolested in their persons. Nor shall their houses or goods be burnt or otherwise destroyed, nor their cattle taken, nor their fields wasted, by the armed force into whose power, by the events of war, they may happen to fall; but if the necessity arise to take anything from them for the use of such armed force, the same shall be paid for at an equitable price. All churches, hospitals, schools, colleges, libraries, and other establishments for charitable and beneficent purposes, shall be respected, and all persons connected with the same protected in the discharge of their duties, and the pursuit of their vocations.

(2). In order that the fate of prisoners of war may be alleviated all such practices as those of sending them into distant, inclement or unwholesome districts, or crowding them into close and noxious places, shall be studiously avoided. They shall not be confined in dungeons, prison ships, or prisons; nor be put in irons, or bound or otherwise restrained in the use of their limbs. The officers shall enjoy liberty on their paroles, within convenient districts, and have comfortable quarters; and the common soldiers shall be dispose(in cantonments, open and extensive enough for air and exercise and lodged in barracks as roomy and good as are provided by the party in whose power they are for its own troops. But if any office shall break his parole by leaving the district so assigned him, o any other prisoner shall escape from the limits of his cantonment after they shall have been designated to him, such individual, officer, or other prisoner, shall forfeit so much of the benefit of this article as provides for his liberty on parole or in cantonment. And if any officer so breaking his parole or any common soldier so escaping from the limits assigned him, shall afterwards be found in arms previously to his being regularly exchanged, the person so offending shall be dealt with according to the established laws of war. The officers shall be daily furnished, by the party in whose power they are, with as many rations, and of the same articles, as are allowed either in kind or by commutation, to officers of equal rank in its own army; and all others shall be daily furnished with such ration as is allowed to a common soldier in its own service; the value of all which supplies shall, at the close of the war, or at periods to be agreed upon between the respective commanders, be paid by the other party, on a mutual adjustment of accounts for the subsistence of prisoners; and such accounts shall not be mingled with or set off against any others, nor the balance due on them withheld, as a compensation or reprisal for any cause whatever, real or pretended Each party shall be allowed to keep a commissary of prisoners, appointed by itself, with every cantonment of prisoners, in possession of the other; which commissary shall see the prisoners as often a he pleases; shall be allowed to receive, exempt from all duties a taxes, and to distribute, whatever comforts may be sent to them by their friends; and shall be free to transmit his reports in open letters to the party by whom he is employed. And it is declared that neither the pretense that war dissolves all treaties, nor any other whatever, shall be considered as annulling or suspending the solemn covenant contained in this article. On the contrary, the state of war is precisely that for which it is provided; and, during which, its stipulations are to be as sacredly observed as the most acknowledged obligations under the law of nature or nations.

ARTICLE XXIII

This treaty shall be ratified by the President of the United States of America, by and with the advice and consent of the Senate thereof; and by the President of the Mexican Republic, with the previous approbation of its general Congress; and the ratifications shall be exchanged in the City of Washington, or at the seat of Government of Mexico, in four months from the date of the signature hereof, or sooner if practicable. In faith whereof we, the respective Plenipotentiaries, have signed this treaty of peace, friendship, limits, and settlement, and have hereunto affixed our seals respectively. Done in quintuplicate, at the city of Guadalupe Hidalgo, on the second day of February, in the year of our Lord one thousand eight hundred and forty-eight.

N. P. TRIST
LUIS P. CUEVAS
BERNARDO COUTO
MIGL. ATRISTAIN